D0941443

The Colour Guide to
BRITISH BIRDS
and their eggs

The Colour Guide to

BRITISH BIRDS

and their eggs

by
Frances Fry

Nimrod Press Limited
15 The Maltings
Turk Street
Alton, Hants GU34 1DL

First edition 1990

Published by
Nimrod Press Limited
15 The Maltings
Turk Street
Alton, Hants GU34 1DL

Produced by
Jamesway Graphics
18 Hanson Close
Middleton
Manchester M24 2HD

Printed in England

ISBN 1-85259-241-9

CONTENTS

PARTS OF THE BIRD

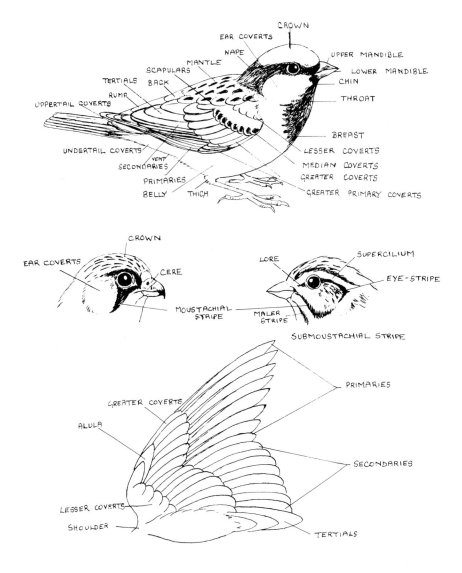

CROWN
EAR COVERTS
NAPE
MANTLE
SCAPULARS
TERTIALS   BACK
RUMP
UPPERTAIL COVERTS
UPPER MANDIBLE
LOWER MANDIBLE
CHIN
THROAT
BREAST
UNDERTAIL COVERTS
VENT
SECONDARIES
PRIMARIES
BELLY   THIGH
LESSER COVERTS
MEDIAN COVERTS
GREATER COVERTS
GREATER PRIMARY COVERTS

CROWN
EAR COVERTS
CERE
MOUSTACHIAL STRIPE
MALER STRIPE

LORE
SUPERCILIUM
EYE-STRIPE
SUBMOUSTACHIAL STRIPE

GREATER COVERTS
ALULA
PRIMARIES
SECONDARIES
LESSER COVERTS
SHOULDER
TERTIALS

WING FROM ABOVE

Birds are among the most successful inhabitants of the planet Earth, with a wide variety of species co-existing with mankind, living in all sorts of habitats. More than any other creatures birds are a part of our daily lives, and can be observed wherever we live. Bird-watching is an absorbing hobby, and is becoming even more popular as economic circumstances and changing patterns of life mean more leisure time for mankind.

But all birdwatching really begins with identification. Our enjoyment is vastly enriched when we can tell different species one from another, and put a name to each kind of bird. Then we can learn more about the bird, its habits, its favourite food and the best places to observe it.

There are many different bird books, all excellent in their own way for aiding identification and informing on bird life, but most of these classify birds according to genera and species. This book is different, basing identification primarily on colour, and should be an easy way for a beginner at birdwatching to recognise birds. Here the first basic question is

'What colour was the bird?' and birds are grouped under headings denoting the dominent colour of the bird. All too often a bird is glimpsed only briefly, leaving a fleeting impression of its general colouring, so here colour is the first reference. Other groupings occur within the main colour groups, like **'tree-climbing birds'** or **'Swallow-like birds'**. When a bird might be found under two headings cross-references state which group it is in.

This book is divided into three sections, each one denoting the habitat where the birds are most likely to be found:

Land Birds
Water-side Birds
Water and Sea Birds.

The section covering land birds includes habitats as diverse as towns and gardens, farms and woodland, moorland and mountains. Waterside habitats include swamps and bogs as well as lakes, streams and rivers. Water and Sea birds are all those which spend most of their lives on water, ranging from Ducks to Seagulls. Birds do not keep rigidly to their categories, but these groupings give a general guide which should help to indentify individual birds quickly.

Within each of the three categories the birds are grouped only according to colour. Since few birds are all one colour it is the general effect that counts towards identification. Where male and female differ greatly in colour both sexes are illustrated, but the bird is grouped under the colour of the males plumage.

270 species are shown in this book. All are illustrated in colour, and fully described in the text, with details of size (in both imperial and metric measurements) distribution, habits, call, nest and eggs. The eggs of all British breeding birds are also shown in colour alongside each species so as to aid identification.

Good birdwatching. I hope this book adds to your enjoyment of birds.

BOOKS

The RSPB Book of British Birds,
Holden, Sharrock, Burns.
Macmillan, London 1982

A Field Guild to the Birds of Britain and Europe
Peterson, Mountfort, Hollom.
Collins, London 1954

The Popular Handbook of British Birds
Hollom.
Witherby, London 1982

British Birds
Gooder, Lambert.
Collins, London 1982

Birds of Britain and Europe
Hammon, Everett.
Pan Books, London 1980

British Birds and their Eggs
MacLair Boraston.
Chambers, London 1933

BIRD SOCIETIES

R.S.P.B.
The Royal Society for the Protection of Birds,
The Lodge,
Sandy,
Bedfordshire SG19 2LD

The British Trust for Ornithology,
Beech Grove,
Tring,
Herfordshire HP23 5NR

The Wildfowl Trust,
Slimbridge,
Gloucester GL2 7BT

The Young Ornithologist's Club, (junior section of the R.S.P.B.)
The Lodge,
Sandy,
Bedfordshire SG19 2DL

PART ONE:
LAND BIRDS

Land Birds covers all the birds that are seen mainly on or over land. This is a wide-ranging category, covering many different habitats – towns, parks and gardens, farmland, heaths and commons, mountain and moorland, and broad-leaved and coniferous woodland. Birds do not keep rigidly to one catergory, and some species would be equally at home in land or waterside environments, but as far as possible the three broad groupings in this book serve as a general guide to location. Where there is overlapping, with birds having habituts that fit two categories, the species is put under the most likely grouping but is also cross-referenced to the alternative grouping. For example: The Curlew frequents both moorland and marshland habitats, so it is listed and described under *Land Birds*, and cross-referenced under *Waterside Birds*.

Many Gulls, particularly Black-headed and Herring Gulls, are seen inland, as they take advantage of the easy pickings of man's refuse tips, but as these species are always associated with the sea they are listed and described under *Water & Sea Birds*.

Land Birds is the largest section in this book, and covers many different families of birds: Crows, Raptors, Gamebirds, Thrushes, Finches, Tits, Buntings, Owls, Doves, Woodpeckers, Swifts, Swallows, Sparrows, Warblers, Wrens, etc . . . and also some members of the Wader family.

Black Grouse

SIZE   Male 21in:53cm. Female 16in:41cm.

DESCRIPTION   Black game-bird with white wing-bar and lyre-shaped tail. Under tail coverts white. Red patch above eye. Female has grey/brown and white barred plumage with forked tail.

SONG/CALL   Male has a 'sneezing' call, female a pheasant like 'kok-kok'. Breeding display song by male of cooing, bubbling and crowing notes.

RECOGNITION   Large black game-bird with red wattle, its distinctive white feathers under its tail are used in courtship display to impress the rather dowdy (grey-hen) female. Resident all year round, favourite habitats are moorland, conifer plantations or birch woods. In spring Black Grouse have a communal display area known as a 'lek' where the males spread their tails, and strut and sing before the females. 'Leks' take place very early in the morning.

FOOD   Buds, shoots, leaves, berries and some insects, and grain. Mainly ground-feeding, but will feed in trees when snow covers their usual haunts.

NEST   A shallow hollow scraped in the ground, lined with grass, plant material and a few feathers. Nest found on the edge of woodland, or on moors, in shelter of low plants.

EGGS   6–10, sometimes more, up to 16. Smooth and glossy, creamy buff or yellow marked with small spots of buff-brown or red-brown. 2.0in x 1.4in:51.3 x 37mm. Eggs laid at 36–48 hour intervals, incubation starting when the clutch is complete, and taking 23–26 days. Young Precocial (downy and active).

BREEDING SEASON   May to June. Single-brooded.

Capercaillie

SIZE   34in:86cm. Female 24in:62cm.

DESCRIPTION   Male dark grey/black, long broad tail, white on flanks, red patch above eye. Female smaller, mottled brown, buff and white.

SONG/CALL   Male has a call reminiscent of a throat being cleared. Female has a Pheasant-like 'kok kok'. During mating season the male has a display song, starting with a rattle and ending with a sound like a cork being drawn from a bottle, followed by a clashing of wing quills on the ground.

RECOGNITION   A large turkey-like bird, but secretive and well-camouflaged in its favourite haunt of forests. The native British species of Capercaillie was exterminated in the 18th century, but Swedish stock was successfully re-introduced into Perthshire and later to other parts of Scotland, and they are now well established in this region.

PLATE 1

Black Grouse (scale 1:8.2)

Capercaillie (scale 1:8.2)

FRANCES FRY

Resident all year round. When alarmed raises hackles on neck.

FOOD   Favourite food – buds and shoots of conifers, also various berries.

NEST   A hollow scratched out of the ground under a tree or bush, lined with plant material.

EGGS   Usually 4–8, but occasionally large clutches of 15 or more. Pale yellow-buff colour, with fine speckles and small blotches of yellow or red/brown. 2.2in x 1.5in:57.3 x 41.5mm. Eggs laid on alternate days, with incubation starting when the clutch is complete and taking 26–29 days. Young are down-covered when hatched and active quickly (precocial nestlings).

BREEDING SEASON   Mid-April to June. Single-brooded.

Carrion Crow

SIZE   18½in:47cm.

DESCRIPTION   All black, including bill and legs.

SONG/CALL   A harsh, croaking 'craah'.

RECOGNITION   Same size and colour as the Rook, but can be distinguished by different behaviour patterns and small plumage differences. The Crow has a feathered base to its bill, but no long feathers on its thighs. It is normally a solitary bird, not gregarious like the Rook, and although it may sometimes be seen in small family groups it is more often found singly or in pairs. Resident all year round, and found throughout the British Isles, although in Scotland and Ireland the all-black form is replaced by the black-and-grey Hooded Crow. Flight is rather heavy, and it walks and sidles with ungainly hops.

FOOD   Carrion, as its name denotes, also small birds and animals or eggs etc.

NEST   A bulky cup made of sticks, bound with earth and moss, and lined with wool, hair or feathers. The nest is usually placed in the fork of a tall tree, but a cliff edge may be used in coastal areas.

EGGS   4–6, occasionally 7. Smooth and slightly glossy, various shades of light green or blue, with spots, speckles and blotches of olive, olive-brown, dark brown or grey/blue. 1.7in x 1.2in:43.3 x 30.4mm. Incubation (by female only) 18–20 days. Fledging 28–30 days.

BREEDING SEASON   March to May, depending on the region, (later in the north.) Single-brooded.

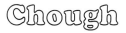

HOODED CROW

Differs from the Carrion Crow only in colour, all other characteristics are the same.

DESCRIPTION   Black head, wings and tail, black bill and legs. Grey nape, back and underparts.

Chough

SIZE   16in:39.5cm.

DESCRIPTION   All black plumage with red bill and legs.

SONG/CALL   'K'chuf' call, giving bird its name, sometimes 'kyow' like a young Jackdaw. Starling-like chattering sub-song is rarely heard.

RECOGNITION   The only all black bird with red bill and legs in Britain. Aerobatic flight; both walks and hops on the ground. Resident all year round, but rare, found only on rocky coasts of western Britain and Ireland.

FOOD   Ants, larvae, insects and spiders. Its long curving bill enables it to probe into the ground for food. It may sometimes form small flocks when searching for food.

NEST   A bulky cup of sticks, grasses and plant stems, lined with wool and hair, usually found on a ledge on rocky outcrops, or in a cave, or in a quarry or deserted building.

EGGS   2–7, but usually 3 or 4. Smooth and glossy, very pale tinged green, cream or buff, and marked with small blothces and spots of olive brown or grey. 1.5in x 1.1in:40.6 x 28.7mm. Incubation, by female alone, 17–23 days. Fledglings leave the nest by 38 days.

BREEDING SEASON   Late April or May. Single-brooded unless the first clutch is lost, then this may be replaced with another.

Rook

SIZE   18 in:46cm.

DESCRIPTION   All black, as crow.

SONG/CALL   Harsh 'caw' or 'caah' call.

RECOGNITION   Large black bird with bare face patch behind bill. Long loose feathers at the top of legs give a 'baggy trousers' effect. The black feathers have a purplish sheen at close range. A very gregarious bird gathering in large flocks. Heavy flight and a sedate, determined walking gait. Resident all year round, and common throughout the British Isles, especially on farmland. Rooks often associate with Starlings and Jackdaws when feeding.

FOOD   Worms, insects, grain or carrion if available. Rooks have an expandable pouch under their bill where food can be stored for feeding the young. A strong bill enables them to probe the ground for insects and larvae.

NEST   A bulky cap made of sticks and earth, lined with grass, roots, moss, wool or hair. Both sexes gather twigs for the nest, but the female does the actual building. The nest is built in a tall tree, often surrounded by many other nests belonging to the same flock. Huge 'rookeries' are sometimes established, and the flocks return and refurbish the old nests each year.

EGGS   Any number from 3 to 9, although 3–5 is usual, 1.6in x 1.15in:40 x 28.3mm. Smooth and glossy, ranging in colour from light blue to green, and marked with blotches and spots, large or small. There is often considerable variation between eggs in the same clutch. Incubation 16–20 days. Fledging 29–30 days.

BREEDING SEASON   Late March to May. Single-brooded.

Raven

SIZE   25in:64cm

DESCRIPTION   All black, including bill and legs.

SONG/CALL   A harsh, gutteral croak. 'kronk', 'kronk'

RECOGNITION   The largest all-black land bird in the British Isles. Wedge-shaped tail, and large head in relation to body size. Massive black bill, and long hanging feathers at the throat forming 'hackles'. Resident all the year in western Britain and Ireland. Found in high moorland regions, mountainous terrain and around sea cliffs. It is often seen performing aerobatics while giving its hoarse 'kronking' call. In olden days the Raven had a grim reputation as a bird of ill omen. Ravens will sometimes feed in flocks.

FOOD   Omnivorous eater, taking small mammals, birds, eggs and carrion.

NEST   A large mass of twigs and vegetable matter, bound with earth and moss, lined with wool and hair. Both sexes build the nest, and each pair of birds usually has several nest sites within their own territory, favoured sites being cliff edges or a tall, inaccessible tree.

EGGS   Usually 4–6, 1.9in x 1.32:49.7 x 33.4 mm, smooth and glossy. Colour tends to be variable, ranging from light blue to greenish blue or pale green, marked with irregular blotches, streaks or lines of olive, brown or grey. Incubation takes 20–21 days, but only begins when the clutch is complete. Fledglings do not leave the nest until they are 5–6 weeks old.

BREEDING SEASON   End of February to Mid-March. Single-brooded.

PLATE 2

Hooded Crow (scale 1:7)

Carrion Crow (scale 1:7)

Chough (scale 1:7)

Rook (scale 1:7)

Raven (scale 1:7)

FRANCES FRY

Black Redstart

SIZE   5½in:14cm

DESCRIPTION   Male all black except for white wing patch and rufous tail. Female and Juveniles greyer.

SONG/CALL   Variety of calls 'tsip', 'tic', 'tucc-tucc'. Song is a staccato warble interspersed with grinding sound.

RECOGNITION   Small Robin-sized bird, with somewhat similar movements, but most distinctive feature is 'tail shivering'. Resident all year round. Likes ruins, waste sites in cities, docks, power stations and similar surroundings. Sometimes winters near the coast.

FOOD   Mainly insects. Spends much of its time ground feeding, searching under debris for small insects.

NEST   Nests in holes, in walls, cliffs, or city buildings. Bomb sites from the second World War were colonised by the Black Redstart and this favourable habitat led to a sizeable increase in numbers of this rare species. The breeding range widened to include industrial sites, and the species is now established in the southern part of Britain. Nest a loose cup of grass and moss lined with hair or wool.

EGGS   Usually 4–6, .8in x .55in:19.6 x 14.4mm smooth, glossy and white. Incubation (by female only) takes 12–16 days. Fledging 12–19 days.

BREEDING SEASON   From late April onwards. 2 or sometimes 3 broods.

Blackbird

SIZE   10in:25cm.

DESCRIPTION   Male bird is glossy black, with a yellow bill and eye-ring. Female is dark brown, often with a slightly spotted breast. Juveniles are red/brown with speckled breast.

SONG/CALL   Alarm call is a loud, ringing, 'Chink Chink'. Song is very melodic and flute-like, tailing off towards the end.

RECOGNITION   The Blackbird is the only jet black bird that hops or runs rather than walking, and that throws up its tail on landing. It is solitary rather than gregarious. Resident all the year round, and common in town or country, it is found throughout the British Isles except in mountainous regions.

FOOD   Berries, fruit, worms and insects. A ground-feeding brid it may often be seen turning over dead leaves in search of worms or millipides.

PLATE 3

Black Redstart (scale 1:4.6)

Blackbird (scale 1:4.6)

Starling (scale 1:4.6)

Jackdaw (scale 1:4.6)

FRANCES FRY.

NEST The Blackbird's nest is a deep cup-shape, made of grass and rootlets plastered together with mud, and lined with fine grass. Hedges and bushes are favoured nest-sites, but tame garden birds will nest almost anywhere – in garden sheds, on piles of garden stakes or even on the window-sill.

EGGS 4–6 eggs are usual, greenish-blue in colour, spotted, streaked or blotched with pale red/brown. Sometimes the larger end of the egg is clouded orangey-brown. 1.1in x .85in:29.4 x 21.7mm. Incubation by female alone, takes 11–17 days. Fledging 12–19 days.

BREEDING SEASON From March onwards. 2 or sometimes 3 broods a year.

Starling

SIZE 8½in:21.5cm.

DESCRIPTION Overall impression black, but plumage is irridescent with green and purple in summer, and spangled with pale spots in winter. Bill yellow, legs reddish brown. Both sexes alike. Juveniles paler and more speckled.

SONG/CALL A wide range of sounds – whistles, chuckling and gurgling notes. An excellent mimic, immitating other birds or more eccentric noises like a whistling kettle or a ringing telephone.

RECOGNITION The starling is the only black bird of thrush size that walks (instead of hopping) and it runs about quickly in a rather ungainly manner. When perching, its wings often droop low at is sides. Highly gregarious, the starling is rarely seen alone, and often forms large flocks. These large packs often perform spectacular flights, wheeling round in perfect unison before returning to communal feeding ground or a general roosting place. Resident all year round, and common throughout the British Isles. A noisy, quarrelsome bird.

FOOD Insects, worms, fruit and berries. Can often be seen on lawns or open ground probing into the ground with slightly open bill searching for leatherjackets (the larvae of craneflies).

NEST A hole-nesting bird. Holes in trees (especially old Woodpecker holes). Holes in walls or cliffs, or under the eaves of houses (under the roof if it can find a suitable entrance. The nest is an untidy mass of straw, twigs and moss, lined with wool and feathers.

EGGS 4–7 average. Pale blue, slightly glossy. 1.2in x 85in:30.2 x 21.2 mm. Incubation (by both sexes) 12–15 days. Fledging 20–22 days.

BREEDING SEASON Begins mid-April. 1 or 2 broods a year.

Jackdaw

SIZE   13in:33cm.

DESCRIPTION   All black, except for grey back to head. Pale eye.

SONG/CALL   A sharp 'jac' call, or a more ringing 'kyow'.

RECOGNITION   A smaller bird than the Rook or the Crow, with a shorter bill. Its flight is quicker than the Crows, and it may frequently perform aerobatics. A gregarious bird, nesting in colonies, and feeding with Rooks and Crows. Resident all year round, and common throughout the British Isles, with habitats as varied as town, woods, cliffs and farmland. It has a liking for bright, shiny objects.

FOOD   Omnivorous, eating young birds, eggs, worms, insects and larvae. Most food is taken from on or near the surface of the ground.

NEST   In holes or in trees, or on cliffs. In open sites the nest is made of sticks, lined with wool, hair and plant fibre; in holes or chimneys the nest is more likely to consist of lodged twigs with more twigs on top. Both sexes build the nest.

EGGS   2–9 although 4–6 is usual. Smooth and glossy, pale blue marked with small blotches, spots and specks of brown or blue-grey. 1.4in x 1in:35.7 x 25.5mm. Markings can vary a great deal. Incubation takes 17–18 days, fledglings leave the nest at 28–30 days.

BREEDING SEASON   From late April. Single-brooded.

Other black birds which are fully described under different sections.

SWIFT The Swift is really dark brown, with a pale chin patch, but often looks black when seen in flight against a light sky. It is described under BROWN BIRDS.

RING OUZEL This mountain cousin of the Blackbird has a bold white cresent on its chest, and is described under BLACK AND WHITE BIRDS.

Snow Bunting

SIZE 6½in:16½cm

DESCRIPTION White underparts and white on wings. In winter male is white with black back and black centre on tail; in summer he is buff-brown above and white below. The female is buff-brown with white on wings and underparts.

SONG/CALL A musical 'teu' call.

RECOGNITION The most northerly breeding songbird, the Snow Bunting is a winter visitor to the coasts and hills of Britain, and is quite plentiful along the east coast where it feeds on the seeds of the coarse grass of the sand dunes. The birds feed in small flocks. A stocky bunting, resembling the Sparrow somewhat in size and shape, the Snow Bunting is always distinguishable by the amount of white in its plumage, particularly on the wings. It is a rare nesting bird in Britain, confined to the mountains of Scotland where numbers are regular but small. During the breeding season the male has a display flight resembling that of the Skylark, hovering in the air and singing loudly.

FOOD Seeds of grasses and weeds, insects in summer, grain, beetles.

NEST A cup of grasses, moss and roots, lined with fine grass, hair and feathers, built by the female in a despression in the ground, or a crevice among rocks.

EGGS 4–6, occasionally 7 or 8, smooth, glossy, pale blue or greenish-blue with reddish-brown blotches or purplish-brown spots, often concentrated at the larger end of the egg. .85in x .70in:21.9 x 16.2mm incubation, by the female alone, takes 10–15 days, fledging 10–14 days.

BREEDING SEASON Late May to July, varying with altitude. Double-brooded.

The Snow Bunting is also listed under BLACK AND WHITE BIRDS.

Ptarmigan

SIZE 14in:35cm

DESCRIPTION Pure white plumage in winter, white and mottled brown in summer, with black tail. In summer plumage the male is a darker brown than the female, and has a large red wattle over the eye. In autumn the male is grey/brown and white, the female dark brown.

SONG/CALL A harsh croak for a call, and a grating alarm call.

RECOGNITION An Arctic gamebird living in high, mountainous country, resident in Scotland all year round. Slightly smaller than the Red Grouse the Ptarmigan is recognisable at all seasons by its white wings and white belly. More trusting than most birds, it is more likely to crouch and 'freeze' when startled than fly away, the mottled

PLATE 4

Snow Bunting (scale 2:5.8)

Snowy Owl (scale 1:7)

Ptarmigan (scale 1:4.6)

plumage blending into the rocks, or the white winter feathers merging into the snow. The Ptarmigan's main natural enemy is the Golden Eagle.

FOOD   Shoots, leaves, berries and seeds

NEST   The nest is a bare hollow scrape made in the shelter of a rock, or a clump of vegetation, and thinly lined with grass or a few feathers.

EGGS   4–12, laid at intervals of one or two days, smooth and glossy, whitish cream in colour with a mottling of dark brown spots 1.7 x 1.1in:43.6 x 31.1mm. Incubation, by the female alone, takes 24–26 days. The young are precocial and downy, and can fly, albeit weakly, at about 10 days.

BREEDING SEASON   Mid-May to June, sometimes later in inclement weather. Single-brooded.

Snowy Owl

SIZE   24in:60cm

DESCRIPTION   White, flecked or barred with brown (more brown markings on the female) with yellow eyes.

SONG/CALL   Usually a silent bird, but during the breeding season has a loud 'krow-ow' call, or a repeated 'rick rick'

RECOGNITION   A large white, round-headed owl, with fierce yellow eyes, the Snowy Owl is one of Britain's rarer birds, being an irregular migrant visitor to Scotland. However, in recent years it has bred in parts of Scotland, particularly the Shetland Islands. Its normal habitat is tundra and barren hills. It is largely diurnal, and solitary, but may perch in the open on a post or rock providing a good vantage point. Every few years the Snowy Owl irrupts from its normal Arctic strongholds and spreads south, and when this occurs its range is extended to include sea shores, dunes and marsh.

FOOD   Carnivorous bird of prey, taking rodents and small birds, but can also take large animals, like an Arctic Hare. Glides silently searching for prey, then makes a swift dash to the kill.

NEST   Ground nesting, usually choosing a mossy hummock on moorland or hillside, but sometimes using a large boulder or ledge of rock. The nest consists of a hollow scrape made by the female, lined with moss and feathers.

EGGS   The size of the clutch varies with the food supply, 4–10, Smooth, slightly glossy, and white. 2.25 x 1.75in:57.4 x 45.2mm. Incubation, by female only, takes 32–37 days, the eggs hatching at 1–2 day intervals, so that a large clutch may take 2 weeks or more. The young are ready to leave the nest-site at 3–4 weeks, but cannot fly well until they are about 8 weeks old.

BREEDING SEASON   From mid-April to June. Single-brooded, but like other Arctic birds may not nest at all some years when severe weather has depleted their food supply.

SIZE   12in:30cm

DESCRIPTION   Black and white, with rounded wings and short tail, crest and long legs. The black feathers on head and back have a greenish sheen, particularly in sunlight, which accounts for the alternative name of Green Plover. Orange feathers underneath the tail.

SONG/CALL   A wheezy, drawn-out 'peewit' call, giving, yet another alternative name – Peewit.

RECOGNITION   The Lapwing is the only British bird with a long crest, except the tiny Crested Titmouse. Resident all year round, and distributed throughout the British Isles, though more plentiful in the north. Principally a bird of farmland or moorland, walking with a rapid gait, or standing motionless for long periods. Its flight is heavy and slow. During the breeding season the Lapwing has a showy courtship display, flying steeply upward, then tumbling down to within a few feet of the ground before straightening out and repeating the manouevre.

FOOD   Insects, grubs, worms, slugs and some seeds.

NEST   A hollow depression in the ground, often with no lining, sometimes with quite a wad of grasses and vegetable matter.

EGGS   3–5, but usually 4, pyriform to oval shape, cream or stone colour tinted brown and marked with blotches. 1.6in x 1.3in:47.1 x 33.7mm. Incubation by both sexes takes 24–29 days. Precocial and downy young, buff and black banded, are independent in about 33 days.

BREEDING SEASON   Late March to April. Single-brooded, but a lost clutch may be replaced.

SIZE   18in:46cm

DESCRIPTION   Black and white, with irridescent blue/green on wing feathers and long wedge-shaped tail.

SONG/CALL   A harsh, metallic 'chack chack' call.

RECOGNITION   The most spectacular member of the crow family the Magpie is conspicuous with its black and white plumage and long tail. Resident all year round, and found throughout the British Isles, its favourite habitat is farmland or open country with plenty of hedges and trees nearby, although it is also found in increasing numbers in towns and cities too. It is a large, noisy bird, often seen in small groups or larger flocks in winter. Likes bright, shiny objects.

FOOD   Omnivorous, eating seeds and berries, insects and fruit, eggs and small mammals, and carrion. Its fondness for taking eggs led to persecution by gamekeepers, but this had little long-lasting effect on the species as the Magpie proved adaptable and spread to other, more industrial areas.

NEST   A large, untidy, domed-shaped structure of sticks, with a cup of fine roots lined with plant fibre or hair. Both sexes help to build the nest which is usually situated in a tall tree or hedge.

EGGS   5–8, sometimes up to 10, smooth and glossy, pale and blue/green, heavily spotted with olive-brown or grey. Sometimes the markings are concentrated at one end of the egg. 1.4 x 1.0in:34.7 x 24mm. Incubation, by female only, 17–18 days, fledging 22–28 days.

BREEDING SEASON   Early April to late May. Single-brooded.

Ring Ouzel

SIZE   10in:25cm

DESCRIPTION   Black plumage, with broad white band under the throat, yellow bill. Female brown with pale cresent under throat.

SONG/CALL   A clear piping song, and a loud 'tac-tac' call.

RECOGNITION   The Ring Ouzel is the Blackbird of the mountain areas. It closely resembles the Blackbird with gestures as well as plumage, sharing the same hopping gait, and throwing up the tail on landing, but the broad white band under the throat is the distinguishing factor. Close viewing reveals that the black feathers are margined with grey. It is a Summer visitor to Britain, arriving in April and departing in the autumn, and is found in hill country and mountains. Numbers seem to be decreasing as the Blackbird has become more numerous and increased its range northwards.

FOOD   Worms, insects, berries or fruit.

NEST   A bulky cup of grass, heather, moss and leaves, plastered with mud and lined with fine grass. Both sexes build the nest which is situated in a tree or shrub if these are available, or in heather or on a ledge in moorland regions.

EGGS   4–5, smooth and glossy, light blue blotched with red-brown, red-purple or red-grey. 1.1in. x 85in:30.4 x 21.5mm. Incubation, by both sexes, takes 13–14 days, and fledging a similar period of 13–14 days.

BREEDING SEASON   Mid-April in southern regions, to early June in the north. Usually single-brooded, but sometimes double-brooded.

LAND BIRDS

PLATE 5

Magpie (scale 1:4.6)

Lapwing (scale 1:4.6)

Ring Ouzel (scale 1:4.6)

Long-tailed Tit (scale 1:4.6)

FRANCES FRY

Long-Tailed Tit

SIZE 5½in:14cm

DESCRIPTION Tiny, round-bodied bird with long tail that it easily recognisable. Black and white plumage save for rosy-pink on wings and underparts.

SONG/CALL A high 'see see' call and a lower-pitched 'truip'.

RECOGNITION Year round resident, and distributed throughout the British Isles, preferring woodland habitat. Long-tailed Tits often travel around in small flocks, and roost together at night, huddling close for warmth in bad weather. A severe winter can have a disasterous effect on numbers, as such a small bird has a job to find enough food to keep up its body-heat in cold conditions. Old nests often provide much-needed shelter, and many birds may seek mutual warmth inside. Shyer than most of the Tits, they do not visit surburban gardens much except when food is scarce – then they may be tempted, especially by fat hung up for them.

FOOD Mainly insects and spiders, seeds or buds.

NEST The Long-tailed Tits nest is one of the most beautiful and elaborate in the bird world. It is an intricate domed structure, oval shaped with a hole at the side, made of moss, wool, spiders' webs, covered with lichen and lined profusely with feathers. 2000 feathers were found in one nest. Both sexes help to build the nest which is usually situated in a bush or tree. When it is completed the fit is so snug that the bird's long tail has to fold back over its head when it is incubating the eggs.

EGGS 8–12, smooth and glossy, white, sometimes finely speckled with small purple/red spots. .53in x .42in:14.3 x 10.8mm. Incubation, mainly by the female, takes 12–14 days, fledging 14–18 days.

BREEDING SEASON Late March to April. Usually single-brooded, but sometimes double-brooded.

Pied Wagtail

SIZE 7½in:19cm.

DESCRIPTION Slim bird, black and white plumage and long tail. White edge to wing feathers, and outer-tail feathers white.

SONG/CALL 'Tschizzik' high-pitched flight call, also given during courtship.

RECOGNITION Most distinctive feature is the long tail, which is constantly wagged up and down, giving the bird its wagtail name. A ground-feeding, walking bird, running swiftly after insects then pausing to wag the tail. Resident all year round, and distributed throughout Britain, sometimes found near water, but also in dry places like car parks or playgrounds. The Pied Wagtail is quite at home in towns, and often roosts in large flocks on buildings, at sewage works or in greenhouses. It seems to have a fondness for tarmac, and often courts disaster walking along roads, flying to safety at the last minute.

FOOD   Insects, including flies and moths, also beetles.

NEST   The Wagtail's nest is made of dried grass and rootlets, lined with hair and feathers, and built in a hole or crevice by the female. The ledge of a building may provide a suitable site in a town, or a thatched roof in the country. Human activity does not seem to disturb the birds.

EGGS   5 or 6, sometimes 7, smooth, glossy, blueish-white or grey freckled with grey-brown spots. .8 x .6in:20.6in x 15.3mm. Incubation, chiefly by the female, takes 12–14 days, fledging 13–15 days.

BREEDING SEASON   Late April to June. Single-brooded in the north, sometimes double-brooded in southern regions.

Pied Flycatcher

SIZE   5in:13cm.

DESCRIPTION   Britain's smallest black and white bird. Male black above, with white forehead, white underparts and white wing-bar. Female and autumn-plumaged male olive-brown in place of black plumage.

SONG/CALL   A two-note song, repeated with a short trill. 'Tac', 'tu' and Swallow-like 'whit' call notes.

RECOGNITION   Small and retiring, the Pied Flycatcher keeps to the upper branches of trees, and is rather difficult to observe except in the breeding season. Then it takes readily to nest-boxes, and has greatly increased its range in recent years as the distribution of such boxes has also increased, and it no longer has to compete with Redstarts and Tits for natural nesting-holes. A summer visitor to deciduous woods, it is now found quite plentifully in Wales, western England and northern England, and parts of Scotland. Most of its food is caught on the wing, but it sometimes feeds on the ground and may sometimes cling to the trunk of a tree like a Tit.

FOOD   Flies, moths etc, sometimes worms and grubs but mostly insects.

NEST   A loose cup of leaves, grass and roots, built by the female in a natural hole, or a man-made nest-box. The nest is lined with grass, hair or bark, and sometimes with wool or feathers.

EGGS   4–7 usually, sometimes up to II, smooth, glossy, and pale blue in colour. .68in x .52in:17.9 x 13.4mm. Incubation, by female only, takes 12–13 days, and fledging 13–16 days.

BREEDING SEASON   Begins May. Single-brooded.

Great Spotted Woodpecker

SIZE 9in:23cm.

DESCRIPTION Boldly marked black upperparts and white underparts, with oval white patches on the wings most noticeable when the bird is perching. White cheeks, black moustachial stripe, crimson feathers beneath the tail, and the male bird has a crimson patch on the nape. A stout, straight bill.

SONG/CALL A repeated 'tchick' call, enlarged into a trill during the breeding season. The sound most associated with all woodpeckers is the drumming produced when hamering on wood.

RECOGNITION The Great Spotted Woodpecker is the most widespread of the three British Woodpeckers, found throughout England, Wales and most of Scotland, but absent from Ireland. Resident all year round, liking woods and forests, and spreading into suburban gardens and parks. It is a very agile climber, and may be seen on the trunks or branches of trees probing into the bark for insect larvae. Flight undulating. Sometimes a ground feeder, and in some districts a regular visitor to birdtables for nuts. During the breeding season there is often a courtship chase around tree trunks, and wing-fluttering displays.

FOOD Larvae of beetles wood wasps and moths, bee grubs, and occasionally young birds or eggs raided from nests.

NEST Both sexes excavate a hole in a tree, usually high up (at least 10ft from the ground) and this is lined only with a few wood-chips. Sometimes a nest box is used. In excavated holes a small entrance of about 2¼in across leads to an elongated nest chamber 1ft x 5in.

EGGS 4–7, smooth, glossy white eggs, .98 x .75in:26.4 x 19.5mm. Both sexes share incubation duties although the female does more than the male, and this takes 16 days, the young are fledged and ready to leave the nest at 18–21 days.

BREEDING SEASON Begins mid-May. Single-brooded.

The Great Spotted Woodpecker may also be found listed under BIRDS WITH RED ON HEAD.

Lesser Spotted Woodpecker

SIZE 6in:14cm

DESCRIPTION Small, Sparrow-sized bird, with black upperparts barred with white, white underparts, and red crown (on male only).

SONG/CALL A high, fast 'pee-pee-pee' song, a quiet 'tchick' call, and a high pitched fast drumming sound made by the bill hammering on wood to establish territory.

BLACK/WHITE BIRDS

LAND BIRDS

PLATE 6

Pied Wagtail (scale 2:5.8)

Pied Flycatcher (scale 2:5.8)

Greater Spotted Woodpecker (scale 2:5.8)

Lesser Spotted Woodpecker (scale 2:5.8)

FRANCES FRY

RECOGNITION Britain's smallest Woodpecker, no bigger than a Sparrow and easily overlooked. Resident all year round, but found mainly in the woodlands and parks of southern England and Wales. It creeps along tree branches, often on the underside probing the bark for insect life, which is then caught with its long tongue. It has an undulating flight, and a moth-like display flight during the breeding season. It may frequent gardens with orchards, and occasionally visit bird-tables in winter.

FOOD Insects and grubs of wood-boring beetles and moths, also grubs of gall-wasps, flies and spiders. Some fruit is also taken, especially soft fruit, like currants or raspberries.

NEST Both sexes help bore out a nest-hole in decayed wood in old trees, at up to almost any height to a limit of about 70ft from the ground. A shaft of 7½ to 10in leads from the entrance hole to the nest chamber, which is lined sparsely with wood chips.

EGGS 4–6 glossy white eggs, .75 x .57in:18.8 x 14.5mm. Incubation, by both sexes, (the male usually sitting at night) takes about 14 days, and the young are fledged and ready to leave the nest at about 21 days.

BREEDING SEASON From early May onwards. Single-brooded.

The Lesser Spotted Woodpecker may also be found listed under BIRDS WITH RED ON HEAD.

Other black birds which are fully described under different sections.

SNOW BUNTING This winter visitor is described under WHITE BIRDS.

HOUSE MARTIN An aerial bird with dark blue and white plumage that often looks black and white when seen in flight against a light sky. It is described under DARK BLUE AND WHITE BIRDS.

GREAT GREY SHRIKE A winter visitor with light grey and black plumage that has a 'pied' appearance. It is described under GREY BIRDS.

WOODCHAT SHRIKE A striking bird of passage with brown, black and white plumage that has a 'pied' appearance. It is described under BROWN, BLACK, AND WHITE BIRDS, but is illustrated under BROWN BIRDS.

Willow Tit

SIZE   4½in:11.5cm.

DESCRIPTION   Dull light-brown upperparts, greyish-white underparts, with dull black cap extending over the nape and small black bib. White outer margins on flight feathers form a pale panel on the closed wing that is absent in the very similar-coloured Marsh Tit.

SONG/CALL   A buzzing 'eez-eez-eez' call, a 'tchay' call, and sometimes a thin 'zi-zi-zi'. The rarely heard song is a lovely liquid warble with almost Nightingale-like qualities.

RECOGNITION   Very similar in appearance to the Marsh Tit. Chief differences are song and calls, plumage differences are dull black cap instead of glossy, slightly larger black bib, and pale patch on flight feathers noticeable when the wings are closed. Resident all year round, it inhabits mixed woodlands, farmland and sometimes gardens, but with a decided preference for damp places as it likes old, rotting timber in which to excavate its nest. It is fairly widely distributed in England and Wales, but scarce in northern Scotland and absent from Ireland.

FOOD   Insects and insect larvae, spiders and some berries.

NEST   The Willow Tit's nest is usually excavated in a rotten tree or stump, although occasionally a natural hollow or an old woodpecker hole is used instead. The female excavates the hole, and lines the nest cavity with wood fibre and fragments, with an inner lining of hair or feathers.

EGGS   6–9 usually, sometimes more, up to 13. Smooth, glossy, white in colour, speckled or blotched finely with reddish-brown markings concentrated at the larger end of the egg. .59 x .45in:15.5 x 12.2mm. Incubation, by the female only, takes 13–15 days, and fledging 17–19 days.

BREEDING SEASON   Mid-April in the south, June in the north. Single-brooded.

Marsh Tit

SIZE   4½in:11.5cm

DESCRIPTION   Dull light-brown upperparts, grey-buff underparts, with glossy black cap extending over the nape and tiny black bib.

SONG/CALL   A loud 'pitchcoo-pitchcoo' call, and variable little song which is rather like an extended call of 'pitcha weeoo', also a scolding 'chicka dee-dee-dee'.

RECOGNITION   Very similar in size to the Coal Tit, but distinguished from it by lack of white nape patch and tiny black bib instead of large bib. The Marsh Tit is very similar in appearance to the Willow Tit, but is distinguished from this bird by its glossy black cap. Resident all year round, and despite its name, it is usually found in wooded areas, or gardens with mature trees. It is widely distributed in England and Wales, but is not found in Scotland or Ireland. A gregarious bird that will join flocks of mixed Tits scouring woods and hedgerows for food, and sometimes coming to birdtables for scraps.

FOOD   Insects and their larvae, weed seeds, and various berries.

NEST   A cup of moss lined with hair and feathers, built by the female alone in a natural hole in a tree, stump or wall – rarely in a nest box.

EGGS   6–9, sometimes up to 11, second clutches tending to be smaller. The eggs are smooth and slightly glossy, white with reddish markings more numerous at the larger end. .61 x 47in:16.2 x 12.4mm. Incubation, by the female only, takes 13–17 days, fledging 16–21 days.

BREEDING SEASON   Begins mid-April. Birds in northern regions tend to be single-brooded, while those in southern climes are double-brooded.

Coal Tit

SIZE   4¼in:11cm

DESCRIPTION   Small bird with a disproportionately large head, with glossy black crown, white cheeks, and large white nape-patch. Grey/brown back and buff coloured belly, thin white cross-bars on wings.

SONG/CALL   A repeated 'seetoo seetoo' song, and a thin 'tsui' call or 'susi'.

RECOGNITION   The smallest British Tit, most easily recognised by its large patch of white on the nape which distinguishes it from the Marsh and Willow Tits, and black bib. Resident all year round, its favourite habitat is woodland or gardens with decorative trees, and it is a frequent visitor to birdtables. It is a gregarious bird and flocks with other members of the Titmouse family. It is widely distributed throughout Britain except for the Hebrides, Orkneys and Shetlands. It is also scarce in the Fen district.

FOOD   Insects and their larvae, spiders, small seeds, also peanuts and food scraps put out in gardens.

NEST   A cup of moss and spiders webs, lined with hair and feathers. The female builds the nest alone, usually in a hole in a tree, wall or bank, or a nest box.

EGGS   7–9 usually, but occasionally up to 12. Smooth and slightly glossy, white slightly speckled with reddish-brown, often concentrated at the larger end of the egg. .7 x .55in:14.9 x 11.6mm. The female alone incubates the eggs, and this takes 14–18 days, fledging 16–19 days.

BREEDING SEASON   Begins late April. Usually double-brooded.

Bullfinch

SIZE   5¾in:14.5cm

DESCRIPTION   A striking bird, with black cap, rose-pink breast, white rump, and grey back with blue-grey wings and tail. Stubby black bill. The female bird is paler and drabber.

SONG/CALL   A soft 'deu deu' call.

RECOGNITION   A handsome but shy bird, resident all year round, and widely distributed throughout the British Isles. Its favourite habitats are woodland, hedges, gardens and orchards. It has a great liking for fruit buds, and is an unpopular bird with commercial fruit-growers due to this habit – even a single bird can do a lot of damage, eating up to 30 buds a minute. Ornamental flowering trees are decimated in a similar manner. Bullfinches seem to pair for life, staying together throughout the year.

FOOD   Fruit tree buds, weed seeds and tree seeds, and berries. Caterpillars are food for young birds.

NEST   The female builds a nest of twigs, moss and lichen, lined with wool and plant down. It is usually situated in a hedge or thicket of brambles, sometimes in a tree, towards the end of a branch with fairly open foliage.

EGGS   3–7, although 4–6 is usual. Smooth and glossy, pale blue colour finely spotted or blotched with purple or pink, with markings concentrated at the larger end of the egg. .73 x .55in:18.3 x 13.4mm. Incubation, by the female, takes 12–14 days, and the young birds are fledged and ready to leave the nest at 12–15 days.

BREEDING SEASON   Late April to May. Double, sometimes treble-brooded.

The Bullfinch may also be found listed under BIRDS WITH RED OR ROSY BREASTS.

Blackcap

SIZE   5½in:14cm.

DESCRIPTION   The easiest Warbler to identify, with its distinctive black cap which gives the bird its name. The underparts are pale grey, the upperparts grey/brown, darker on the wings. The female has a chestnut-brown crown in place of the black cap of the male bird. Legs and bill are blackish.

SONG/CALL   A beautiful, rich warbling song, loud and clear – worthy rival to the Nightingale. Also a sharp little 'tac-tac' call or churring.

RECOGNITION   Most Blackcaps are summer visitors, arriving in April and departing October, but in recent years there has been evidence of some birds overwintering in the warmer south-west of England. The species is widespread in most of England and Wales, but more sparsely distributed in Scotland and Ireland. Favoured habitat is woodland, heaths and gardens with undergrowth and brambles which provide good nest sites. The birds tend to skulk in the undergrowth as they feed, but in some gardens they can be tempted to the bird table in cold weather. The male has a vigorous courtship display, raising its cap feathers, flapping its wing and spreading its tail, and the beautiful song helps to establish territory.

FOOD   Insects, flies and caterpillars, also fruit and berries.

NEST   A rather frail structure, built mainly by the female, consisting of a cup made of grass, roots and moss, with fine material binding the rim of the nest to supporting stems with basket-like 'handles'. It is lined with fine grass and hair.

EGGS   4–6, smooth, glossy, with colour varying from white to pink of olive/buff, with sparse markings of darker spots. .73 x .58in:19.6 x 14.8mm. Incubation, shared by both sexes, takes 12–15 days, and fledging 10–14 days.

BREEDING SEASON   Late April to May. Single or double-brooded.

The Blackcap may also be found listed under GREY BIRDS.

Reed Bunting

SIZE   6in:15cm

DESCRIPTION   Sparrow-sized bird, rather similar at first glance to the House Sparrow, but much brighter coloured and with clear differences in plumage. Black head and throat with white collar around nape. Dark brown streaked back, grey rump, white outer tail feathers and greyish underparts. The female bird lacks the black head markings, having only a black and white moustachial stripe.

SONG/CALL   A 'chink, chink tititick' song, and a 'tseep' call.

RECOGNITION   Most Reed Buntings are resident all year round in Britain, but some more visit in the summer and some Northern European birds visit in the winter. The species is widespread throughout the country, with numbers still on the increase. At one time it was regarded as a wetland species, but in recent years has changed its habitat to include drier areas such as conifer plantations and chalk downs. Often found in company with other Buntings and Finches flocking together over farmland in search of food. In some districts The Reed Bunting has become a common visitor to gardens and bird tables.

FOOD   Mainly seeds, but also beetles, caterpillars, insects and freshwater snails.

NEST   The female builds the nest which is made of grass and moss, cup-shaped and lined with fine grass and hair. It is usually situated low down in a bush or on the ground

PLATE 7

Willow Tit (scale 1:2.3)

Marsh Tit (scale 1:2.3)

Coal Tit (scale 1:2.3)

Bullfinch (scale 1:2.3)

Blackcap (scale 1:2.3)

Reed Bunting (scale 1:2.3)

FRANCES FRY.

in a clump of vegetation or a tussock of grasses, or among the reeds which gave the bird its name. Both sexes will divert attention from the nest if danger threatens by feigning a broken wing, shuffling along the ground with wing trailing.

EGGS 4–5, sometimes more, up to 7. Smooth, glossy, lilac coloured, with bold scrawling marks of blackish purple often with a blurred outline. .77 x .59in:19.9 x 14.7mm. Incubation, chiefly by the female, takes 12–14 days, fledging 10–13 days.

BREEDING SEASON Late April onwards. Double or sometimes treble-brooded.

The Reed Bunting is also listed under BROWN BIRDS WITH SPECKLED BREASTS

Other black-headed birds which are fully described under different sections.

BLACK-HEADED GULL *Although this bird is widespread inland the species is listed in the SEA BIRD section, under WHITE SEA BIRDS.*

BRAMBLING *This member of the Finch family is listed under BIRDS WITH RED OR ROSY BREASTS.*

STONECHAT *This member of the Thrush family is listed under BIRDS WITH RED OR ROSY BREASTS.*

GREAT TIT *This member of the Titmouse family is listed under BRIGHT COLOURED BIRDS : BLUE AND YELLOW BIRDS.*

LAPLAND BUNTING *(in breeding plumage). This winter visitor is listed under BROWN AND WHITE BIRDS.*

Crested Tit

SIZE 4½in:11.5cm.

DESCRIPTION Brown upperparts, white underparts shaded buff, with prominent black-and-white crest, white cheeks and black eye-stripe, black chin patch extending round neck to nape.

SONG/CALL 'zee-zee-zee' purring call, or a 'choorr' churring sound.

RECOGNITION A small, plumpish brown bird, easily distinguished by its distinctive crest. Resident all year round, but only found in Scotland. The Crested Tit is a bird of mature pine forests, preferably with some decaying wood to provide suitable nest sites. Re-forestation in Scotland has led to this species increasing its range somewhat, but the advance is slow. The Crested Tit is shyer than most of the Titmouse family, less gregarious by nature, and not a garden visitor.

FOOD Insects and their larvae. Conifer seeds and berries, especially juniper berries.

NEST The female builds the nest, although the male may help to gather material. Usually a natural hole is used, but sometimes she will excavate a hole in a rotten tree or stump. The nest consists of a cup made of moss and lichen, lined with deer hair, wood or feathers.

EGGS 4–8, sometimes up to 11. Smooth, slightly glossy, white speckled with reddish brown or purple markings more dense at the larger end of the egg. .62 x .47in:16.4 x 12.5mm. Incubation, by the female alone, takes 13–18 days, and fledging 17–21 days.

BREEDING SEASON Mid-April to May. Usually single-brooded, but sometimes double-brooded in southern areas.

Sand Martin

SIZE 4¾in:12cm

DESCRIPTION Small Swallow-like bird, with brown upperparts and white underparts broken by a conspicious brown band across the breast, and forked brown tail. Aerial in habit.

SONG/CALL A 'Tchurrup' call, extending to a twittering song.

RECOGNITION This summer visitor is the smallest member of the Swallow family, with a more dashing, erractic flight, and distinctive brown and white plumage. Sand Martins are very gregarious and are always found in colonies, feeding, breeding, roosting and migrating together. Always found near to water, and nesting in sandy cliffs. Widely distributed throughout the British Isles, with numbers increasing again after a recent decrease with the excavation of more sand pits and gravel quarries opening up new habitat. In autumn large flocks congregate in reedbeds prior to migration back to Africa in September.

FOOD   Almost entirely insects caught on the wing.

NEST   Sand Martins nest in burrows which both sexes dig out in river banks or sea cliffs, or man-made environments like sand or gravel pits. Colonies of birds nest in the same sites, in numbers ranging from a few pairs to several hundred. The rounded nest-chamber at the end of the tunnel is lined with feathers, straw or grass which the birds have gathered in flight.

EGGS   4–5, sometimes up to 7, non-glossy white eggs, slightly elongated, .7 x .48in:18 x 12.6mm. Incubation, by both sexes, takes 12–16 days, and the young are fledged and ready to leave the nest at around 19 days.

BREEDING SEASON   Begins mid-May. Usually double-brooded.

The Sand Martin will also be found listed under WATERSIDE BIRDS : BROWN AND WHITE BIRDS.

Barn Owl

SIZE   13½in:34cm

DESCRIPTION   A long-legged, pale-coloured Owl, with white facial disc bordered by a fine, heart-shaped black edging. Light golden-brown upperarts, finely speckled, and white underparts. The long legs are feathered white, and the eyes are dark black.

CALL   An eerie, wild shriek, giving rise to the country name of 'screech owl', and various yapping and snoring notes given when the bird is at rest.

RECOGNITION   This beautiful Owl has a ghost-like appearance, especially noticeable at dusk which, with dawn, is its favourite hunting time, and the eldrich screech given during flight adds to this expression. Many old tales of ghost-haunted churchyards probably owe their origins to Barn Owl activities. Resident, and distributed throughout most of Britain except for northern Scotland and outlying islands, the Barn Owl is mainly nocturnal, but may be seen hunting in daylight in winter when food is short, or in summer when feeding young. Its natural habitat is farmland and open country. The species got its name through roosting and nesting in farm barns, but modern farm buildings offer little scope for such activities, and this together with loss of habitat due to changing farming methods and the use of toxic chemicals on the land has led to a drastic decline in numbers.

FOOD   Mainly small rodents, although small birds are also taken. The Barn Owl is a good friend to the farmer eating harmful rats and mice, and it is to be hoped that places will exist on modern farms for this useful, attractive bird.

NEST   The Barn Owl builds no nest as such, using a convenient hole in a tree, or ledge in a building. The eggs are sometimes cushioned on owl pellets, but no nesting material is used.

PLATE 8

Sand Martin (scale 1:2.3)

Crested Tit (scale 1:2.3)

Barn Owl (scale 1:3.5)

Tree Creeper (scale 1:2.3)

EGGS   4–7, occasionally up to 11, non-glossy white eggs are laid. 1.6 x 1.2in x 39.7 x 31.6mm. Incubation, by the female alone, takes 32–34 days, and the young have a lengthy fledging period of 64–86 days. The eggs are laid at 2-day intervals, and the young hatch at similar intervals and thus vary in size. When food is scarce the largest youngsters get fed first, and the smaller ones may die of starvation.

BREEDING SEASON   Usually begins in April, but can be earlier. Often double-brooded.

Tree Creeper

SIZE   5in:12.5cm

DESCRIPTION   Striped brown upperparts with barred wings, and white underparts. Thin curved bill, and stiff pointed tail-feathers.

SONG/CALL   A high, thin 'tsit' call, and a repeated 'tsee-tsee-tsee' song.

RECOGNITION   The Tree Creeper lives up to its name, climbing agilely up tree trunks and branches, creeping round the trunk, starting at the base and working upwards in spirals, seeking food from bark crevices, probing with its thin curved bill. A quiet, mouse-like bird, it is often overlooked unless its call draws attention to it. When under observation it will move round behind the tree trunk, or else 'freeze' becoming invisible as its mottled plumage blends in with the bark. When climbing the tree it moves upwards in short jerky spurts, using its stiff tail feathers to balance itself against the trunk. The Tree Creeper is a resident bird, found throughout the British Isles in wooded country.

FOOD   Insects and their larvae, spiders and their eggs.

NEST   A neat cup of twigs and grasses, roots and moss, lined with wool and feathers. It is usually situated in a tree crevice, behind a loose piece of bark, or sometimes in a hole in a wall, or the plank walls of a shed. Both sexes help to build the nest.

EGGS   3–9, but more usually 6, non-glossy white eggs, finely speckled with reddish-brown spots at the larger end. .62 x .47in: 15:6 x 12.2mm. Incubation, by the female only, takes 14–15 days, and fledging 14–16 days. The young can fly only weakly on leaving the nest, but they can climb well from the start.

BREEDING SEASON   From April onwards. Double-brooded.

Other brown, black and white birds which are fully described under different sections.

REED BUNTING This Sparrow-sized bird is described under BLACK-HEADED BIRDS.

Red Kite

SIZE   22–24in:61cm.

DESCRIPTION   Slim elegant raptor, with long wings and long forked tail. Rusty brown plumage with greyish streaked head.

CALL   A high-pitched 'wee-oo wee-oo'.

RECOGNITION   One of Britain's rarer nesting birds, resident all year round, but found only in central Wales where a small breeding population is gradually expanding. At one time this species was widespread throughout Britain, but persecution by man led to the breed coming to the edge of extinction here. Special protection by conservationists have had good results, and the numbers are slowly building up. The Red Kite is a very agile flyer, circling effortlessly for hours when looking for prey – indeed it was this remarkable flying that led to the name 'kite' for children's flying toys. The graceful flight and forked tail provide easy recognition.

FOOD   Rabbits, small mammals, carrion, fledgling birds, sometimes worms and frogs.

NEST   The Kites nest is built high in a tree, often on the base of an old nest belonging to a Buzzard or Raven. Both sexes help in the construction, using sticks and twigs, and decorating it with old bits of rag or polythene.

EGGS   2–3 usually, sometimes, 4 or 5. Non-glossy, white, spotted with reddish brown 2.25 x 1.75in:56.8 x 45.1mm. Incubation, usually by the female, takes about 30–40 days, and the young can fly the nest at about 45–50 days.

BREEDING SEASON   April. Single-brooded. A lost clutch is seldom replaced.

Kestrel

SIZE   13½in:34cm.

DESCRIPTION   A long-winged, long-tailed falcon, upperparts rust/brown with black markings, underparts lighter and streaked with dark brown or black. The male has blue/grey head, rump and tail, with black band at the end of the tail; the female has a barred tail, also with a black band at the end. Yellow legs.

CALL   A high-pitched 'kee-kee-kee-kee' in the breeding season only.

RECOGNITION   Resident all year round, the Kestrel is the most widespread bird of prey in Britain, being common throughout the country. Its long pointed wings and long tail, and its ability to 'hover' during flight when looking for prey are the easiest means of identification. It is at home in most kinds of habitat, from farmland, heaths, moors and marshes to parks, suburbs and even city centres. The Kestrel has proved a very adaptable bird, and since the coming of the motorways it has used the wide verges and central reservations as new hunting grounds, free from human interference.

FOOD   Mainly mice, voles and rats, also frogs, earthworms and insects, and in towns small birds (like House Sparrows). The Kestrel hovers over its prey with tail fanned out and wings flapping, then pounces down for a quick kill.

NEST   No proper nest is built, eggs are laid on cliff ledges, in old buildings, in a tree hole, or the abandoned nest of another bird. Little or no nesting material is used.

EGGS   4–5, although up to 9 occasionally. Smooth, non-glossy, yellowish white colour heavily speckled with dark red/brown. 1.6 x 1.25in:39.7 x 31.8mm. Eggs are laid at intervals of 2–3 days, and incubation, mainly by the female, begins with the first egg, and takes 27–29 days. The young are feathered at 12–20 days and ready to leave the nest at 27–39 days, but remain dependent on their parents for several weeks afterwards.

BREEDING SEASON   From mid-April onwards. Single-brooded.

Buzzard

SIZE   20–22in:51–56cm.

DESCRIPTION   Large, chunkily-built bird of prey (raptor) brown above, with streaked or barred brown plumage below. Smallish head, broad rounded wings and rounded tail are distinguishing features at flight. The female is often larger than the male.

CALL   A 'mewing' call.

RECOGNITION   This resident bird favours wooded country, moorland, mountains or farmland. It is widespread in Wales, western England and Scotland, less plentiful in central and eastern England, and scarce in Ireland, being found only in the north. Never popular with gamekeepers, pesticides, and myxomatosis amongst rabbits which were an important part of its diet, all contrived to bring a sharp decrease in numbers in the 1950s, but now the species is on the increase again. The Buzzard is most often seen lazily quartering the sky over grassland or moorland in search of prey. Sometimes it resembles a small Eagle, and there are several similarities in its display flight too, but size is the determining factor. It may often 'mew' as it flies, and may sometimes be mobbed by crows or gulls.

FOOD   Rabbits, small mammals, carrion, sometimes earthworms and beetles or berries.

NEST   A bulky structure of twigs, sticks and branches, lined with green material and decorated with leaves or seaweed. Both sexes help build the nest, usually in a tree, but sometimes on a cliff ledge or rocky outcrop. The nest is often re-used annually, with more sticks and new decorations added each year.

PLATE 9

Red Kite (scale 1:7)

Kestrel (scale 1:4.6)

Golden Eagle (scale 1:8.2)

Buzzard (scale 1:7)

EGGS   2, 3 or 4, laid at 2–3 day intervals. Non-glossy, white with chocolate brown markings. 2.25 x 1.75in:56.8 x 45.5mm. Incubation, mainly by the female but sometimes both sexes, can take up to 42 days for a clutch. The young vary in size, with the smallest often dying if food is short. Fledging takes 12–30 days, but they do not fly the nest until 40–45 days.

BREEDING SEASON   April or May. Single-brooded.

Golden Eagle

SIZE   35in:88cm.

DESCRIPTION   Very large all brown bird, easily distinguished by its sheer size. Light golden-brown feathers on nape, yellow on beak and legs, heavy feathering on legs. Broad wings, large head and tail clearly visible during flight.

CALL   Usually a silent bird, but occasionally gives a thin yelping 'twee-oo'.

RECOGNITION   Large solitary bird, resident all year round, found mostly in the Scottish Highlands. Widespread persecution from gamekeepers drastically reduced numbers, but in recent years legal protection has led to a recovery, and the Golden Eagles has increased its breeding range to the English Lake District. It is most usually seen soaring lazily over the hillsides searching for prey. Eagles pair for life, and sometimes perform spectacular courtship display flights, soaring and then plunging earthwards with half-closed wings, rolling over in mid-air and briefly linking talons.

FOOD   Grouse, Ptarmigan, Hares, carrion and sometimes weakly lambs.

NEST   Both sexes build an imposingly high basket of sticks, known as an eyrie, placed on a mountain crag, cliff, or tall tree. A pair of Eagles will usually have several nest sites which are used in rotation, old nests being repaired before the breeding season starts, with more sticks added and fresh greenery for decoration. After several years re-use the nest becomes a massive structure of branches and twigs. The site is usually as inaccessible to enemies as possible.

EGGS   Usually 2, sometimes just 1, rarely 3. Non-glossy white, spotted or blotched brown, with great variations in a clutch. 2.98 x 2.4in:76.7 x 59.4mm. Incubation, usually by the female although the male sometimes assists, takes 43–45 days. The young takes 30–50 days to get fully feathered, and if food is scarce the smaller chick may die. It is 63–70 days before the young are strong enough to fly the nest.

BREEDING SEASON   Around late March. Single-brooded.

Swift

SIZE 6½in:16.5cm.

DESCRIPTION Totally aerial bird, with dark brown/black plumage except for white chin-patch. Long scythe-shaped wings, thin body and forked tail.

CALL A shrill screaming. The Swift was once known to countrymen as the 'devil bird' because of its habit of flying screaming around houses during the spring and summer.

RECOGNITION The Swift is a summer visitor that can only be confused with the Swallow family (represented in Britain by the Swallow, the House Martin and the Sand Martin) but it can be distinguished from them by its higher, more gliding flight, and its shrill screeching, as well as its thin sickle-shaped wings and streamlined body. The Swift is the only bird with very long pointed wings that appears dark all over during flight. Swifts eat, drink, sleep and mate on the wing; the only time they are not airborne is during the nesting season when they are laying or incubating eggs. With such a totally aerial life their legs are very tiny, useless for walking or hopping, with all four toes facing forwards enabling the bird to cling to vertical surfaces like walls and roofs when nest-building. If a Swift becomes stranded on the ground it has great difficulty getting airborne again. Swifts are gregarious, and are usually seen in flocks, wheeling and screaming as they search for insect food.

FOOD Almost entirely insects caught on the wing, the Swift's broad beak opening to a wide gape enabling it to fill its chin pouch with food.

NEST A rudimentary cup of straw, feathers and grasses glued together and stuck to the nest site with a saliver secretion. It is built under eaves, or in church towers, always somewhere high up so that the parent birds can launch themselves downward in flight.

EGGS 3, sometimes 4 elongated white eggs are laid – 1in x .65in:25 x 16.3mm. Incubation, mainly by the female, takes 14–20 days and fledging about 35 days.

BREEDING SEASON Begins late May. Single-brooded.

Nightingale

SIZE 6½in:16.5cm.

DESCRIPTION A small brown bird, with buff underparts and rounded rufous tail.

SONG/CALL The prima donna of the bird world, with a beautiful rich and varied song that is its most outstanding feature, with repeated notes and a bubbling 'chook-chook-chook'. The song is often given at dusk when most other birds have ceased to sing and gone to roost, and to hear a Nightingale singing on a summers evening is a marvellous experience. It also has a number of less attractive calls – a 'hweet', a 'tac' and a rather grating 'chaaa'.

RECOGNITION   The Nightingale is a shy retiring bird, preferring to remain in deep woodland cover, and although it is a regular summer visitor to Britain it is more often heard than seen. The lovely song is the best means of identification. Shrinking woodlands with the resultant loss of habitat has meant that numbers have declined quite sharply over the last 30 years, and it is now found only in southern and eastern England. Its flight and attitude while feeding on the ground is similar to the Robin, but unlike that very familiar bird the Nightingale is given to skulking and solitary behaviour.

FOOD   Mainly ground insects, also spiders and beetles.

NEST   The Nightingale conceals its nest carefully, building close to the ground among thick undergrowth. The female builds the nest, which is a loose cup made of dead leaves and grass and lined with fine grass and hair.

EGGS   4–5 usually, sometimes varying from 3–7, smooth and slightly glossy, basically blue/green or olive brown colour with fine reddish markings so plentiful as to give a rusty tint to the whole egg. .8 x .6in:20.8 x 15.6mm. Sometimes there is a chalk-white slash or smear mark on the eggs. Incubation, by the female only, takes 13–14 days, and fledging 11–12 days.

BREEDING SEASON   Around mid-May. Single-brooded.

Red-backed Shrike

SIZE   6¾in:17cm.

DESCRIPTION   Smallest of the shrikes, becoming rare in Britain. The male has chestnut back, grey head and rump, black mask, black tail with white base to outer feathers, and stubby hooked bill. The female has chestnut back and tail, greyish head, and cream underparts barred brown on breast and flanks.

SONG/CALL   A harsh 'chak-chack' call note, and a warbling song containing some harsh notes and also some mimicry.

RECOGNITION   This attractively coloured summer visitor is now quite rare in most of Britain, found mainly in southern and eastern England in small numbers. The species has suffered a drastic decline over many years, although the cause is not certain – some habitat has been lost through land improvement, and egg-collectors have also contributed to the damage, but climatic changes may also be a factor. The Red-backed Shrike likes heathland, or commons with gorse and thorny trees, and overgrown gardens, or orchards and parks. It hunts in a similar manner to a small hawk, locating its prey from a look-out post or while hovering in flight, then swooping down to the kill Surplus prey is impaled on thorns, or sometimes barbed wire, and kept in this grisly 'larder' until required, giving the bird a country name of 'Butcher Bird'.

FOOD   Small birds, small mammals and amphibians, but mainly insects.

PLATE 10

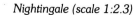

Nightingale (scale 1:2.3)

Swift (scale 1:2.3)

Red Backed Shrike (scale 1:2.3)

FRANCES FRY.

Woodchat Shrike (scale 1:2.3)

NEST   A bulky cup of grasses, plant stems and moss, lined with hair, rootlets and wool or down, built in a tree or shrub about 3–9 feet from the ground.

EGGS   5–6, rarely more but sometimes up to 7, glossy eggs are laid, very variable in colour, ranging from green or pink to cream or white, usually with a zone of spots forming a band around the larger end. .82 x .69in:22.9 x 17.1mm. Incubation, usually by the female, takes 14-16 days, and fledging 12-16 days.

BREEDING SEASON   May to June. Single-brooded.

Woodchat Shrike

SIZE   6¾in:17cm.

DESCRIPTION   Striking black, white and brown bird, with bright chestnut cap and nape, black frontal band on head, black back, wings and tail with conspicious white scapulars and white rump, and white breast and underparts. The female is similar but duller.

SONG/CALL   Harsh chattering 'kiwick-kiwick' notes, and a song containing melodious phrases and imitations of other birds.

RECOGNITION   The Woodchat Shrike is a regular passage migrant to Britain, seen in Spring in coastal areas of southern and eastern England. It is a strikingly handsome bird, easily identified by its pied plumage and typical Shrike behaviour, perching freely on tree tops, bushes, posts and wires, although it tends to sit in trees amongst the foliage more than other shrikes. Otherwise its habitat and lifestyle is very similar to that of the Redbacked Shrike, with typical 'larders' of prey used regularly and similar hunting methods.

FOOD   Small birds, small mammals, and invertebrates like earthworms.

The Woodchat Shrike does not breed in Britain or Ireland.

Wren

SIZE   3¾in:9.5cm.

DESCRIPTION   A tiny, plump bird, with barred brown plumage and short cocked tail.

SONG/CALL   A loud warbling song ending with a flourishing trill. It always seems surprising that such a small bird can produce so much sound, but this attractive trilling is given from song posts or from within deep cover, and draws attention to an otherwise inconspicuous bird. When alarmed the Wren gives a scolding 'tic-tic-tic' call.

RECOGNITION   The Wren is resident all year round and widely distributed throughout the British Isles, occupying a varied range of habitats from woodland to high mountain land. It is found in hedgerows, gardens, city centres, heaths and cliffs. It is an extremely active little bird with mouse-like habits of foraging amongst ground litter when searching for food. Although it is a popular garden visitor it often keeps out of sight under cover of undergrowth or shrubs, but it sings throughout the year, even in the depths of winter, and is a regular user of nestboxes when these are available. In winter the nestbox is used as a communal roost, with many Wrens huddling together inside for warmth – up to 60 birds have been recorded in a single box. Hard winters take a heavy toll on numbers, and when the weather is particularly severe the population may fall drastically, taking several years to recover again.

FOOD   Insects and their larvae, spiders and moth larvae.

NEST   The male bird builds several nests (known as 'cock' nests) and the female decides which one to use, and lines it with feathers and fine grasses. The nest is dome-shaped, made of grass, moss and leaves, and well hidden in a tree hole, a crevice in rocks, or a cavity in a wall or bank, or in a nestbox. Extra nests are not always wasted, as males are often polygamous and have several females in different nests.

EGGS   5–8 usually, although large clutches of up to 16 have been known. The eggs are glossy, white with a few spots of black or reddish brown at the larger end. .67 x .5in:17.6 x 13.3mm. Incubation, by the female alone, takes 14–17 days, and fledging 16–18 days.

BREEDING SEASON   April onwards. Single or double-brooded.

Dartford Warbler

SIZE   5in:12.5cm.

DESCRIPTION   Small, rare warbler taking its name from Dartford Heath in Kent where the species was first identified. The male has dark brown upperparts, reddish underparts and grey head, with a long tail that is frequently held cocked over its back. The female (and juveniles) are much paler. The eye is red-ringed.

SONG/CALL   Chattering, warbling song, rather similar to that of the Whitethroat, usually given during a bouncing display flight. Also a harsh metallic 'tchirr', and an abrupt 'Tuc' call note.

RECOGNITION   The Dartford Warbler is resident all year round, but it is now a rare species in Britain, found mainly in Hampshire and Dorset, Sussex and Surrey, and a few heaths in southern England. Sadly it is no longer found at Dartford. It is a bird of specialized habitat – heather-clad heathland with plenty of gorse – and this has contributed to its decline as much of such land has been 'improved' for more intensive farming. Severe winters also take their toll as Dartford Warblers are mainly insectivorous and food is hard to find in bad weather. It is a bird with skulking habits, disappearing quickly into cover, and difficult to observe closely. Its flight tends to be weak, with rapidly whirring wings and much tail-bobbing.

FOOD   Mainly insects and their larvae, also spiders, and blackberries in autumn.

NEST   The Dartford Warbler nests in low, dense cover, like gorse. The female does most of the building, making a neat cup of grasses and moss with wool, plant down and spiders cocoons, lined with roots, fine grass and hair, placed low down near the ground. The male bird often constructs rather insubstantial 'cock' nests, but these are rarely used.

EGGS   3–4, occasionally up to 6, glossy white eggs finely speckled with dark or greyish brown markings. .75 x .55in:18.6 x 13.9mm. Incubation, mainly by the female, takes 12–13 days, and fledging 11–13 days.

BREEDING   SEASON From   mid-April   onwards.   Double,   sometimes treble-brooded.

Garden Warbler

SIZE   5½in:14cm.

DESCRIPTION   A small plumpish brown bird with a greyish tinge, slightly darker on the wings, and with light buff underparts. It has no real distinguishing features save for a rather short stubby bill compared to other members of the Warbler family.

SONG/CALL   A warbling song, rather similar in a way to that of the Blackcap, but softer and lacking the higher-pitched notes, and usually longer too. Also a 'check-check' call and a 'churr'.

RECOGNITION   The Garden Warbler is a summer visitor to Britain, found fairly widely in England and Wales, but scarcer in Scotland and rather rare in Ireland. It is an inconspicuous little bird, easily overlooked, and is chiefly identified by its sustained and beautiful song, usually given from the cover of undergrowth, or bushy scrubland, with plenty of brambles and ground cover, or overgrown hedges. It is a shy, retiring bird, keeping under cover for much of the time, but sometimes darting out to catch insects on the wing in the manner of a Flycatcher.

FOOD   Mainly insects, moths, spiders, also caterpillar larvae, and berries in autumn.

NEST   A cup of dried grasses and moss and fine twigs, lined with fine grasses, hair and rootlets usually situated in a low shrub or tree, or an overgrown hedge or bramble patch. Both sexes build the nest.

EGGS   4–5, sometimes 3–7, glossy whitish eggs with variable tinges of buff, green or pink, and irregularly blotched with dark spots of reddish brown or purple. .75 x .6in:18.6 x 14.8mm. Incubation, by both parent birds, takes 11–12 days, and fledging 9–10 days.

BREEDING SEASON Late May or early June. Single, sometimes double-brooded.

Grasshopper Warbler

SIZE   5in:13cm.

DESCRIPTION   A dull brown little bird with strongly streaked upperparts, and lightly streaked buffish-white underparts, and graduated rounded tail with faint barring on the feathers.

SONG/CALL   A carrying song consisting of a repeated churring of one high note, reminiscent of the winding of a fishing reel, and continuing for some minutes at a time. Also a quiet 'twitt' or 'pitt', produced in a chatter when alarmed.

RECOGNITION   A summer visitor with very skulking habits, keeping well concealed in undergrowth in hedgerows, marshes and heathland and reedbeds. It is farily widely distributed throughout the British Isles, but usually keeps within dense cover, and is usually identified by its song with its distinctive 'fishing-reel' sound. It arrives in Britain about mid-April and remains here until September when it migrates back to its winter quarters in Africa.

FOOD   Insects and their larvae, also spiders and woodlice.

NEST   Both sexes build the nest, a cup of dead leaves, plant stems and grasses, lined with fine grasses and hair, sometimes with feathers also. It is usually situated on the ground or close to ground level, in thick undergrowth, rushes or long grass – constant comings and goings by the parent birds often leave a discernable flight path through the vegetation by the end of the breeding season.

EGGS   6, sometimes 4–7, glossy white eggs, densely speckled with purplish or lilac spots, sometimes so thickly covered that the whole egg shell is tinted, sometimes with a dark cap of speckles at the larger end. .7 x .54in:18.1 x 13.8mm. Both sexes share the incubation of the eggs, which takes 13–15 days. Fledging takes 10–12 days.

BREEDING SEASON   Early May to June, depending on climate. Single or double-brooded.

Whitethroat

SIZE 5½in:14cm.

DESCRIPTION Small warbler with brown upperparts rusty-coloured wings, grey head, white throat, pale pink breast fading to white belly, with narrow white eye-ring and white outer tail feathers. The female is similar, except that her head is brown. Legs and feet pale horn colour.

SONG/CALL A vigorous chattering song, given during flight or from a prominent perch. Call notes – a scolding 'tcharr', and a quiet 'wheet, wheet, whit-whit-whit' ending hurriedly.

RECOGNITION The Whitethroat is a summer visitor to Britain, arriving in April and departing September. It is widely distributed throughout most of the British Isles except the far north of Scotland and its outlying islands, but numbers have declined drastically in recent years, due it is thought to drought in its wintering grounds in Africa. The population is now increasing again, but is still well below previous levels. Favoured habitats are heaths and commons, woodland edges, hedgerows and conifer plantations. The Whitethroat is a restless bird, darting in and out of cover with raised crest and cocked tail, but also tends to skulk within vegetation, and may be overlooked when silent.

FOOD Insects and their larvae, ants and spiders, fruit and berries in autumn.

NEST The male Whitethroat builds several rudementary nests of grasses for the female to choose from, and then she lines the chosen one with roots and hair (usually dark) plant down or wool. Occasionally all the male's nests are rejected and the female builds her own. The nest is usually situated in a low shrub, or amongst dense vegetation, about a foot above ground.

EGGS 4–5 usually, occasionally 3–7, glossy pale blue or green eggs, very finely speckled with light green or olive spots or dark grey blotches. .75 x .55in:18.6 x 13.9mm. Incubation, by both sexes, takes 11–13 days, and fledging 10–12 days.

BREEDING SEASON Begins in May. Usually double-brooded.

Ortolan Bunting

SIZE 6½in:16.5cm.

DESCRIPTION An attractive brownish finch from the Continent. The male has brown upperparts streaked black, orange underparts, greenish head and breast and yellow throat with moustachial stripe, and white outer tail feathers. The female is duller and darker, with heavier streaking. Both sexes have yellow eye-ring giving 'spectacle' effect and pink bill.

PLATE 11

Dartford Warbler (scale 1:2.3)

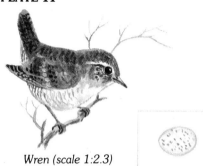

Wren (scale 1:2.3)

Grasshopper Warbler (scale 1:2.3)

Garden Warbler (scale 1:2.3)

Ortolan Bunting (scale 1:2.3)

Whitethroat (scale 1:2.3)

FRANCES FRY.

SONG/CALL   A 'zit' and a louder 'tseu' call. A rather melancholy song, consisting of several 'tseu' notes ending with the last note at a different pitch from the preceding ones – either higher or lower.

RECOGNITION   The Ortolan Bunting is a regular passage migrant from the Continent, seen at spring or autumn along the southern coasts of England, north Norfolk, and at Fair Isle. Numbers are small, with single birds most often observed, but small flocks are sometimes recorded. It is usually seen in open country with low vegetation, agricultural land, sometimes hedges and gardens, but most frequently on plough, where its colours blend into the earth making it easy to overlook. It is a quiet secretive bird, quick to fly away when even slightly disturbed.

FOOD   Mainly seeds, but some insects are also taken, and snails.

The Ortolan Bunting does not breed in Britain or Ireland.

Short-eared Owl

SIZE 15in:38cm

DESCRIPTION Mottled brown owl with short ear-tufts. Upperparts tawny-brown streaked with dark brown, underparts buff and boldly streaked with dark brown. Prominent facial disc with dark markings around the pale yellow eyes, and long barred wings. The short ear-tufts are inconspicuous, and the expression is fierce.

CALL A harsh, barking 'kee-kaw', and a triple-hoot of 'boo-boo-boo', usually given during flight.

RECOGNITION The Short-eared Owl is resident, and fairly well distributed throughout the British Isles except for the far north of Scotland and the west of Ireland. It hunts at dusk or in daylight in open countryside, quartering the ground rather like a Harrier, and it is occasionally mistaken for a female Hen Harrier at a distance. Unlike most owls it perches on the ground a lot of the time. It has a slow display flight, low and rolling, and occasional wingclaps. Its favourite habitat is moorland hills or marshes, but in winter it extends its territory to include arable fields.

FOOD Mainly field voles, but many other rodents are taken, also young rabbits and small birds.

NEST A shallow hollow in the ground serves as a nest, with no lining, in open country sheltered by grass, reeds or heather.

EGGS 4–8 usually, sometimes up to 14 if food is very plentiful. White and non-glossy, the eggs are laid at 2 day intervals. 1.6 x 1.25in:40.2 x 31.8mm. Incubation, by the female alone and beginning with the first egg, takes 24–28 days, and fledgling about 24 days. The young leave the nest early before they can fly, at 12–17 days, flying about 10 days later.

BREEDING SEASON Usually begins in April. Normally single-brooded, but may be double-brooded when food is plentiful.

Little Owl

SIZE 8½in:22cm

DESCRIPTION Small, squat, flat-headed owl, with dark brown upperparts spotted and barred with white, and whitish underparts streaked with brown. prominent facial disc with dark area around the yellow eyes. The flattened head and fierce yellow eyes give the bird a cross 'frowning' expression.

CALL A plaintive 'kiu' is the most common call, frequently heard by day. Also a barking 'werro'. When nesting the 'kiu' note may be repeated to form a song.

RECOGNITION The Little Owl is the smallest owl resident in Britain, and well distributed throughout England, Wales and Scotland. It is not found in Ireland, or out-lying Scottish islands. It is often seen in daylight, perching on fences or telegraph poles with upright stance and suspicious stare. If alarmed it will bob and move from side to side. It has low, rapid, undulating flight, somewhat similar to a woodpecker. Originally introduced from Europe in the nineteenth century it adapted well, and is now found in many different habitats, including farmland, open country, hedges, etc., even in towns.

FOOD   A wide variety of prey, ranging from small rodents to birds, even small rabbits sometimes, insects and worms. Most hunting takes place at dawn or dusk.

NEST   An unlined hole in a tree (pollarded willows are favoured) or wall, an old building or a hayrick, sometimes in a rabbit burrow. Man-made owl nest-boxes may also be used. Many sites are used on successive years.

EGGS   3–5 usually, sometimes 2–8, non-glossy white eggs. 1.45 x 1.29in; 35.6 x 29.6mm. Incubation, starting with the first egg, and by the female alone, takes 28–29 days, and fledgling about 26 days. The male brings food at first, later both parent birds tend the young.

BREEDING SEASON   Mid-April to May. Usually single-brooded, but occasionally a second brood is reared.

Long-eared Owl

SIZE   14in:36cm

DESCRIPTION   Mottled brown owl with long ear-tufts. Upperparts brown or grey-brown streaked with dark brown, underparts buff streaked dark brown with fine cross-barring. Orange eyes, prominent facial disc edged with black, and two long ear-tufts which can be raised conspiciously or held flat against the head. Long wings, and overall slender shape.

CALL   A low, moaning 'oo-oo-oo', usually given only during the breeding season. Occasional yelping or wailing notes. Outside the breeding season it is normally a silent bird.

RECOGNITION   The Long-eared Owl is the only British owl with long ear-tufts, and when raised these provide instant recognition. It is a resident bird, breeding throughout the British Isles but nowhere near so widespread as the Tawny Owl. It is a secretive bird, preferring the cover of coniferous woodland, although deciduous woods are also used. It is the most common owl in Ireland. Because it hunts mainly at night, and keeps well under cover by day, the Long-eared Owl is usually identified by its moaning call, although during the breeding season it may be seen on a display flight over the tree trops, or indulging in vigorous wing-clapping.

FOOD   Small mammals and birds, particularly mice and voles. Birds as large as a Jay may sometimes be taken.

BROWN BIRDS (speckled breast)

LAND BIRDS

PLATE 12

Short-eared Owl (scale 1:3.5)

Little Owl (scale 1:3.5)

*Long-eared Owl
(scale 1:3.5)*

Tawny Owl (scale 1:3.5)

FRANCES FRY

NEST   The Long-eared Owl usually takes over the old nest of another bird, such as a Crow or Magpie, or a Squirrel's drey. Sometimes, if an old nest is not available, the original owners are forceably evicted by the Owls. Alternatively a hollow in the ground may sometimes be used.

EGGS   4–5, occasionally 3–8, moderately glossy white eggs are laid on alternate days. Sometimes the surface is slightly pitted. 1.6 x 1.3in; 41.0 x 32.7mm. Incubation, normally by the female and beginning with the first egg, takes 25–30 days, and fledging 23–24 days. If disturbed at the nest the young adopt a defensive posture with raised ear-tufts and half-spread wings, and give a cry like an un-oiled hinge.

BREEDING SEASON   Starts in March or early April. Usually single-brooded, but sometimes double-brooded.

SIZE   15in:38cm

DESCRIPTION   A round-headed owl, with bulky rounded body. Upperparts brown or grey-brown barred with black, underparts buff-brown streaked with arrows of dark black-brown. Dark eyes, and prominent facial disc with 'eye-brows' extending from the eyes upwards. Basic colour can vary from chestnut brown to grey.

CALL   A shrill 'ke-wick', and a deep 'who-hoo-hoo', followed after an interval by a tremulous 'oo-oo-oo-oo'. The traditional 'twit-twoo' owl call of fiction is produced when two Tawny Owls answer each other.

RECOGNITION   The Tawny Owl is the most common British owl, resident, and widely distributed throughout most of the country, but absent from Ireland and out-lying Scottish islands. It is strictly a nocturnal bird, hunting only by night on silent wings, but may sometimes be seen during the day roosting in a tree, close-up to the trunk. The mottled and barred plumage provides good camouflage, and often hides the bird, sparing it the vociferous attentions of small songbirds should they discover its daytime roost. Its habitat includes woodland, parks and large gardens, and it can even be found in towns and cities where there are suitable trees or buildings to provide roosting places. The hooting call is frequently heard in the autumn when territories are being established prior to the breeding season.

FOOD   Small rodents, particularly field mice, voles and shrews, also small birds and fish. Urban Tawny Owls prey on House Sparrows as well.

NEST   A shallow unlined hollow serves as a nest, usually in a natural hole in a tree or rock crevice, or sometimes the old nest of a Crow or Magpie is used. Special nest-boxes for owls are also used.

EGGS   2–4 usually, occasionally up to 7, rounded white eggs are laid, at intervals of 2–7 days. 1.8 x 1.5in:46.7 x 39.1mm. Incubation, by the female alone and starting with the first egg, takes 28–30 days, and the young are ready to leave the nest at 32–37 days. When food is short larger nestlings survive at the expense of the smaller ones.

BREEDING SEASON   Starts in March or April. Single-brooded.

The Tawny Owl is also listed under BROWN/GREY BIRDS (speckled breast).

SIZE   7in:18cm

DESCRIPTION   Brown and buff coloured bird with heavily streaked upperparts and breast. Longish tail with conspicuous white outer feathers, and prominent rounded crest. The legs and feet are pale, with extra-long hind claws.

SONG/CALL   A high musical warbling song, uttered in flight while hovering or ascending, and sustained for a considerable period. Also a clear 'chir-up' call. The Skylark sings throughout the year to some extent, but most prolonged singing occurs from February onwards until June, and again in the autumn. It sings at dawn, giving rise to the old saying 'up with the lark'.

RECOGNITION   Somewhat surprisingly for a bird with sky in its name the Skylark spends much of its time on the ground, on moors, fields, marshes or sand dunes. It is one of the most widespread British resident birds, found in most open landscapes. On land it has a rather crouching walking gait, and its flight is strong and undulating. Skylarks often form sizeable flocks when searching for food. Its mottled plumage merges into the vegetation, and the lovely song given from soaring heights is often the best identification.

FOOD   Weed seeds and cereal crops, insects and their larvae, spiders and slugs.

NEST   The Skylark is a ground-nesting bird, choosing a slight depression in the land sheltered by a tuft of grass or heather. The female usually builds the nest, constructing a shallow cup of grasses, lined with finer grass and hair. In very open sites the outside of the nest is surrounded by small pebbles.

EGGS   3–4 usually, sometimes more – up to 7, fairly glossy greyish-buff eggs, heavily spotted overall with brown or olive markings. Sometimes the markings are heavy enough to mark the original ground colour of the eggs. .94 x .68in:23.8 x 17.1mm. Incubation, by the female only, takes about 11 days, and fledgling about 10 days. The young leave the nest before they can fly, and if danger threatens hide by crouching motionless. Parent birds will feign injury to draw predators away from the nest or the young.

BREEDING SEASON   Starts in April. Double- or treble-brooded.

SIZE   6in:15cm

DESCRIPTION   Small brown and buff bird with streaked back and breast. A first glance rather similar in appearance to the Skylark, but there are several important differences, namely short tail without white sides, and conspicious white eye-stripes joining on nape, and finer bill. It also has a black and white mark just below the bend of the wing.

SONG/CALL   A very melodious song consisting of short phrases interspersed with trilling, but rather less powerful and less sustained than the Skylark's. Also a liquid 'toolooeet'. The song is given in flight, or from a perch in a tree or shrub.

RECOGNITION   This attractive resident songster is unfortunately a declining species in Britain, being found usually only in southern England, and occasionally in Wales. It likes heathland habitat, or grassland with scattered trees and bushes which provide suitable song-posts. Loss of habitat may have caused the recent decline in numbers. Like the Skylark the beautiful song, given while ascending or hovering in its circling flight. draws attention to the ground-loving Woodlark. The Woodlark tends to be solitary in its habits.

FOOD   Insects and their larvae, and various seeds in autumn.

NEST   Both sexes help build the nest, which is situated on bare ground, or sheltered by a tuft of grass or vegetation. A substantial cup is made of grasses and moss, with an inner lining of fine grass or hair.

EGGS   3–4 usually, sometimes up to 6, moderately glossy buff-grey eggs, profusely speckled with brown or purplish spots. .83 x .63in:21.6 x 16.4mm. Incubation, by the female alone, takes 12–16 days, and fledgling 11–12 days. The young cannot fly when they leave the nest, and crouch motionless to avoid danger.

BREEDING SEASON   Starts in March. Double- or sometimes treble-brooded.

Song Thrush

SIZE   9in:23cm

DESCRIPTION   Upperparts brown, pale underparts with lines of clear spots. The breast is pale orange-yellow fading to white on the belly.

SONG/CALL   A flute-like, musical song with short varied phrases repeated 3 or 4 times with brief pauses inbetween. The Song Thrush is a renowned songster, and this ability is reflected in its country names of 'Mavis' or 'Throstle'. It also has a soft 'sip' flight call, and a loud 'thuck' alarm call.

RECOGNITION   The Song Thrush is a familiar resident bird, widespread throughout the British Isles, with comparatively tame habits. Habitat includes woodland, hedgerows, parks, and it is a frequent visitor to gardens and birdtables. Garden lawns are good hunting ground for worms, and rockeries or paths provide 'anvils' for the Song Thrush to use to break the shells of snails, beating them against the hard surface to extract the snail. The Song Thrush often stands upright and motionless looking for signs of a worm, then darting upon it and drawing it from its hole. The lovely song is usually given from a prominent perch, particularly at sunrise and sunset.

PLATE 13

Woodlark (scale 2:5.8)

Skylark (scale 2:5.8)

Song Thrush (scale 2:5.8)

Redwing (scale 2:5.8)

FOOD   Worms, slugs, insects and their larvae, ants, spiders and snails. Soft fruits are often raided when in season, and elder, holly or yew berries provide autumn food. Birdtable scraps are also appreciated.

NEST   The female builds the nest, a deep cup made of roots, grass and twigs and leaves with the inside plastered with mud or cow-dung. The nest is situated fairly low in a tree or bush, usually close to the trunk, or in ivy or other vegetation growing over a tree or building.

EGGS   4–6, sometimes 3–9, slightly glossy light blue eggs sparingly speckled with black or purplish blotches. 1.0 x .78in:27.4 x 20.8mm. Incubation, by the female alone, takes 11–15 days, and fledgling 12–16 days.

BREEDING SEASON   From March until June. Double- or treble-brooded.

Redwing

SIZE   8½in:22cm

DESCRIPTION   Rather like a small Song Thrush with distinctive red patch under the wings which gives the bird its name. Brown upperparts, cream supercilium (eye-brow) and moustachial streak, and streaked (not spotted) breast are other distinguishing features.

SONG/CALL   A thin 'see-ip' flight note, an abrupt 'chup' and a harsh 'chittuc' call. The song consists of a repeated phrase of 4–6 flute-like notes, rising and falling, but lacking the variety and strength of the Song Thrush.

RECOGNITION   The Redwing is a common winter visitor to Britain, with large flocks of birds from northern Europe arriving each autumn. Much shyer than the Song Thrush, preferring open country or woodland to garden environments. Redwings are gregarious birds, flocking together or with Fieldfares to seek food in hedgerows and grassland. Feeding posture is similar to the Song Thrush, with the same upright stance. The red wing patch is the most obvious means of identification, but small size and flocking habits also help to distinguish the Redwing from other Thrushes. In recent years small but significant numbers have become resident all year round in parts of Scotland and norther England, and breeding has been established since the 1960s.

FOOD   Worms, insects and their larvae, slugs, snails, and a large variety of berries.

NEST   The female builds the nest, a thick cup of grass, fine twigs, moss and lichen, usually lined with an inner cup of mud, this in turn lined with fine grass. Usually situated in a tree, close to the trunk, or in a shrub, or in creeper on trees or buildings, or in a bank.

EGGS   4–6, sometimes 2–8, glossy blue-green eggs, prousely marked overall with reddish-brown speckles. 1.0 x .70in: 27.1 x 19.1mm. Incubation, by the female alone, takes 11–15 days, and fledgling 10–15 days.

BREEDING SEASON From April or May onwards. Usually double-brooded.

Tree Pipit

SIZE 6in:15cm

DESCRIPTION Sparrow-sized bird with speckled breast, superficially rather similar to the Meadow Pipit, but distinguished from it by warmer brown colouring, and pale legs and feet with short hind claws. Upperparts warm olive-brown streaked black, underparts warm buff shading to white, clearly streaked with black. Cream chin and supercilium. More stocky in build than the Meadow Pipit, and with slightly longer tail.

SONG/CALL A rather hoarse 'teez' call, and a musical song given during display flight – a trill terminating in a 'seea-seea-seea' as the flight ends in a parachute-like descent, returning to a prominent perch.

RECOGNITION The Tree Pipit is a summer visitor to Britain, fairly well distributed throughout England, Wales and Scotland, but not found in Ireland. It is less a ground-dwelling bird than the Meadow Pipit, and frequently takes refuge in trees. Habitat includes heathland and open woods with plentiful growth of small trees. The Tree Pipit's song is often given from a perch like a telegraph pole or fence post; or the bird starts its display flight from such a perch, returning to it afterwards.

FOOD Mainly insects and their larvae, also spiders, beetles or grasshoppers, and some seeds in autumn.

NEST The Tree Pipit is a ground-nesting bird, constructing a large cup made of dried grasses and plant material, lined with fine plant material or hair. The nest is usually well hidden beneath a tussock of grass or bracken.

EGGS 3–5 usually, sometimes up to 7, glossy eggs, very variable in colour, ranging from pale grey to buff, pink of green, finely speckled with darker shades of brown or grey. Sometimes the markings are so profuse that the whole egg takes on a darker hue. .82 x 60in:20.8 x 15.6mm. Incubation, by the female alone, takes 11–15 days, and fledging 12–14 days.

BREEDING SEASON Starts in mid-May. Often double-brooded.

Meadow Pipit

SIZE 5¾in:14.5cm

DESCRIPTION Rather like a smaller Sparrow-sized, streaked thrush, the Meadow Pipit has olive-brown upperparts streaked with black, and buff-white breast and underparts streaked with dark brown. The outer-tail feather are white, and it has a white supercilium. Legs and feet are brownish, with long hind-claws.

SONG/CALL A 'tseep' or a 'tissup' call, repeated rapidly when alarmed. The song, usually given during display flight, is a trill of 'tseeps', and ends with a parachute-like descent to the ground.

RECOGNITION The Meadow Pipit is a common resident British bird, widely distributed throughout the country, but especially plentiful in moorland areas. Numbers increase in winter when Scandinavian and Icelandic birds arrive to join the residents. In open country it is often the most common bird, and in winter its range also extends to coastal areas, riverbanks and sewage works. It is a gregarious bird, and large flocks are frequently seen on moors and during migration.

FOOD Mainly insects, but also spiders, worms or plant seeds.

NEST The Meadow Pipit is a ground nesting bird, building a neat cup of dry grasses and plant material, lined with hair or plant fibre. The nest is usually well concealed from view, under cover of a clump of heather or grass.

EGGS 3–5 usually, sometimes up to 7, glossy eggs of grey or brown hue, finely mottled with darker brown or grey. Sometimes the markings are so profuse that the whole egg takes on a darker shade. .78 x .57in:19.8 x 14.6mm. Incubation, by the female alone, takes 11–15 days, and fledging about 14–16 days. The young leave the nest early, at 10–14 days, before they can fly well.

BREEDING SEASON Starts in April. Usually double-brooded, but occasionally three broods are raised if food is plentiful.

Twite

SIZE 5¼in:13.5cm.

DESCRIPTION Small brown finch with rather Linnet-like appearance. Dull brown-buff upperparts streaked with black and brown, and lighter brown underparts with slightly streaked breast. White wing and tail flashed noticeable in flight. The male has a dark pinkish rump, the female buff streaked black. Short, thick bill.

SONG/CALL A nasel 'chweet' call, and constant twittering in flight, rather morre metallic than the Linnet's song, and given at a slower pace.

RECOGNITION Some Twites are resident all year round (mainly in Scotland) but many birds seen in coastal areas of England and Ireland are winter visitors from Scandinavia, arriving in October and staying until March or April. In Scotland, the Twite takes the place of the more southerly-based Linnet, but in some areas the two species inter-mingle and form mixed colonies. Twites have the bounding flight typical of many small finches, and a hopping gait on the ground. Heather moors and grassland are favoured habitats, and coastal areas in winter. They are gregarious birds, forming flocks with other finches to search for food. In spring courtship display consists of the male opening and drooping its wings to show off its pink rump.

FOOD Weed and grass seeds, cereals, seeds of rushes and salt-marsh plants, and insects for feeding the young.

NEST　The Twite's nest is a bulky cup of grasses and plant stems, lined with wool, hair and feathers. The female builds the nest, which is situated on the ground, amongst heather or rough herbage, or in a hollow of a bank or hole in a wall.

EGGS　5–6 usually, sometimes 4–7, non-glossy pale blue eggs, spotted or scrawled with dark brown or purplish markings. Sometimes the markings are largely confined to the larger end of the egg. .7 x .5in:17.3 x 12.8mm. Incubation, by the female alone, takes 12–13 days, and fledging about 15 days.

BREEDING SEASON　Starts in April or May. Single- or double-brooded.

Corn Bunting

SIZE　7in:18cm

DESCRIPTION　Predominantly buff coloured, chunky bird, with large head and stout bill. Upperparts buff-brown, underparts buff, with bold streaks of dark brown, and a blurred moustachial streak. Flesh-coloured legs and feet, with a yellowish tinge.

SONG/CALL　A 'quit' call note, a rasping 'zeep', and a song reminiscent of a jangling bunch of keys.

RECOGNITION　The Corn Bunting is the largest member of the bunting family, and the heavy build and lack of white in its tail are the best means of identification. It is resident all year round, and found in open, arable country throughout most of Britain, although numbers are low in Wales and Ireland. It has a heavy, slow flight, and often dangles its legs when flying. The song is usually given from a prominent post, with head held back. From most of the year Corn Buntings are solitary birds, but in winter they flock together searching for food. Farmland, cornfields, hedgerows and grassland are all favoured habitats, but always somewhere that offers a selection of suitable song-posts.

FOOD　Weed seeds, grasses, cereal crops, berries in season, and wild fruits. Insects are also taken during the breeding season to feed the young.

NEST　A loosely constructed cup of grass, lined with finer grass, roots and hair. Sometimes a ground-nester, with the rest hidden in grass or herbage, sometimes in thick bushes or hedges at heights up to 5ft from the ground.

EGGS　4–6 usually, but numbers can vary greatly, from 1–7. The eggs are only slightly glossy, white tinted pale blue, purple or buff, and very finely speckled with grey and bolder blotches of black or purplish-brown. The markings are often much more concentrated at the larger end of the egg. 1in x .7in:23.3. x 17.8mm. Incubation, by the female alone, takes 12–14 days, and fledging 9–12 days, with the young leaving the nest before they can fly. The male is often polygamous, leaving his various females to tend the young on their own.

BREEDING SEASON　From April onwards. Single- or double-brooded, and occasionally treble-brooded when food is plentiful.

LAND BIRDS

PLATE 14

Tree Pipit (scale 1:2.3)

Meadow Pipit (scale 1:2.3)

Twite (scale 1:2.3)

Corn Bunting (scale 1:2.3)

FRANCES FRY.

Quail

SIZE 7in:18cm

DESCRIPTION The smallest British game-bird. Sandy-brown plumage, with strong streaks of black and white, dark brown crown with cream stripe down centre and cream stripe above the eye. The male has a black chin and throat band.

SONG/CALL The male has a 'whic, whic-ic' call with the accent on the first syllable; the female has a wheezing 'queep-queep'. The Quail's voice tends to have deceptive ventriloqual qualities, and may be heard at night, but perhaps most frequently at dawn or dusk.

RECOGNITION The Quail is like a diminutive partridge, dumpy and short-tailed, often very difficult to spot as its favourite habitat is cornfields or rough grassland, wasteland or dunes, where it can hide secretively in the vegetation. Its presence is usually first indicated by its distinctive call. Quails are very difficult birds to flush, particularly in the breeding season, and if successfully roused will fly low over the ground. Its flight is slower, and usually much briefer in duration than the Partridge's. The Quail is a summer visitor, arriving from the mediterranean in May and leaving in September. It is rather scarcely distributed in Britain, with most birds concentrated in southern and central England, particularly chalkland areas.

FOOD Grass seeds, cereal seeds, and some insects.

NEST The female makes a shallow hollow in the ground, which she lines with grass or plant material. The male is polygamous, and leaves all nesting and rearing duties to the female.

EGGS A large clutch of 7–12, sometimes up to 18 eggs are laid, glossy cream-yellow, usually heavily speckled or blotched, with red-brown or chocolate brown markings. 1.1 x .9in:30.4 x 23.0mm. Incubation, by the female alone, takes 16–21 days. The young are precocial, ready to leave the nest a few hours after hatching, and feather rapidly, flying at about 19 days.

BREEDING SEASON May to June. Usually single-brooded, but occasionally double-brooded.

Corncrake

SIZE 10½in:27cm

DESCRIPTION A dumpy, yet slim bird with buff plumage barred and streaked with chestnut and black, greyish head and breast. Flanks and under-tail coverts are barred with chestnut, and chestnut wings are conspicuous in flight. Legs and feet yellowish, as is thick, stubby bill. Resembles large buff-coloured Moorhen.

SONG/CALL A grating 'crerrp-crerrp' call, frequently repeated. Calls by night as well as day.

59

RECOGNITION The Corncrake is a summer immigrant to Britain, becoming increasingly rare as modern agricultural methods destroy its habitat of moist grassland and meadows. Mechanical harvesting of hay crops early in the season conflicted with the Corncrake breeding season and also contributed to its decline. It still breeds in small numbers in England and Wales, but is most plentiful in Scotland and Ireland. it is a secretive, skulking bird solitary by nature, well-camouflaged with its barred plumage, and is more often identified by voice than sighting. It hides determinedly in long grass, refusing to flush if disturbed, and is very difficult to observe. Sometimes known as Land Rail.

FOOD Insects, worms and snails, also weed and other seeds.

NEST A pad of grasses forms a nest for the Corncrake, hidden away in hay crops or other vegetation.

EGGS 8–12, sometimes 6–14, greenish-grey eyes, blotched with red-brown or purple. 1.45 x 1.1in:37.4 x 26.8mm. Incubation, usually by the female alone, takes 15–18 days. The young are precocial, and leave the nest soon after hatching, being fed by the parent birds for 3–4 days then feeding themselves. They are fully fledged by 7–8 weeks.

BREEDING SEASON May or June. Usually single-brooded, but occasionally double-brooded.

Curlew

SIZE 21–23in:53–58cm

DESCRIPTION The largest European Wader, easily identified by size, long down-curving bill. Buffish-brown plumage, streaked and mottled with darker brown, with whitish rump and long slender legs.

SONG/CALL A very distinctive 'coor-lee', which gives the species its name, and a bubbling song given in flight, particularly in spring, although the Curlew sings almost all the year.

RECOGNITION The Curlew is resident throughout most of Britain, with a migrant population from the Continent swelling numbers in the autumn. Most waders are coastal birds, feeding on crustaceans founds in estuaries and similar territory which they obtain by probing in the mud with their long bills, but the Curlew is often found inland in dry areas. Curlews are gregarious birds, and form large flocks when feeding. Grassland, heather moors, arable fields, marshes and sand-dunes are all favoured habitats, and in winter estuaries and shorelines also. Flocks seen in flight fly high, in lines or chevron formation, with a measured gull-like beat.

FOOD Lugworms, fish, molluscs, crustaceans, insects and their larvae, also berries and grass-seeds when available.

NEST The Curlew breeds in open country such as moorland, grassland or dunes. A shallow hollow serves as a nest, with a lining of plant material.

EGGS 3,4 or 5 eggs are laid, oval to pyriform shape, glossy olive-green in colour spotted or blotched with various shades of brown or purple. The markings are usually very plentiful. 2.75 x 1.9in:54.7 x 37.3mm. Incubation, by both sexes but mainly by the female, takes 22–24 days. The young are precocial, ready to leave the nest soon after hatching, and are tended by both parents to begin with, but later by the male alone. They can fly at about 5–6 weeks.

BREEDING SEASON April or May. Single-brooded.

Stone Curlew

SIZE 16in:41cm

DESCRIPTION Long-legged, ground-dwelling bird with hunched posture. Normally classed with Waders, but distinguished from them by round-headed appearance, and large yellow eyes. Upperparts sand-brown streaked with black, underparts buff-white streaked with brown. Short, stout yellow and black bill, and pale yellow legs and feet. Two white wing-bars show up clearly during flight.

SONG/CALL A thin, curlew-like 'coo-ree', or a higher 'kee-rrr-eee' with the middle syllable dropping lower. The evening is the time when the Stone Curlew is most vocal.

RECOGNITION The Stone Curlew is the only British member of the bird family with the distinctive name 'thick-knees', and although allied to the Waders it prefers dry, open ground such as heaths and downland, or areas of ploughed land, or coastal shingle. It is a summer visitor to Britain, and is becoming increasingly rare as more and more of its habitat is lost. Intensive farming was responsible for some lost habitat, but the startling decrease of the rabbit population in the 1950s due to myxomatosis was another cause, as without the close grazing from rabbits scrubland rushes encroached on the open grassland favoured by the Stone Curlew. It is now mainly confined to southern and eastern England in chalky areas. It runs in a furtive manner on the ground, with head low and body hunched, and when resting flattens itself to the ground as much as possible laying its head down low to hide. It is often active at night, when its mournful call can sound quite eerie. Stone Curlews form flocks in autumn prior to migration.

FOOD Insects and their larvae, worms and snails.

NEST A shallow scrape on bare ground, unlined save for a scattering of plant debris or rabbit droppings.

EGGS 2, sometimes 3, slightly glossy buff-cream eggs speckled, spotted or blotched with dark brown or purple-grey. 2.1 x 1.5in:53.8 x 38.4mm. Eggs laid on alternate days. Incubation, by both sexes, takes 25–27 days. Young are precocial, leaving the nest soon after hatching. Independent in about 6 weeks.

BREEDING SEASON Begins April or May. Single-brooded usually, but occasionally double-brooded.

Other brown birds which are fully described under different sections.

REED BUNTING This bird is described under BLACK-HEADED BIRDS.

The category of BROWN BIRDS is a large one, with many colour variations, and the two sections covering BROWN AND WHITE BIRDS and GREY/BROWN BIRDS are also wide-ranging, but if the bird you seek does not appear in any of the BROWN groupings then it may be the female of another coloured species. A list of such BROWN coloured females is given below:–

FEMALE
CAPERCAILLIE
BLACK GROUSE
BLACKBIRD
BLACK REDSTART
All described under BLACK BIRDS

RING OUZEL
PIED FLYCATCHER
Both described under BLACK AND WHITE BIRDS

HEN HARRIER
MONTAGUE'S HARRIER
MERLIN
All described under GREY BIRDS

WHEATEAR
Described under BLUE/GREY BIRDS

REDSTART
WHINCHAT
STONECHAT
LINNET
All described under BIRDS WITH RED/ORANGE ON HEAD, OR ROSY BREASTED

PHEASANT
LADY AMHERST'S PHEASANT
GOLDEN PHEASANT
BLUETHROAT
All described under BRIGHT COLOURED BIRDS

JUVENILES
CUCKOO
Described under GREY BIRDS

ROBIN
Described under BIRDS WITH RED ON HEAD OR BREAST

BLUETHROAT
Described under BRIGHT COLOURED BIRDS

BROWN BIRDS (speckled breast)

PLATE 15

LAND BIRDS

Corncrake (scale 1:3.5)

Quail (scale 1:3.5)

Stone Curlew (scale 1:5.8)

FRANCES FRY

Curlew (scale 1:5.8)

Lesser Whitethroat

SIZE 5½in:14cm

DESCRIPTION An unobtrusive little warbler, with grey upperparts, white throat, and pink-buff underparts. Most distinguishing feature is black mask extending from beak through eyes and over ear coverts. Legs and feet are black, and tail has white outer feathers.

SONG/CALL Song starts with a subdued warble followed by a repeated rattling on one note. Call notes similar to the Whitethroat's – a 'tac-tac' and a 'tcharr'.

RECOGNITION The Lesser Whitethroat is a summer visitor to Britain, found mainly in southern and eastern England. It has skulking habits, and is easy to overlook when silent. Habitat includes woodland, hedgerows with tall trees, large gardens and conifer plantations, but it essentially needs good ground cover with dense vegetation or plenty of trees. Like the Whitethroat it is a restless bird, darting in and out of the undergrowth, but quick to return to cover if danger threatens.

FOOD Larvae and eggs of insects, spiders, small worms, and berries in autumn.

NEST A loosely-built cup of dry grass and roots, lined with roots and hair, plant down or wool, or downy catkins. Both sexes build the nest which is usually hidden in dense dark cover, like a thick hedge or shrubby undergrowth. The nest is usually situated low down, about 2–3ft from the ground, occasionally higher.

EGGS 4–6 usually, sometimes 3–7, glossy creamy white eggs, sparingly marked with olive or grey, with most markings tending to be concentrated at the larger end. .70 x .52in:17.6 x 13.1mm. Incubation, by both sexes, takes 10–11 days, and fledging 10–11 days, the young leaving the nest as soon as they can flutter but before they can fly.

BREEDING SEASON May to June. Single-brooded usually, but sometimes double-brooded.

Lapland Bunting

SIZE 6in:15cm

DESCRIPTION A small, ground-loving bird, superficially similar to the Reed Bunting (particularly females and juveniles). The male in summer breeding plumage has black head and breast bordered by white line that extends to form a white eye-stripe. Chestnut nape, brown upperparts streaked black, and whitish underparts streaked black on flanks. Females are duller, with no black on head.

SONG/CALL A 'teeu' and a 'ticky-tick-tick' call, and a short warbling song given in flight rather like the Skylark's.

RECOGNITION   The Lapland Bunting is an arctic bird (as its name suggests) and is mainly seen in Britain as a winter visitor or a passage migrant on the east coast. Recently however small numbers have been recorded as breeding in Scotland. In winter small flocks of Lapland Buntings may be seen on coastal marshes or saltings, and sometimes they may join up with flocks of finches and other buntings, but care is needed in identification as their winter plumage is easily confused with the more common Reed Bunting.

FOOD   Grass seeds and other seeds in winter, insects and their larvae in summer.

NEST   The Lapland Bunting normally breeds on open tundra or similar mountain habitat and the few birds recorded here have been in bare northern terrain. The nest is a cup of grasses, moss and roots placed in a depression in the ground beside a hummock or bank. There is a lining of finer grass, hair and feathers.

EGGS   5–6, sometimes 2–7, glossy, pale greenish eggs, with the ground colour largely obscured by brown mottling. .87 x .57in:20.7 x 14.99mm. Incubation, mainly by the female, takes 10–14 days, and fledging 11–15 days. The young leave the nest at 8–10 days shortly before they can fly.

BREEDING SEASON   End of May to June. Single-brooded.

Tree Sparrow

SIZE   5½in:14cm

DESCRIPTION   Close relation to the House Sparrow, superficially similar in appearance, but distinguished by significant plumage differences. Brown upperparts streaked black, buff-white underparts like House Sparrow, but chestnut crown, much smaller black bib, black 'comma' mark on cheeks and partial white collar. Sexes alike.

SONG/CALL   A sharp 'tek' call note, and a 'chip' or 'chip-tchup'.

RECOGNITION   The Tree Sparrow is the country cousin of the House Sparrow, found in agricultural areas, woodlands, hedgerows, orchards or around cliffs. Although it is resident and quite widely distributed (throughout England and Wales, but rarer in Scotland and Ireland) it is often overlooked or confused with the House Sparrow. Tree Sparrows are gregarious birds, often forming loose colonies, or flocking together with House Sparrows when feeding over stubble-fields. They will vist gardens and bird tables, and sometimes use nestboxes. The Tree Sparrow population seems subject to considerable variations, with rapid increases or decreases in numbers for no obvious reason. The species nearly became extinct in Ireland in 1959–60, but quickly recovered again with 50 colonies recorded in 1966. Overall the population appears to be continuing to expand.

FOOD   Weed seeds and grain, insects and their larvae.

NEST   Both sexes build the nest, which can be cup-shaped or domed according to site. It may be situated in a hole in a tree, cliff or wall, or in a bush or haystack, or in a nestbox. Tree Sparrows sometimes evict Bluetits from their nestboxes and take over their nest. Generally speaking the nest is domed if out in the open, cup-shaped in a hole. Materials include plant stems and twigs, with feathers and down for lining.

EGGS   4–6, although it can vary from 2–9, white eggs heavily blotched with brown. .75 x .57in:19.3 x 14.0mm. Incubation, by both sexes, takes 11–14 days, and fledging 12–14 days.

BREEDING SEASON   Begins in April. Double- or treble-brooded.

Great Grey Shrike

SIZE   9½in:24cm

DESCRIPTION   Grey and white bird, comparable in size to Blackbird, with long tail and undulating flight. Upperparts grey, black mask, black wings with white bar, and pale underparts. The long, rounded tail has black central feathers and white outer feathers. In outline the Shrike resembles a small bird of prey, and its habits are similar too.

SONG/CALL   A warbling song interspersed with harsh notes and occasional mimicry. Also a harsh 'sheck-sheck' alarm call.

RECOGNITION   The Great Grey Shrike is a winter visitor to Britain, seen mainly in the east of the country, particularly the coast. Habitat includes heaths and common land with scattered trees for cover, hedgerows and wooded countryside. The Shrikes lifestyle is similar to a hawks in that it can hover during flight and then swoop down to kill its prey, returning with it to the launching perch. Sometimes the prey (small birds, small animals or large insects) is eaten at once, otherwise the Shrike has the gruesome habit of storing surplus food by impaling it on thorns (or barbed wire if thorns are not available). This 'larder' of spare food gave the Shrikes the country name of 'Butcher Birds'. Great Grey Shrikes arrive in Britain in October, and soon establish regular winter hunting territories, perching upright out in the open on a post or on top of a bush watching for prey. In early spring they return to their breeding grounds on the continent, where the species is well established from France to the north of Scandinavia.

FOOD   Small birds, small mammals and amphibians, beetles and other insects.

The Great Grey Shrike does not breed in Britain or Ireland.

House Sparrow

SIZE   5¾in:14.5cm

DESCRIPTION   Brown upperparts streaked with black, grey crown and rump, black bib which widens out over the chest, white cheeks and white wing-bar. The female is much duller, with brown upperparts streaked black, buff cheeks and supercilium, and buff underparts.

PLATE 16

Lesser Whitethroat (scale 1:2.3)

Lapland Bunting (scale 1:2.3)

Great Grey Shrike (scale 1:2.3)

Tree Sparrow (scale 1:2.3)

House Sparrow (scale 1:2.3)

FRANCES FRY.

SONG/CALL A 'cheep' call note, and a chirpy little song.

RECOGNITION To town-dwellers the House Sparrow must seem to be the most numerous bird in Britain, but in fact it is plentiful mainly around human settlements and overall birds like the Chaffinch and the Blackbird are more widespread. Nevertheless, there can be few people who do not know the cheeky, chirpy Sparrow. It is resident and widespread throughout the country; concentrated in towns, cities and villages, but also found on farmland or in hedgerows. Bold, gregarious and noisy, the House Sparrow has always been closely associated with man, feeding on scraps and human refuse, and nesting in buildings. In autumn however many Sparrows desert city habitats and move out into the countryside in large flocks to feed on cereal crops in agricultural districts. They are regular visitors to bird tables where they will imitate Tits and hang on to nutstrings or other food suspended from the table. Sparrows are resourceful and adaptable, and this is the reason for the great success of the species throughout the world.

FOOD A wide variety of foods – grain and weed seeds, insects and their larvae, and in built-up areas bread and scraps.

NEST The House Sparrow has a wide variety of nest sites, ranging from a natural hole in a tree, wall or building to old nests of other species – House Martins' nests are often taken over in this way. The nest is a domed structure made of straw, plant stems and any handy rubbish such as paper, string or rags lined with feathers and down. In trees it is often a neat construction with compact side entrance, but if an old nest is used or when the site is in a building then a very untidy nest can result. Both sexes help build the nest with the male doing most of the work.

EGGS 3–5, occasionally up to 8, white eggs speckled with purplish-grey markings. .85 x .61in:22.5 x 15.7mm. Incubation, chiefly by the female, takes 11–14 days and fledging 15 days.

BREEDING SEASON Usually May–August, but can nest throughout the year. Usually treble-brooded.

BARRED WARBLER
Vagrant autumn visitor from central and eastern Europe. Grey/brown plumage, with domed head and heavy bill, light underparts barred dark. Bright yellow eyes. Skulking behaviour, rather clumsy movements on ground.

This species is not illustrated.

Dunnock

SIZE 5¾in:14.5cm

DESCRIPTION Small, self-effacing bird with drab plumage that is often overlooked. Upperparts brown streaked black, with chestnut on wings, underparts grey-brown with streaked flanks. Fine, pointed bill, and orangish iris to eyes.

SONG/CALL A thin, high 'tseep' call, and a pleasant but undistinguished warbling song.

RECOGNITION The Dunnock is resident and widely distributed throughout The British isles with the exception of the Scottish Highlands and Shetland Islands, but its rather skulking habits and dull colouring make it easy to overlook, although it is found in many varied habitats, from hedgerows and open country to gardens. It often comes to birdtables, but usually feeds on the ground beneath them, picking up discarded scraps rather than join battle with rivals on the table. Dunnocks are unobtrusive birds, creeping over the ground, usually in a crouched position, searching for seeds or insects, but they are usually quite easy to approach. The species is also known as the Hedge Sparrow, but it is quite unrelated to the sparrow family, and belongs to the accentor group.

FOOD Insects, spiders and worms, and seeds in autumn and winter.

NEST Both sexes help build the nest, a cup of twigs, stems, leaves, moss and plant material, lined with hair, wool or moss, occasionally with feathers. The nest is usually well hidden in a tree or bush. Occasionally the old nest of another species is used.

EGGS 4–5, sometimes 3–6, glossy bright blue eggs are laid. .77 x .57in:19.9 x 14.7mm. Incubation, by the female alone, takes 12–13 days, and fledging is usually completed in 12 days.

BREEDING SEASON Begins late March or early April. Double, sometimes treble-brooded.

Spotted Flycatcher

SIZE 5½in:14cm

DESCRIPTION A small, upright-perching bird, with grey-brown upperparts, and buffish underparts streaked with dark brown on throat and breast. The crown is flecked buff and brown. Long wings, forked tail, and short bill.

SONG/CALL A thin 'tzee' call, and a song consisting of a short series of rather squeaky 'sip-sip-sreet-sreet-sip' notes.

RECOGNITION The Spotted Flycatcher is a summer visitor to Britain, arriving late in April and departing in September. It is widely distributed throughout the country, in wooded areas, parkland, farmland and gardens. It feeds exclusively on flying insects and is often seen perched on a convenient post in an upright position watching for its prey. An established watching post is used for a considerable length of time, the Flycatcher making repeated sallies after insects, catching them (often with a clearly audible snap of its bill), and returning to the original perch again and again. While it is busy in this way it is often possible to approach quite close to the bird, but care should be taken not to disturb its feeding so much as to force it to seek new territory. It is a creature of habit, and will return year after year to a favoured nest-site.

FOOD   Almost entirely flying insects, chiefly flies but also butterflies, craneflies, wasps, and very occasionally earthworms or rowan berries.

NEST   Both sexes help build the nest, although the female does most of the work. The nest consists of an untidy cup of grass, twigs roots plant down, fibres and spiders webs, with a lining of feathers, hair, fibres and dead leaves, and is usually situated against a tree-trunk, on a ledge, or in creeper or in an open hole. Flycatchers also take readily to nestboxes of the open-fronted type.

EGGS   Usually 4–5, occasionally 2–7, non-glossy pale blue eggs, blotched with red-brown .72 x .52in:18.5 x 14.1mm. Incubation, usually by the female, takes 11–15 days, and fledging 12–14 days.

BREEDING SEASON   May to June. Sometimes double-brooded.

Fieldfare

SIZE   10in:25.5cm

DESCRIPTION   Handsome member of the thrush family, with blue-grey head, nape and rump, chestnut back, dark tail, and warm orange breast striped with arrow-shaped markings in typical thrush pattern. The bill has an orange-yellow base but the overall colour is dark. Sexes alike.

SONG/CALL   A harsh-sounding 'cha-cha-cha-chack', given during flight as a contact call. The song is a poor imitation of the Blackbird's, with some whistling notes.

RECOGNITION   The Fieldfare is a common winter visitor to Britain, widely distributed throughout the countryside, in wooded habitat or hedgerows, parks and gardens. Large numbers arrive from northern Europe each autumn and stay until March or April, but in recent years small numbers have remained here to breed, mainly in Scotland. Fieldfares are noisy, gregarious birds, and form large flocks, sometimes with Redwings, to search for food along hedges or in grassland areas. They have a particular fondness for rotting apples, and will visit orchards or large gardens with fruit trees.

FOOD   Berries, fallen fruit (especially windfall apples) also worms, insects and their larvae, and spiders.

PLATE 17

Dunnock (scale 2:5.8)

Spotted Flycatcher (scale 2:5.8)

Fieldfare (scale 2:5.8)

Mistle Thrush (scale 2:5.8)

FRANCES FRY.

NEST In established breeding grounds in Scandinavia, Fieldfares usually nest in colonies in woodland or town surroundings, but at present only a few birds nest in Britain, in conifers or woodland, or moorland scrub areas. The female builds the nest, a bulky cup made of grass, twigs, moss and roots, with a mud lining which has an inner lining of fine grass.

EGGS 5–6 usually, sometimes 3–8, glossy eggs, light blue with reddish markings that sometimes obliterate the ground colour. The eggs are very similar to those of the Blackbird or the Ring Ouzel. 1.12 x .80in:29.1 x 21.3mm. Incubation, by the female alone, takes 11–14 days, and fledging 12–16 days.

BREEDING SEASON Usually May or June. Often double-brooded.

Mistle Thrush

SIZE 10½in:27cm

DESCRIPTION Greyish-brown thrush with upright stance. Upperparts grey-brown, with creamy underparts – the breast heavily marked with rounded dark brown spots. The outer tail feathers show white in flight, which is undulating, more like a woodpecker than a thrush, with a long, slow glide on landing.

SONG/CALL A chattering rattling call, and a loud, clear song rather like that of the Blackbird. The song is usually given from the top of a tall tree, and often during gales and stormy weather, and this habit gave the species the old country name of 'stormcock'.

RECOGNITION The Mistle Thrush is resident throughout the British Isles except for the far north, and is found in open country with hedges and corpses, large gardens and parkland. Numbers are nowhere so abundant as the Song Thrush, but each bird tends to hold unusually large territories. The Mistle Thrush is larger, greyer and more upright than the Song Thrush, and has bolder spots on its breast. In autumn Mistle Thrushes gather together in noisy flocks seeking berries and fruit to feed on. Individuals will visit gardens for windfall fruit.

FOOD Fruit and berries such as rowan, yew or holly. The Mistle Thrush gets its name from its particular fondness for Mistletoe berries, and the species helps propagate the parasitic plant by spreading its seeds, either by wiping surplus from its bill or passing them through its digestive system. Worms, snails, ants, insects and their larvae are also eaten.

NEST The female builds the nest, usually in the fork of a tree, but occasionally in a shrub or hedge. A bulky cup of grass, plant stems and moss and dead leaves, with earth mixed in consolidating it, lined with fine grass.

EGGS 4–5, sometimes 3–6, glossy pale blue eggs spotted or blotched with reddish-purple 1.25 x .88in: 31.2 x 22.3mm. Incubation, by the female alone when the clutch is completed, takes 12–15 days, and fledging 12–16 days.

BREEDING SEASON Begins in March. Double-brooded.

Dotterel

SIZE 8½in:22cm

DESCRIPTION   Colourful plover, seen mainly in mountainous regions. In summer the upperparts are brown, the chest dove-grey bordered by a band of white seperating it from chestnut belly deepening to black. White undertail coverts, white cheeks and white supercilium. Overall shape is rotund, with round head, short bill and long yellow legs. The male is duller than the female, and slightly smaller. Plumage is greyer in winter.

SONG/CALL   A 'ting' contact note, and a 'titi-ri-titi-ri' which becomes a trill.

RECOGNITION   The Dotterel is the plover that frequents Arctic regions and northern Europe, but in Britain it is found in small numbers in the mountainous areas of Scotland, the border hills and parts of north Wales, and passage migrants occur in other districts (particularly East Anglia) in spring and autumn. Although it prefers high stony ground for breeding it can be seen on lowland heaths and coastal fields during migration. Although colourful the plumage pattern merges in with the rocks and flora of hillsides, making the bird difficult to locate, even at fairly close quarters, but once found it is remarkably tame. Outside the breeding season Dotterels are gregarious birds and may form small flocks. Migrating birds often have traditional stopover places to which they return each year in small groups known as 'trips'.

FOOD   Insects and their larvae, spiders, and some seeds in winter.

NEST   A shallow hollow on the ground, unlined or with a sparse lining of vegetation. Unusually the female is the dominant partner, and when she has laid her eggs joins up with other females leaving nesting duties and most of the rearing of the young to the male.

EGGS   3 usually, sometimes 2 or 4, buffish oval eggs heavily blotched with dark brown or black, laid at 1–2 day intervals. 1.75 x 1.15in:44.1 x 28.9mm. Incubation, usually by the male alone, takes 21–26 days. The young are precocial, ready to leave the nest the day after hatching, and are tended by the male for about 4 weeks until they are fledged and independent. The male will feign injury to distract attention from the nest or the young.

BREEDING SEASON   Late May or June. Single-brooded.

Red Grouse

SIZE   15–16in:38–41cm

DESCRIPTION   Stocky rust/brown bird, heavily barred with black. Wings and outer tail feathers dark brown/black. Male bird has red patch over eyes; the female lacks this, and is generally paler.

CALL   A 'go-back go-back' call, usually given to challenge a rival bird.

RECOGNITION   The Red Grouse is a species unique to Britain, its closest relation being the Willow Grouse which is found in Norway and northern Europe. Resident all year round, and found in moorland habitat in Scotland, Ireland, Wales and parts of England (not midland or southern counties). A secretive bird, which will hide in heather or undergrowth only flushing from cover at the last possible moment when disturbed. This habit makes it a favourite gamebird, and the opening of the Grouse-shooting season – 'the glorious twelfth' is eagerly awaited by the sportsmen. Good conservation of heather moors is necessary to build up numbers each year for a shoot, and if it were not for good gamekeeping the species would soon decline.

FOOD   Almost entirely ling heather, with some fruits and shoots of cranberry, and some insects for the young.

NEST   The female makes a scrape in the ground and lines it with grass and heather.

EGGS   6–11, sometimes 4–17 eggs are laid, smooth, glossy, cream/yellow heavily blotched all over with dark red-brown. 1.75 x 1.2in:45.8 x 32.1mm. Incubation, by the female only beginning when the clutch is completed, takes 20–26 days. The young are precocial, ready to leave the nest soon after hatching and find their own food, and able to fly in 12-13 days. Both birds help to guard the young, and will feign injury to distract intruders.

BREEDING SEASON   Late April or May. Single-brooded.

Red-legged Partridge

SIZE   13½in:34cm

DESCRIPTION   A plump ground-dwelling gamebird with distinctive black and white markings on the head, and red legs and bill. Chestnut brown upperparts, pinkish breast and grey flanks barred with chestnut, black and white. Short tail and rounded wings.

SONG/CALL   A 'chuck-chuck-er' call, or a slow, rather harsh 'tschreck-tschreck', often given from a low perch. Also a 'kuk-kuk' alarm call when flushed from cover.

RECOGNITION   Similar shape to the common Partridge, but easily distinguished from it by red bill and legs, and very different voice. The Red-legged Partridge was introduced into Britain from France in the late eighteenth century, and in some districts it is still known as the French Partridge or 'Frenchman'. It is now resident in similar habitat to the common Partridge (arable land, dunes or downland) and is quite common in southern and eastern England – in fact in some areas it is more plentiful than the native species. Like the Grey Partridge it is difficult to flush, preferring to run away rather than fly, and is usually seen in small flocks or 'coveys'.

FOOD   Cereals, seeds, leaves and other vegetable matter, and some insects and spiders.

LAND BIRDS

PLATE 18

Dotterel (scale 1:4.6)

Red Grouse (scale 1:4.6)

Red-legged Partridge (scale 1:4.6)

Grey Partridge (scale 1:4.6)

FRANCES PRY.

NEST A shallow hollow in the ground, usually situated in good cover such as growing crops, or under a hedgerow or bush. The nest is scantily lined with plant material.

EGGS 10–16, sometimes many more (20, even up to 28), glossy eggs are laid at intervals of about 36 hours, yellowish-white to pale yellow-brown in colour, with fine reddish markings. 1.6 x 1.25in:41.4 x 31.1mm. Occasionally the female may lay two consecutive clutches in different nests, and when this happens one will be incubated by the female, the other by the male, the two broods being cared for separately. Incubation takes 23–25 days, and the chicks are precocial, ready to leave the nest quickly after hatching, and fly at an early stage. The brood stays together on maturity, and may join up with other youngsters to form large bands.

BREEDING SEASON April or May. Single-brooded, or two broods laid consecutively and raised separately.

Grey Partridge

SIZE 12in:30cm

DESCRIPTION Brown upperparts streaked black and white, grey underparts, barred with chestnut on flanks, and with dark brown 'horseshoe' on the breast. The female is duller, with less distinct markings. A plump, dumpy bird with short tail with chestnut outer feathers.

SONG/CALL A grating 'kerric-kerric-krrr-ick', often heard at dusk or after dark.

RECOGNITION The common Partridge is a rotund, chicken-like bird with short rounded wings and rufous tail, frequenting farmland, pasture and wasteland, moors and sand dunes. Once a popular resident gamebird with wide distribution throughout Britain, the species has suffered a serious decline in the last 30 years, due to pesticides and changing agricultural methods which have resulted in loss of habitat. Late, wet springs also take their toll of chicks, and prevent numbers increasing, but the Partridge is still found in most parts of England, although it is scarce in northern Scotland, parts of Wales and the south of Ireland. Partridges are gregarious birds, generally found in small groups known as 'coveys'. When alarmed they will squat motionless, relying on camouflage, or run swiftly rather than fly, but if flushed will fly low over the ground, with alternate spells of whirring wing-beats and gliding.

FOOD Weed seeds, shoots of cereals or weeds, and insects.

NEST A shallow hollow, lined with dead grasses and leaves, usually sheltered by vegetation, or beneath a hedgerow, or in growing crops.

EGGS A large clutch of 9–20, sometimes up to 23, eggs are laid at 1–2 day intervals, glossy buff, brown or olive in colour. 1.45 x 1.15in:36.5 x 27.3mm. Incubation, by the female alone but with the male in close attendance, takes 23–25 days. The young are precocial, ready to leave the nest soon after hatching. Both parents tend them, and although the young are fully fledged in about 28 days the family group stays together until the following spring.

BREEDING SEASON April to June. Single-brooded.

Woodcock

SIZE   13½in:34cm

DESCRIPTION   A large chunky wader, with rounded appearance and long, downward-pointing bill. Chestnut brown upperparts barred black, and buffish underparts finely barred with brown, broad rounded wings.

SONG/CALL   A soft, croaking 'orrrt-orrrt' call, usually given during slow display flight (known as 'roding'), and a sharp 'tsiwick' call that carries for a considerable distance.

RECOGNITION   The Woodcock is a solitary bird of woodland habitat. It is resident all year round, and quite well distributed throughout the British Isles except the outlying Scottish islands. Its barred plumage makes perfect 'dead-leaf' camouflage in woodland, and enables the bird to escape detection at close quarters. Woodcock are most often seen 'roding' over the tree-tops at dawn or dusk, when their call draws attention to them. The flight is rapid and dodging, and the bird looks stout and 'neckless' with the bill pointing downward distinctively.

FOOD   Largely earthworms, extracted by the long, probing bill, but also insects and their larvae, plant seeds and freshwater molluscs.

NEST   The Woodcock's nest is a hollow in the ground, often at the foot of a tree, lined with dead leaves or plant material. A bird sitting on the nest is well camouflaged blending in with the dead leaves, and will usually sit tight hoping to escape notice, but if this fails and the bird is flushed she will distract the intruder from the nest by feigning injury.

EGGS   4, sometimes 3–5 eggs, oval to pyriform shape, slightly glossy cream-buff eggs, speckled with brown or purplish markings, large and small. 1.75 x 1.3in:44.2 x 33.5mm. Eggs are laid at 2–3 day intervals. Incubation, beginning with the last egg, is by the female alone, and takes 20–23 days. The young are precocial, and leave the nest immediately after hatching, as soon as they are dry. They are independent at about 5–6 weeks. It is believed, but not completely proven, that the female will carry her young in flight, one at a time between her legs, to safety if danger threatens them.

BREEDING SEASON   Begins in March, and is often prolonged. Double-brooded.

Golden Plover

SIZE   11in:28cm

DESCRIPTION   Dark upperparts speckled with gold, black face, throat, breast and belly bordered by broad white line. Typical rotund plover shape, with small bill and long legs, dark blackish in colour.

SONG/CALL   Flight call note of 'tlui', and a rather melancholy 'tlu-i'. The song given during display flight in the breeding season is a rippling trill with repeated 'toori' and 'tirr-peeoo's.

RECOGNITION The Golden Plover is a gregarious moorland bird with very distinctive gold-flecked plumage. Britain has a sizeable resident population, and a much larger number of birds arrive each autumn to overwinter here. The resident birds are essentially moorland in their habits, found in hilly areas of the north and west, but migrants overwinter in coastal areas or on farmland. In spring Golden Plovers may be seen displaying in chase or 'switchback' flight as they establish territories for breeding. Outside the breeding season flocks of Golden Plovers often associate with Lapwings, particularly in winter when both species tend to gather on grassland.

FOOD Insects and their larvae, spiders and worms, grass seeds and berries in autumn.

NEST A shallow scrape in the ground, lined with plant material, usually hidden in heather.

EGGS Usually 4, sometimes 3, stone-coloured eggs, heavily blotched with blackish-brown markings. The eggs are oval or pyriform in shape, and are laid at intervals of 2–3 days. 2.1 x 1.4in:52.1 x 35.5mm. Both sexes help incubate the eggs, but the female takes the dominant role. The young hatch in 27–28 days, and are precocial, leaving the nest quickly. If danger threatens the parents will feign injury to draw attention away from the nest or the young. The parents tend the chicks for 4 weeks until they are fledged and independent.

BREEDING SEASON Begins in mid-April. Single-brooded.

SIZE 6½in:16.5cm

DESCRIPTION Dull coloured member of the woodpecker family that is often overlooked. At a distance the bird looks uniformly grey-brown with pale underparts, but really the plumage is a mixture of buff, browns and greys rather like the Nightjar's. It has a distinctive 'V' of cream on its back. The short bill is sharply pointed, and the feet resemble all the woodpeckers with two toes forward and two behind. The crown feathers are erectile, and the head can turn through 180 degrees, hence the name – Wryneck.

SONG/CALL A repeated 'kyee-kyee-kyee' call, given in early spring but ceasing when the first clutch of eggs is laid.

RECOGNITION The Wryneck is a summer visitor to Britain, becoming increasingly rare with only a few breeding birds and some passage migrants. Numbers have decreased rapidly in the last 50 years, and its survival as a breeding species here looks precarious. Its habitat is parkland or gardens with old trees or orchards, and sometimes woodland edges. It is more often heard than seen. Although it is classed as a woodpecker the Wryneck does not climb the trunks of trees like true woodpeckers, but clings to the trunk or perches across branches. It is predominantly a ground-feeder, and hops along with raised tail.

FOOD Largely ants taken from the ground, but also other insects and their larvae, and beetles.

NEST The Wryneck lays its eggs in an unlined cavity, natural or artificial, in a tree, building or wall, often quite low down.

EGGS 7–10, sometimes 5–14, numbers vary considerably, non-glossy oval white eggs, with thicker shells than most woodpeckers. .79 x .60in:20.8 x 15.4mm. Incubation, by both sexes but mainly by the female, takes 12–14 days, and fledging 19–21 days.

BREEDING SEASON Begins late May. Usually single-brooded, but occasionally two broods may be raised.

Nightjar

SIZE 10½in:27cm

DESCRIPTION Nocturnal bird with large dark eyes, large gape, tiny bill, small feet, and long wings and tail, its general appearance is elongated, with flattened head. The plumage is grey-brown, speckled and barred to produce perfect camouflage. The sexes are alike save for three white spots near the wing-tips, and on the outer-tail feathers, in the male.

SONG/CALL The song, given at night, is a loud, fast churring, rising and falling in pitch, and sustained for a considerable period, often with a ventriloquial effect as the head is turned from side to side, with a few clucking notes when the song is running down. Also a 'goo-ek' alarm call, and a high 'cui-ic' note.

RECOGNITION The Nightjar is a summer visitor to Britain, arriving late, in May, and departing early, in August. Numbers have declined drastically this century, but it is still found throughout England and Wales in small numbers, although it is scarce in Scotland and Ireland. It is more often heard than seen, as it usually spends the day crouched motionless along a branch or on the ground hidden among dead vegetation, where its mottled plumage blends perfectly with the surroundings. It emerges at dawn and dusk to hunt owl-like on silent wings, pursuing moths and insects, scooping them up in its large gape. During the breeding season the male indulges in 'wing-clapping' to impress the female, but otherwise the Nightjar tends to be silent in the daytime. Habitat includes woodlands, moors, commons, areas of bracken and gorse, and sand dunes.

FOOD Nocturnal-flying insects, particularly moths.

NEST The Nightjar lays its eggs on the bare ground; sometimes in a scraped hollow, often next to a piece of dead wood which may act as a marker.

EGGS 2 greyish-white eggs, speckled and blotched with yellow-brown markings. 1.25 x .80in:31.9 x 22.5mm. Incubation, by both sexes with the female sitting by day, the male by night, takes about 18 days. The young are partly precocial, with a light covering of down and are tended by both parents until the female lays a second clutch. They can fly at 16–18 days, and are fully independent at 31–34 days.

BREEDING SEASON Begins mid-May. Double-brooded.

GREY/BROWN BIRDS *(barred plumage)*

PLATE 19

Woodcock (scale 1:4.6)

Golden Plover (scale 1:4.6)

Wryneck (scale 2:5.8)

Nightjar (scale 1:3.5)

FRANCES FRY.

Rock Dove

SIZE 13in:33cm

DESCRIPTION The ancestor of the Feral Pigeon, distinguished from it and the somewhat similar Stock Dove by its whitish rump, white underwings, and two broad black bands across secondary flight feathers. Grey-blue plumage with glossy green and lilac on sides of neck, and black terminal band on tail. Long wings and swift flight.

SONG/CALL 'oo-roo-coo', sometimes a quiet 'ooo'.

RECOGNITION The true Rock Dove is now quite a scarce resident in most of Britain, being found mainly on northern and western coasts. In many areas Feral pigeons have interbred with Rock Doves, and some of these birds are also found in coastal regions. Rock Doves inhabit rocky cliffs and adjoining fields, and often form flocks. They sometimes roost with cliff-nesting seabirds. They are fast, skilful flyers, gliding about the cliff faces and over the sea.

FOOD Weed seeds, cereal crops and small molluscs.

NEST Rock Doves usually nest colonially, in caves and crevices of seacliffs or on rocky outcrops. Both sexes help build the nest, but little material is used, just a thin layer of twigs or roots.

EGGS Usually 2, slightly glossy white eggs are laid. 1.56 x 1.16in:39.4 x 29.2mm. Both sexes help incubate the eggs, and hatching takes about 12–17 days. The young are fed on special 'pigeon's milk' regurgitated from the crop of both parents, and are fledged and ready to fly in about 35 days.

BREEDING SEASON March to September. Double- or treble-brooded.

The Rock Dove is also listed under BIRDS WITH ROSY BREASTS.

Feral Pigeon

SIZE 13in:33cm

DESCRIPTION City-dwelling descendents of the Rock Dove. Some birds retain similar colours to their ancestors, but there are many plumage variations, from white through chequered patterns to black. Their beaks are shorter and stouter than the Rock Dove.

SONG/CALL Familiar 'oo-roo-coo', like domestic or racing pigeon.

RECOGNITION The Feral Pigeon must surely be familiar to every city-dweller, and is also widespread in towns and villages, industrial areas, farms, and even on the seashore. No bird has a closer association with man, nesting in and roosting on his buildings, and often depending on him for food. Despite assuming pest status in some areas where their droppings may cause damage Feral Pigeons have proved very difficult to discourage, and indeed in some places (like Trafalgar Square) they have become an essential part of the scene, and always find people to feed them.

FOOD   Weed, seeds and grain, also bread, cake and scraps from the public.

NEST   The Feral Pigeon is not over-faddy about its nest site, and will use ledges on buildings, holes in or on man-made structures, or sometimes nest right inside dis-used buildings. A scanty layer of twigs is usual, but sometimes other material is used if available, like thin pieces of wire. Both sexes help to build the nest.

EGGS   Usually 2 slightly glossy white eggs are laid. 1.55 x 1.14in:39.3 x 29.1mm. Incubation is by both sexes, and takes 17–19 days, and the young are fed on 'pigeon's milk' regurgitated from the crop of both parents. Fledging takes about 35 days.

BREEDING SEASON   Very long and varied, but most usual from March to September. In urban situations it may be longer. Several broods may be raised each year – 3 or 4 are usual. The special 'pigeon's milk' for feeding the young means that the breeding season is not curtailed by food shortages as is the case for most birds, and for this reason pigeons are very successful breeders although each clutch is small.

Stock Dove

SIZE   13in:33cm

DESCRIPTION   Superficially rather similar in appearance to the Rock Dove, but lacking that species white rump and broad black wing-bars. The Stock Dove has blue-grey plumage, with rosy breast, glossy green patch on side of neck, and two short, broken black wing-bars, and black terminal band on tail.

SONG/CALL   'ooo-roo-ooo' with stress on the first syllable.

RECOGNITION   The Stock Dove is resident throughout most of the British Isles except the Scottish Highlands and islands, and northwestern Ireland. Its habitat includes woodland, parkland, large gardens and dunes, as well as cliffs. It is a gregarious bird, usually seen in flocks, sometimes in company with the larger woodpigeons. Its behaviour is similar to the Woodpigeon, but its flight is more rapid. In spring the male postures before the female, puffing out his chest, or gives a slow display flight with wing-clapping on ascent and a gliding return to ground.

FOOD   Mainly grain, but clover, root vegetables and shoots are also taken, as are leaves from peas and beans.

NEST   The Stock Dove is a hole-nester, choosing a natural hole in a tree, cliff or quarry, or sometimes a hole in a building; very occasionally a rabbit hole in very open areas. Sometimes the cavity is lined with twigs, roots or dead leaves, but sometimes it is left unlined. Sometimes the old nest of another species is used.

EGGS Usually 2, slightly glossy white eggs are laid, sometimes with a slight creamy tint. 1.5 x 1.1in:37.9 x 29.0mm. Incubation, by both sexes, begins with the first egg and takes 16–18 days. The young (known as 'squabs') are fed on pigeon's milk'. Fledging takes around 27–28 days, sometimes less.

BREEDING SEASON Begins in March, and may extend to September. Double- or treble-brooded.

The Stock Dove is also listed under BIRDS WITH ROSY BREASTS.

SIZE 16in:41cm

DESCRIPTION The largest British pigeon, with grey upperparts, pink breast, black primaries and black terminal band on tail. Best identified by bold white bar across wings and white neck bar. Yellow bill, and yellow iris in eyes.

SONG/CALL The well-known 'coo-coo-coo'.

RECOGNITION The Woodpigeon is the most common British pigeon, widespread throughout all the country with the exception of the Scottish highlands, the Outer Hebrides and Shetland. Most birds are resident, but numbers increase in the autumn with immigrations of Continental birds. It has a wide range of habitat, from agricultural land to parks, gardens and towns, but it is in the countryside that Woodpigeons are most noticeable, forming large flocks foraging over farmland. Such a large population makes the species a menace to agriculture, with its fondness for grain, root crops and peas, but control by shooting or doped grain has had little effect.

FOOD Mainly grain, but also root crops, peas and beans, fruits and seeds, and sometimes worms and slugs.

NEST A flimsy platform of twigs placed in a tree or bush, sometimes on a rocky ledge or building, occasionally on the ground in treeless country. Sometimes the old nest of another species may be used as a base. The female does most of the building, but the male helps gather material.

EGGS Usually 2, slightly glossy white eggs are laid. 1.75 x 1.2in:44.1 x 29.8mm. Incubation, by both sexes, starts with the first egg and takes about 17 days. The young squabs are fed on 'pigeon's milk', and fledge in 29–35 days.

BREEDING SEASON Begins in April and is very extensive, lasting until October usually, although some birds nest even in winter. Treble-brooded usually.

The Woodpigeon is also listed under BIRDS WITH ROSY BREASTS.

Rock Dove (scale 1:3.5)

Feral Pigeon (scale 1:3.5)

Stock Dove (scale 1:3.5)

Woodpigeon (scale 1:3.5)

Hobby

SIZE   12–14in:30–36cm

DESCRIPTION   Long-winged falcon with superficial resemblance to the Kestrel, but distinguished from it by longer, narrower wings, moustachial stripe, and chestnut on thighs and under tail. Slate-grey upperparts, white cheeks, dark moustache, and white underparts streaked with black. In flight the Hobby can resemble a large Swift.

CALL   A repeated 'kew' or 'ket', and a rapid 'ki-ki-ki', often with variations in pitch.

RECOGNITION   The Hobby is a summer visitor, arriving in May from its wintering grounds in Africa and departing back there in early autumn. It is fairly rare in Britain, being usually found only in southern England, and parts of the south Midlands, and numbers of breeding pairs are small although there are encouraging signs of a slow gradual increase, and a few birds have been recorded in Scotland. The Hobby is perhaps the most aerial of the falcons, with such powerful flight that it can catch other aerial masters such as Swifts and Swallows, and hawk for large insects which are consumed on the wing. It frequents dry heaths and downland with scattered trees or light woodland.

FOOD   Flying insects and small birds such as Larks or Swallows.

NEST   The Hobby breeds in open country with scattered woodland cover, and usually takes over the old nest of another species, situated high in a tree, conifer for preference. No lining is added, indeed if the nest taken over is new then part of a thick lining may be removed.

EGGS   2–3, non-glossy yellowish-brown eggs are laid at 2–3 day intervals. They are densely speckled with red-brown spots which may originally obscure the ground colour but tend to fade rapidly. 1.69 x 1.31in:41.8 x 32.6mm. Incubation, mainly by the female, begins with second egg and takes around 28 days. The young are close-brooded by the female for the first week. They feather in 2–3 weeks and fly at 28–32 days, but continue to be dependent on their parents for some time after leaving the nest.

BREEDING SEASON   May to June. Single-brooded.

Peregrine Falcon

SIZE   15–19in:38–48cm

DESCRIPTION   Crow-sized falcon with long pointed wings and rapid pigeon-like flight. Dark slate-grey upperparts, with prominent dark moustaches on white cheeks, and buff-white underparts narrowly barred with black. Yellow cere, eye-ring, and legs and feet. The female is larger and darker than the male. Juveniles brownish.

CALL A wide range of calls, particularly during the breeding season – a high 'kek-kek-kek', a short 'kiack', and a repeated 'we-chew'.

RECOGNITION The long wings and short tapered tail are characteristic of the Peregrine Falcon, and when it folds its wings in a stooping dive on to its prey it has tremendous speed. It is resident, and patchily distributed in Britain, being found in small numbers in Scotland, Wales, the west country, and parts of Ireland, but scarce in north eastern and midland and southern England. The species suffered a serious decline in the 1950s due to accidental poisoning from agricultural chemicals, and its great popularity for falconry also put the Peregrine at risk. Increased protection has now helped, and numbers show a slow but steady increase. Peregrine habitat is wild, open country such as cliffs, mountains and moors, or occasionally quarries or marshland.

FOOD Largely medium-sized birds such as pigeons. The Peregrine dives on its prey at great speed, killing it quickly with a blow from its feet.

NEST A hollow, unlined scrap serves as nest, with sites being re-used year after year. The nest site is usually situated on a cliff ledge, or a rocky outcrop.

EGGS 3–4, sometimes 2–6, non-glossy cream eggs, heavily marked with fine red or chestnut speckles or reddish brown blotches. 2.0 x 1.6in:52.0 x 40.0mm. The eggs are laid at 2–3 day intervals, and incubation, by both sexes, begins with the second or third egg, and takes 28–29 days. The female close broods the young for the first fortnight. The young start to feather at about 18 days, and can fly at 35–42 days, but remain dependent on their parents for several weeks more.

BREEDING SEASON Starts around April. Single-brooded.

Goshawk

SIZE 19–24in:48–61cm. The female is much larger than the male.

DESCRIPTION Large hawk with long tail and rounded wings, rather similar in colouring to the female Sparrowhawk but much larger. Dark slate-grey upperparts with pale supercilium, and white underparts barred black. The undertail coverts are white, and the tail is broadly barred. Legs and feet yellow.

CALL A Buzzard-like, mewing 'hi-aa', and a harsh 'gig-gig-gik'.

RECOGNITION The Goshawk is a rare resident in Britain. In the nineteenth century it was well established in Scotland and found sporadically elsewhere, but a decline set in and it ceased to breed in Britain. Now, due to escapees from falconry and introduced birds it is beginning to re-establish itself, and small breeding populations are found in Scotland and the north midlands. In spring the Goshawk has a soaring display flight to establish territory, and this is when the bird is most likely to be seen – normally it is a self-effacing bird, keeping within the cover of trees. The hunting flight through the trees is fast and low.

FOOD   Mainly woodland birds, larger than those taken by the Sparrowhawk.

NEST   A large, shallow, untidy structure of twigs and branches, lined with bits of bark and leafy twigs. The male bird does nearly all of the building. The nest is usually situated high up in a tree, supported by a strong forked branch. Sometimes an old nest may be re-used, and an established pair of birds will have several alternative sites within their territory.

EGGS   2–3 is usual, but numbers can vary from 1–5. The eggs are laid at 3 day intervals and are non-glossy and pale blue-white. 2.25 x 1.75in:57.4 x 44.2mm. Incubation, mainly by the female, takes 36–41 days. The female broods the young closely for 8–10 days, with the male bringing food. Fledging takes 18–38 days, and the young can fly at about 45 days, but they remain dependent on their parents for up to 70 days.

BREEDING SEASON   April to June. Single-brooded.

Sparrowhawk

SIZE   11–15in:28–38cm. The female is considerably larger than the male.

DESCRIPTION   Agile, small hawk with long tail, broadly barred, and rounded wings. The smaller male has dark slate-grey upperparts with rufous cheeks and white spot on nape, and pale underparts finely barred with reddish-brown, and tail banded grey and brown. The female has dark blackish-brown upperparts, white stripe over eye, and white underparts barred with dark brown. The female may occasionally be confused with the lighter-coloured Cuckoo, but is distinguished by feathered thighs and different flight – rapid-wing beats between long glides.

SONG/CALL   The Sparrowhawk has quite a large vocabulary in the breeding season – a 'kek-kek-kek', a 'keeow', a 'kew' and other similar variations.

RECOGNITION   The Sparrowhawk is a resident woodland bird, widely distributed throughout the country. Woods are its favourite habitat, but farmland, hedgerows and plantations are also used, and more open land provided there are sufficient trees to give cover. The Sparrowhawk is a specialized hunter, taking mainly small birds, and cruises above woods and hedges searching and pouncing on its prey. In the 1950s and 60s over-enthusiastic use of pesticides on the land poisoned much of the Sparrowhawk's prey and led to a drastic decline in numbers, but fortunately the danger was recognised just in time and protection and a ban on the most dangerous chemicals has enabled the species to make a gradual recovery.

FOOD   Largely small woodland birds.

NEST   An unitdy, flattish structure made of twigs and sticks, roughly lined with leafy twigs. The female does most of the building, with a little help from the male, and the nest is usually situated high in a tree. Often the old nest of another bird provides a base for the Sparrohawk's nest.

PLATE 21

Hobby (scale 1:5.8)

Peregrine Falcon (scale 1:5.8)

Coshawk (scale 1:5.8)

Sparrowhawk (scale 1:5.8)

FRANCES FRY

EGGS   4–5, sometimes 2–7, non-glossy blue-white eggs blotched with dark red-brown markings 1.6 x 1.25in:39.8 x 31.8mm. The eggs are laid at intervals of 2–4 days, and incubation, by the female alone, starts with the second or third egg, and takes 32–42 days. The female broods the young closely for the first 4–5 days. Fledging takes 13–28 days, but the young remain dependent on parental feeding for some weeks.

BREEDING SEASON   April to June. Single-brooded.

Cuckoo

SIZE   13in:33cm.

DESCRIPTION   Slim, hawk-like bird with barred grey plumage. Upperparts grey, with black primaries and black tail marked with white spots, underparts whitish barred dark grey. Long, rounded tail, long pointed wings, yellow legs, bill and eye. Juveniles brown-barred.

SONG/CALL   The unmistakable 'cuc-koo', so eagerly awaited each spring. As summer advances the call changes, to 'cuc-cuc-koo', then 'cuc-cuc'. The female has a 'bubbling' call.

RECOGNITION   The Cuckoo is perhaps Britain's best known summer visitor, easily identified by voice. It is widely distributed throughout the countryside, and the familiar call, given from a perch or during flight, draws attention to its presence. It is less easy to see, keeping largely to the cover of trees or shrubs, but can be observed flying from perch to perch with shallow wing-beats, gliding a little before landing. The long wings and tail are quite distinctive in flight.

FOOD   Insects and their larvae, spiders and worms, also hairy caterpillars, which most birds reject.

NEST   The Cuckoo is a brood parasite – the only British bird that has no nest of its own and lays its eggs in other bird nests. Each female chooses a territory containing suitable foster parent nests (such as Pipits, Dunnocks, Robins, Wagtails) and keeps watch until the unwilling hosts clutch is nearly complete. She then removes one of the eggs and lays one herself to replace it.

EGGS   The Cuckoo lays 8–12 eggs, each one in a different nest, and the colour varies considerably, blending in each time to the host birds eggs. Average size is about .85 x .75in:22.7 x 16.9mm. Incubation, by the foster mother, takes about 12 days. On hatching the young Cuckoo instinctively ejects the other eggs or young in the nest, wriggling under them and positioning them in a special hollow in its back, rearing up against the side of the nest and throwing them out. The Cuckoo is fledged and ready to leave the nest at 20–23 days, but will continue to be fed by its foster-parents (and other birds feeding young) for some weeks.

BREEDING SEASON   May. Only one clutch of eggs is laid.

Merlin

SIZE 10½–13in:27–33cm. The female is larger than the male.

DESCRIPTION A small, agile falcon, long-winged and fast-flying. Male has slate-blue upperparts, rufous-striped underparts, with broad black terminal band on its tail. The larger female has dark brown upperparts, and barred cream and brown tail. The wings are very long, reaching to the tip of the tail when folded at rest. Legs, feet and cere are yellow.

CALL A high-pitched 'ki-ki-ki-ki' by the male. The female has a lower, plaintive 'eep-eep' call.

RECOGNITION The Merlin is one of the smallest falcons. In Britain it is a resident bird, found in hilly districts, particularly in the north and west. Its habitat is mainly moorland, but marshy ground, young forestry plantations and sea cliffs are also part of its range. It is a very fast hunter, with a bouyant, erratic flight with occasional short glides, and preys on small birds, particularly Meadow Pipits, but its small size does not restrict the Merlin to only small prey – it is an aggressive hunter and can down a bird nearly as large as itself.

FOOD A wide variety of small birds, with Meadow Pipits featuring prominently in its diet. Small mammals and insects are also taken.

NEST The Merlin usually nests on the ground, choosing a bare hollow amongst heather or dunes, but occasionally cliff ledges are used, or the nests of other birds in trees. Nests among dunes sometimes have a grass lining pulled in by the sitting bird, otherwise no lining is used unless it is already present in an old nest.

EGGS 5–6 usually, sometimes 2–7, non-glossy pale buff eggs with a heavy sprinkling of red or brown markings. Sometimes the markings are so profuse that the egg takes on a darker hue. 1.5 x 1.2in:40.2 x 31.2mm. The eggs are laid at 2 day intervals, and incubation, mainly by the female, begins before the clutch is completed, and takes 28–32 days. The young are closely brooded by the female at first with the male bringing food. Fledging takes about 18 days, and the young can fly at 25–30 days, but they remain dependent on their parents for about 6 weeks.

BREEDING SEASON April to June. Single-brooded.

Hen Harrier

SIZE 17–20in:43–51cm.

DESCRIPTION Long-winged, long-tailed bird of prey. The male is ash-grey with black wing-tips and white rump, grey throat and chest fading to white on flanks. The female is brown with streaked buff underparts, and strongly barred tail. Both sexes may be confused with the somewhat similar Montagu's Harrier, but are slightly larger and more heavily built, and have larger and more distinctive white rump.

91

CALL   A high-pitched 'kee-kee-kee', and a wailing 'Pee-e'.

RECOGNITION   The Hen Harrier is resident, although numbers increase in the autumn due to the passage of Continental birds, some of which overwinter in coastal or moorland areas. The species has always been fairly well established in Scotland, but was in danger of extinction in England and Ireland by the turn of the century. Happily numbers have increased steadily since then, and it now breeds over much of Scotland, northern England, north Wales and Ireland. It inhabits open moorland, marshes, bogs or young forestry plantations. Its flight is one of the Harriers most distinctive features, very low and gliding with the wings held in a shallow 'V'.

FOOD   Small mammals, young rabbits, and birds up to Lapwing size, taken on the ground from cruising flight.

NEST   The Hen Harrier is a ground-nesting bird, choosing moorland, a thicket or even crops to nest in. On dry sites the nest consists of a thin layer of twigs or reeds lined with grass, but on wet ground the whole structure is larger and much more substantial. The female does most of the building although the male may help gather material.

EGGS   4–6 usually, although occasionally clutches of up to 12 have been recorded. The eggs are laid at intervals of 2 days or more, and are blueish-white, rarely blotched with light brown. The inside of the shell is green. 1.81 x 1.42in:46.2 x 35.3mm. Incubation, by the female alone, begins with the second or third egg, and takes 29–39 days. The female broods the young closely for the first two weeks, the male bringing the food and passing it to the female in mid-air. The young are fledged at about 35 days, when they leave the nest and hide in nearby vegetation, returning when the parent brings food. They remain dependent on their parents for some time.

BREEDING SEASON   Late April to June. Single-brooded.

Montague's Harrier

SIZE   16–18in:41–46cm.

DESCRIPTION   Lightly built bird of prey, superficially similar to the Hen Harrier, but with narrower, more pointed wings, and more buoyant flight. The male has pale grey upperparts, grey throat and chest and white underparts streaked with chestnut. A black transverse bar across the wings shows up well in flight. The female has dark brown upperparts and buff underparts streaked with brown.

CALL   A shrill 'kek-kek-kek'.

RECOGNITION   Montague's Harrier is a rare summer visitor to Britain, arriving from Africa in April and departing in September. Numbers in Britain have declined steadily since the 1950s, and only a small breeding population survives in south-west England. Its flight is much buoyant than the Hen Harrier's, but both birds catch their prey by cruising low over the ground, then pouncing to kill. Favoured habitat is rough moorland, heaths or marshland. As breeding is rare in Britain not many young birds

PLATE 22

Cuckoo (scale 1:5.8)

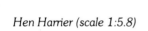

Merlin (scale 1:5.8)

Hen Harrier (scale 1:5.8)

Montague's Harrier (scale 1:5.8)

FRANCES FRY

are seen, but they are very similar in appearance to the Hen Harrier's with brown plumage and rufous streaked underparts, and the boldly barred tail that gives juveniles of both species the name 'ring-tails'.

FOOD   Birds and small mammals.

NEST   The female does most of the nest building, choosing a site on the ground amongst vegetation. The nest is a flat structure made of reed stems, twigs and grasses, lined with finer grass. During the nesting season the vegetation surrounding the nest tends to get beaten down by the frequent comings and goings, and so sometimes reveals a carefully hidden nest.

EGGS   Usually 4–5, although it can vary from 3 to 10. The eggs are laid at intervals varying from 1½ to 3 days. They are non-glossy blue-white, with very occasional red-brown markings, and the shell is green on the inside. 1.65 x 1.27in:41.5 x 32.7mm. Incubation, by the female alone, begins with the first egg and takes 27–40 days, depending on the size of the clutch. With intervals between the laying of the eggs the young vary considerably in size, and the smallest often die soon after hatching. The female close broods her young for the first 3 weeks, the male bringing food to her on the nest. The young fledge at 4 weeks and fly at 30–40 days.

BREEDING SEASON   May or June. Single-brooded.

Other grey birds which are fully described under different sections.

BLACKCAP   **This warbler is described under BLACK-HEADED BIRDS.**

Swallow

SIZE 7½in:19cm.

DESCRIPTION Most familiar of the Swallow family – upperparts a dark iridescent blue, underparts creamy/white, with blue collar round throat, and red chin and forehead. Long pointed wings, sharply angled in flight, and deeply forked tail, the long outer feathers forming 'streamers' – the most distinctive feature when the bird is in flight.

SONG/CALL A 'chirrup', or a high 'tseep' alarm call, and a quiet twittering song.

RECOGNITION The Swallow is one of the most eagerly awaited of summer visitors, being widely regarded as a harbinger of spring. An essentially aerial bird, its gliding flight with extended tail streamers make it easy to recognise. Although nesting in solitary pairs, Swallows are gregarious birds and feed, roost and migrate together in sizeable flocks. Large numbers are often seen perching on phone wires prior to migration back to Africa in the autumn. Swallows are widely distributed throughout the British Isles, and closely associated with man, often nesting in buildings and houses; but they are usually absent from city centres.

FOOD Almost entirely insects caught on the wing.

NEST Both sexes help build the nest – a shallow cup made of mud pellets mixed with vegetable fibre, grass and straw, and lined with feathers. The birds gather globules of mud from stream banks or puddles (even from pails of water) and build up the nest in layers, letting the mud harden before the next course is added. Natural nest sites are ledges in caves or on cliffs, but man-made sites like rafters or girders in a building are used readily, or sometimes the whole structure is supported by a stout nail on a wall. Barns and garages with suitable supports for the nest are also favoured sites.

EGGS 4–5, sometimes up to 8, smooth, glossy, slightly elongated eggs are laid, white sparingly marked with reddish-brown spots. .82 x .54in:20 x 13.7mm. Incubation, mainly by the female, takes 14–16 days, and the young are fledged and ready to fly at 17–24 days, although they often return to the nest to roost for a while.

BREEDING SEASON From mid-May onwards. Double or treble-brooded.

The Swallow is also listed under BIRDS WITH RED ON FACE OR BREAST.

House Martin

SIZE 5in:12.5cm.

DESCRIPTION Swallow-like aerial bird, with dark blue/black plumage above, white below, with conspicuous white rump and dark forked tail.

CALL/SONG A 'chirrup' or high-pitched 'tseep' of alarm. A quiet twittering song.

RECOGNITION   A summer visitor, arriving in March and leaving for Africa in September or October. The House Martin is smaller than the Swallow, with distinguishing white rump and shorter forked tail. It is gregarious and closely associated with man, forming small colonies and nesting on houses, or larger colonies on bridges. Originally cliff or cave dwellers, House Martins have adapted to man's buildings, and their mud nests under the eaves are found in towns and villages throughout Britain. In late summer large numbers of House Martins gather with Swallows and Sand Martins prior to migrating back to Africa.

FOOD   Almost entirely insects caught on the wing.

NEST   Both sexes build the round globe-shaped nest from pellets of mud mixed with grass or roots, situated under the eaves of buildings with the entrance hole at the upper rim. The nest is lined with straw and feathers. Many nests may be built on the same building, forming quite large colonies.

EGGS   Any number from 2–6, but usually 4–5, glossy white and rather elongated. .79 x .52in:19.4 x 13.4mm. Incubation, by both sexes, takes 13–19 days, and the young are fledged and ready to fly in 19–25 days. When all the broods have been raised the nest may continue to be used for roosting purposes – as many as 13 birds have been recorded in a single nest.

BREEDING SEASON   From May onwards. Double or sometimes treble-brooded.

The House Martin is also listed under BLACK AND WHITE BIRDS

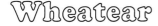

SIZE   6in:15cm.

DESCRIPTION   Small member of the Chat family, with conspicious white rump. Male has blue/grey back, broad white supercilium and bold black eye-stripe widening out over the ear coverts. Underparts are pale orange shading to white, and white tail has black centre and tip. The female has a brown back, and creamy-buff underparts, and lacks the black eye-stripe.

SONG/CALL   A hard 'chack', 'chack-weet' or 'Weet-chack' call, and a lark-like warbling song uttered in display flight or from a low perch, but containing wheezy, rattling notes.

RECOGNITION   The Wheatear is a summer visitor to Britain, frequenting heath and moorland areas, or coastal shingle. It is somewhat patchily distributed throughout the British Isles, being most plentiful in Scotland and northern areas of England and Wales. It is a ground-feeding bird, active and restless, flitting across open ground with tail fanned out and waving, or 'bobbing' up and down. It can also hover briefly like a hawk, and dive to the ground after insects. In spring the male has a dance-like courtship display, involving spread wings and tail and leaping up and down with puffed-out feathers.

PLATE 23

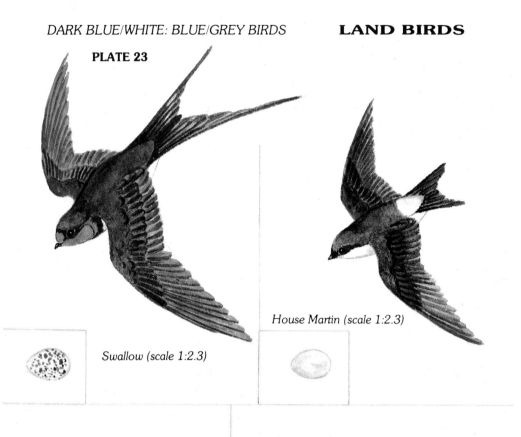

House Martin (scale 1:2.3)

Swallow (scale 1:2.3)

Nuthatch (scale 1:2.3)

Wheater (scale 1:2.3)

FRANCES FRY.

FOOD   Mainly insects and their larvae, also spiders, snails or centipedes or ants.

NEST   The Wheatear is a hole-nester, choosing a natural hole in rocks, walls, quarries, or a rodent burrow, or even a hollow pipe. The nest consists of a large loose cup of grasses, moss, plant stems, roots and leaves, lined with grass, hair, wool or feathers. The female does most of the building, but occasionally the male assists.

EGGS   5–6 usually, sometimes 4–7, non-glossy pale blue eggs. .8 x .6in:20.8 x 15.8mm. Incubation, by both sexes but mainly by the female, takes about 14 days, and fledging about 15 days.

BREEDING SEASON   Late March to June. Single-, sometimes double-brooded.

The Wheatear is also listed under BIRDS WITH ORANGE ON BREAST.

Nuthatch

SIZE   5½in:14cm.

DESCRIPTION   Small tree-climbing bird, with blue/grey upperparts, buff-orange underparts, white throat and bold black eye-stripe. Thick bill, short and sharply pointed, and strong, sharp-clawed feet.

SONG/CALL   A clear, ringing whistle 'chwit-chwit', or a loud 'twee' repeated several times, or a 'pee-pee-pee'.

RECOGNITION   The Nuthatch is the only British bird that can climb down trees head first. Resident all year round, and widespread in southern England and Wales, becoming scarcer in the north. It is not found in Scotland or Ireland. A rotund little bird, a very agile climber, but not restricted just to tree-climbing – the Nuthatch will also fly after insects from a perch like a Flycatcher. Although small enough to be overlooked its loud whistling call often draws attention to the bird, particularly during the breeding season. During courtship the male often displays before the female with feathers fluffed out and tail and wings outspread. A woodland bird by nature, but also seen in gardens and parks as well.

FOOD   Hazel nuts, acorns and beechmast, also beetles, seeds and insects and caterpillars. Its name Nuthatch derives from 'nut-hack' refering to its ability to break open nuts by hacking them with its bill after wedging them in a tree crevice. In recent years the Nuthatch has become a regular visitor to birdtables for nuts and seeds.

NEST   The nest, made of bits of bark and dead leaves, is always in a hole – in an old tree, an old Woodpecker hole, or in a wall, with the entrance hole plastered up with mud until it is the correct size to admit the Nuthatch and keep out larger birds or predators. Nest-boxes are sometimes used, and these too are plastered to fit the bird. The female does most of the building, but the male helps with the plastering.

EGGS   6–9, occasionally up to 13, smooth, slightly glossy white eggs speckled with red-brown markings concentrated at the larger end. .77 x .56in:19.3 x 14.8mm. Incubation, by the female only, takes 14–18 days, and fledging 23–25 days.

BREEDING SEASON   Begins late April to May. Single-brooded usually, but sometimes double-brooded.

The Nuthatch is also listed under BIRDS WITH ORANGE ON BREAST.

Blue Tit.   This attractive blue and yellow tit is described under BRIGHT COLOURED BIRDS.

Great Tit.   This blue and yellow tit is described under BRIGHT COLOURED BIRDS.

Bluethroat.   This colourful passage migrant is described under BRIGHT COLOURED BIRDS.

Waxwing

SIZE 7in:18cm.

DESCRIPTION Plump pinkish-brown bird with crest. Chestnut upperparts, pink-brown underparts, stubby bill, black eye-stripe and black bib, and grey-black tail boldly tipped with yellow. The wings are tipped with yellow and white, and have red wax-like appendages on the secondaries which give the species its' name. Sexes alike.

SONG/CALL A soft 'sirrr'. Waxwings are very sociable birds and call frequently, and where once known as Bohemian chatterers.

RECOGNITION The Waxwing is one of Britain's most exotic winter visitors, rare most years but occasionally widespread when the species has a population explosion and irrupts out of its' normal range in northern Europe. When this occurs, or when food crops fail, many birds arrive in the autumn and Britain has a 'Waxwing winter' with sizeable flocks descending on its berry crops. 'Waxwing winters' have been recorded since the end of the seventeenth century, with a particularly massive invasion noted in 1965–6. Waxwing habitat normally is coniferous forest, but in winter they will frequent any areas of open country with suitable berries, and they will often visit suburban gardens in search of ornamental berries. A small flock of hungry Waxwings can consume an amazing amount of berries in a short time. They are very tame and confiding birds, and may be closely observed without difficulty.

FOOD Mainly berries, although some insects are taken in summer. Rowan berries are the mainstay of their diet, but privet, yew and holly are also taken, as are ornamental species like cotoneaster, viburnum and pyracantha.

The Waxwing does not breed in Britain, but returns to its native Scandinavia.

Hawfinch

SIZE 7in:18cm.

DESCRIPTION Chunky, heavily built finch with large head and massive bill. Tawny head, chestnut brown back and pinkish-brown underparts, with black throat bib and lores, and black wings barred white, chestnut tail tipped with white. The female is paler than the male.

SONG/CALL A loud 'ptik' or 'Ptik-it', a thin 'tzeep', and a seldom heard song – 'tchee-tchee-tur-whee-whee' with variations. The song is usually given from treetops.

RECOGNITION The Hawfinch is the largest British finch, resident all year round, but shy and elusive and difficult to observe closely. Its large head and bill provide easy recognition in the field, but it is chiefly arboreal in habit, frequenting mixed woodlands with plentiful wild fruiting trees. However large gardens with orchards and parks are also visited. The Hawfinch has a rapid, 'bounding' flight, and on the ground walks with an upright gait or hops powerfully. In winter Hawfinches may form flocks feeding on the ground in woodland areas, but they are always extremely wary, even when raiding the vegetable garden for peas or fruit.

FOOD   Insects in summer, buds and fruit, and peas. However most of its diet consists of the hard seeds of fruits than other finches cannot utilize – the Hawfinches powerful bill can crack a cherry stone.

NEST   A cup made of twigs, roots and lichens, lined with finer roots, plant fibre and hair. The nest is usually built in a fruiting tree fairly high up from the ground.

EGGS   Usually 5, sometimes 2–7, glossy pale blue or greenish eggs, sparsely marked with spots and scrawls of dark brown. .96 x .69in:24.2 x 17.4mm. Incubation, mainly by the female but with occasional help from the male, takes 9–14 days, and fledging 10–14 days.

BREEDING SEASON   Begins late April or May. Usually single-brooded, but occasionally two broods are reared.

Hoopoe

SIZE   11in:28cm.

DESCRIPTION   Pale pinkish-brown plumage, with boldly barred black and white wings and tail, and long, black-tipped erectile crest and long de-curved bill.

SONG/CALL   A carrying 'poo-poo-poo', also a quiet chattering when alarmed, and some 'mewing' notes.

RECOGNITION   The Hoopoe is a summer visitor to Britain. It has a wide Continental range, but passage migrants are seen regularly in southern England, and small numbers stay and breed here. Its distinctive black and white and pink plumage is unmistakable. It frequents open country with woods and hedgerow cover, and will also visit parks, orchards and large gardens. It feeds chiefly on the ground in the open, probing with its long curved bill for insects like grasshoppers or crickets. Its flight is lazy and undulating, with a 'slow-motion' wing-action.

FOOD   Insects and larvae, grasshoppers and crickets, occasionally lizards.

NEST   The Hoopoe is a hole-nester, choosing a natural cavity in a tree or stump, in a wall or old building, or a rock crevice. Sometimes however it will use a nestbox. Often the cavity is not lined, but sometimes there is a sparse lining made up of plant material, feathers, wool or old rags. During the nesting period droppings are allowed to accumulate in the nest, and a distinctive foul smell develops.

EGGS   6–8 usually, although sometimes up to 12 eggs may be laid, non-glossy and conspiciously marked with pores, and greyish-green in colour. The colour changes as the eggs become stained by the accumulated droppings. 1.0 x .70in:25.9 x 17.9mm. The eggs are laid on consecutive days, and incubation, by the female alone, begins before the clutch is completed, and takes 16–19 days. The young hatch at intervals and vary considerably in size. The female broods the chicks when small with the male bringing food. The chicks are fledged at 20–27 days, but continue to be fed by their parents after leaving the nest.

BREEDING SEASON Begins in April. Usually single-brooded, but sometimes double-brooded.

Jay

SIZE 13½in:34cm.

DESCRIPTION Noisy, woodland member of the crow family. Pinkish-brown body with black tail and rounded black wings with bright blue-and-white-and black barred primary coverts, most noticeable during flight. White, streaked black, crown which can be raised as a crest, black moustachial stripe, and prominent white rump. Stout, shortish bill.

SONG/CALL Harsh, carrying 'skaark' and 'keeuw' call notes, and (seldom heard) a quiet warbling song.

RECOGNITION The Jay is resident throughout most of the British Isles with the exception of high treeless regions, but despite its showy plumage it is more often heard than seen, being secretive in its habits. Once strictly a woodland species, the Jay has extended its range to include parks and gardens and sometimes city areas too. At one time the species suffered considerable persecution as its bright wing feathers were popular ornaments for fashionable ladies at the turn of the century, and today it is unpopular with gamekeepers due to its fondness for eggs and chicks of game birds; but the species has successfully colonised new areas and is becoming more numerous in towns, adapting to its new surroundings and even visiting bird tables in some districts to take food put out for smaller birds.

FOOD A wide variety of nuts and berries, but particularly acorns. Jays feed well on acorns in autumn, storing any surplus under leaf litter and thus helping to regenerate oak woodlands. Worms and insects are also eaten, as are eggs and young of other birds.

NEST A cup of twigs and barks, placed in the fork of a tree usually, and lined with fine roots and hair.

EGGS 5–7, occasionally 3–10, glossy pale green eggs finely speckled with deeper green markings. 1.2 x .9in:31.6 x 22.9mm. Incubation, by both sexes, begins with the first egg, and takes 16–17 days. The young are fledged and ready to leave the nest at 19–20 days.

BREEDING SEASON Late April or May. Single-brooded.

Turtle Dove

SIZE   11in:27cm.

DESCRIPTION   Slim dove, with red-brown and black upperparts with scalloped-effect markings, pink breast, black and white striped patch on neck, and long dark tail with white tip. The sexes are alike.

SONG/CALL   The 'voice of the turtle' is a purring 'roor-r-r', repeated soporifically.

RECOGNITION   The Turtle Dove is a summer visitor to Britain, widespread in England and Wales but scarce in Scotland and Ireland. Habitat is mostly open ground, woods or hedges, and arable land. It may often be seen in parks and gardens. It feeds mainly on fumitory seeds, and arrives late in April or May when this food supply is available. The scarcity of the fumitory plant in Scotland and Ireland may account for the Turtle Dove finding difficulty in colonising these countries. Turtle Doves are gregarious birds, flocking together to feed on agricultural land. In spring they give territorial display flights, climbing steeply with clapping wings and then gliding down to the launch perch, and like many members of the dove family males court females by bobbing up and down with puffed-out chest.

FOOD   Mainly seeds of fumitory, but also grain and cereal seeds, chickweed, charlock and grass.

NEST   the female builds a flimsy platform of twigs, with a scanty lining of roots, plant stalks and grass, situated in a shrub, hedge or small tree, often quite low down, occasionally the old nest of another bird is used as a base.

EGGS   Usually 2, though occasionally only 1, slightly glossy white eggs are laid. 1.22 x .92in:30.7 x 23.0mm. Incubation, by both sexes, takes 13–14 days, and fledging 19–21 days. If danger threatens the young the parent birds will flutter helplessly to distract attention from the young. The chicks are fed on 'pigeons' milk'.

BREEDING SEASON   May–July. Usually two broods are raised.

The Turtle Dove is also listed under BIRDS WITH ROSY BREASTS.

Collared Dove

SIZE   12½in:32cm.

DESCRIPTION   Distinctive pinkish dove, with warm buff upperparts, and pink-buff head and breast, black edged white half-collar around back of neck, and long black tail with white tip. Sexes alike.

SONG/CALL   A repeated 'coo-coo-cuk', with stress on middle syllable.

RECOGNITION The Collared Dove is a recent newcomer to Britain. Once confined to Asia and southeast Europe a population explosion in the 1930s caused a rapid expansion of range north-westwards. It reached Britain in 1955, and spread quickly, colonizing the whole country in a few years, and is now widespread everywhere except mountainous areas. It associates closely with man, particularly where grain is available, and is found in towns and villages and on farmland. Collared Doves are sociable birds, gathering together at feeding grounds. They will also visit gardens and birdtables. In spring they give display flights similar to those of the Turtle Dove, and they share the same sort of courtship ritual too.

FOOD Chiefly grain, but also weed seeds, fruit such as elderberries, and they also have a fondness for poultry food.

NEST A flimsy platform of twigs and plant stems, usually situated in a tree, often an evergreen, but rarely on a ledge on a building.

EGGS 2 glossy white eggs are laid. 1.20 x .93in:30.1 x 23.2mm. Incubation, by both sexes, takes about 14 days, and fledging 18 days. The young are fed on 'pigeons' milk'.

BREEDING SEASON March to September. Double-brooded, but often more – up to five broods can be raised in a year sometimes, and this fast breeding rate has helped the extraordinary population increase of this species.

The Collared Dove is also listed under BIRDS WITH ROSY BREASTS.

Female Chaffinch   This bird is described under BIRDS WITH ROSY BREASTS.

PLATE 24

Waxwing (scale 1:3.5)

Hawfinch (scale 1:3.5)

Hoopoe (scale 1:3.5)

Jay (scale 1:4.6)

Turtle Dove (scale 1:3.5)

Collared Dove (scale 1:3.5)

Goldcrest

SIZE   3½in:9cm.

DESCRIPTION   The smallest British bird (together with the closely related Firecrest). Upperparts olive-green, underparts pale olive-buff. The male has an orange crown flash bordered with yellow and black; the female has a similar crown marking of yellow and black. Juveniles lack the bright crown markings.

SONG/CALL   A high, thin 'tsee-tsee-tsee' call, and a repeated double-note song ending with a flourish – 'steeng-steeng-steeng-stichipi-steeng'. The call note is rather similar to that of the Coal Tit.

RECOGNITION   The Goldcrest's diminutive size and bright crest mark set it apart from other small birds except for the Firecrest, which is very similar in every way save for a deeper red-orange crest mark. Goldcrests are active, gregarious little birds, and small flocks may be seen in trees or bushes searching for insect food, and sometimes hovering briefly to pick food from the underside of leaves. Resident all year, and found mainly in coniferous woodland although deciduous woods are also visited. They are quite widespread throughout the British Isles, and may visit gardens if there is sufficient tree and shrub cover. Goldcrests do not appear to have a great fear of man, and be quite tame. As with all very small birds severe winters take a heavy toll, but overall the population appears to be increasing.

FOOD   Mainly insects and their larvae, spiders and their eggs.

NEST   Both sexes help build the nest which is a deep cup-shape, suspended from the outer branches of a conifer (for preference) or other suitable tree. The nest is made of moss and lichen, bound together with spiders webs to the supporting twigs, and lined with feathers.

EGGS   7–10, sometimes up to 13, non-glossy white or pale buff eggs, finely speckled with brown or purplish markings, often confined to the larger end. .52 x .4in:13.6 x 10.7mm. Incubation, by the female alone, takes 14–17 days, and the young leave the nest at 16–21 days.

BREEDING SEASON   From late April onwards. Double-brooded.

Firecrest

SIZE   3½in:9cm.

DESCRIPTION   Shares with the Goldcrest the distinction of being Britain's smallest bird. General appearance similar to the Goldcrest – olive-green upperparts and olive-buff underparts – but with dark eye-stripe and broad white line above eye, and thin moustachial stripe. The male has bright orange-red crest stripe edged black.

SONG/CALL   A high-pitched 'zit-zit' call pitched lower than Goldcrest, and a song consisting of repeated 'zit' notes, given with increasing rapidity but ending suddenly.

RECOGNITION　The Firecrest is a much rarer bird than the superficially similar Goldcrest, and is usually found only in southern England. Most of these are summer visitors, or continental birds on passage through England, but a few birds overwinter here, forming a small resident population. Coniferous woodland is the most favoured habitat, but deciduous woods are also visited. Firecrests are active little birds, flitting and hovering amongst the foliage seeking food, but they tend to be rather shy and secretive, and are often revealed only by their calls or song. Numbers seem to be increasing slowly.

FOOD　Insects and their larvae, spiders and their eggs.

NEST　The Firecrest's nest is very similar to that of the Goldcrest, maybe just a little more compact. Situated in a conifer (for preference) or other tree, suspended under the branches, and made of moss and spiders webs, and lined with feathers.

EGGS　7–11 or perhaps 12, non-glossy white eggs, often with a pinkish-buff tinge, finely speckled with reddish-purple markings. .51 x .83in:13.5 x 10.3mm. Incubation, by the female alone, takes 14–15 days, and fledging 19–20 days.

BREEDING SEASON　Begins in May. Double-brooded.

Greenfinch

SIZE　5¾in:14.5cm.

DESCRIPTION　A small, heavily built finch, predominantly green in colour, with yellow-green rump and conspicious yellow on wings and tail, especially noticable during flight. A heavy, light coloured bill and pinkish legs, and deeply forked black-tipped tail are other distinctive features. The female is duller than the male.

SONG/CALL　A nasal 'dweee' given in spring during the breeding season, a short 'chup', and a loud rapid trill. The actual song consists of a mixture of twittering notes and call notes, given from tree-tops or during flight.

RECOGNITION　The Greenfinch's colouring lives up to its name, and this colourful member of the Finch family, resident all year, is widespread throughout Britain, except in the northern offshore islands of Scotland. Its favoured habitat is open woodland, farmland, gardens and parks, and it is a frequent visitor to bird tables for nuts. In spring the male gives a beautiful display flight, circling slowly before his chosen female with slow deliberate wing movements and tail feathers spread wide showing off the bright yellow flashes to best advantage. At other seasons Greenfinches are gregarious birds and often form flocks with other finches.

FOOD　Weed seeds, insects, spiders, cereals, fruit and berries. Peanuts if available.

NEST　A bulky cup made of grasses, plant stems and moss, lined with plant fibres, roots hair and feathers. The female does most of the building, situating the nest in a bush or tree, usually in the fork of a branch.

EGGS　4–6, sometimes 3–8, glossy pale blue eggs, finely marked with purple or black spots or blotches and some paler lilac markings. Markings are sometimes sparse, and concentrated at the larger end of the egg. .83 x .55in:20.6 x 14.8mm. Incubation by the female alone, takes 12–14 days, and fledging 13–16 days.

BREEDING SEASON Begins in April. Single or double-brooded.

Green Woodpecker

SIZE 12½in:32cm.

DESCRIPTION Bright green plumage distinguishes this Woodpecker from all other British tree-climbing birds. A sizeable bird, with strong pointed bill, bright green upperparts and lemon-green underparts, conspicous yellow rump and lower back. Both sexes have a crimson-crown; the male has a crimson moustachial stripe edged with black, the female has a black moustachial stripe. Pale yellow iris to the eye.

SONG/CALL A loud, laughing cry – 'quee-quee-quee', with a shriller, more extended version acting as a song in the breeding season. This ringing cry gives the bird its country name of 'yaffle'.

RECOGNITION Resident all year round and widely distributed throughout England Wales, but scarcer in Scotland and absent from Ireland. Its loud ringing laugh and bright colour make it easy to recognise together with its tree-climbing habit. It frequents open woodland and heaths, parks and gardens, and is often seen on suburban lawns probing the grass with its long bill searching for ants. The Green Woodpecker seldom 'drums' like other Woodpeckers, and often feeds on the ground, moving in clumsy hops. Its flight is very undulating, with long wing-closures between each upward bound.

FOOD Larvae of wood-boring insects, ants, caterpillars and spiders. Sometimes grain, acorns, apples and other fruit. Has been known to raid beehives trying to get at the bee grubs.

NEST Both sexes help make the nest, boring a hole in a tree – rotting wood is preferred, but if this is not available quite sound wood is utilised. An elongated cavity is excavated a small entrance (about 2½in across) leading to a nest chamber roughly 15in x 6in. The hole is not lined.

EGGS 5–7 usually, sometimes 4–9, glossy white eggs. 1.3 x .88in:31.8 x 23.0mm. Incubation, by both sexes, takes 18–19 days, and the young are fledged and ready to leave the nest at 18–21 days.

BREEDING SEASON Late April to May. Single-brooded.

Chiff-Chaff

SIZE 4¼in:11cm.

DESCRIPTION A small plump greenish-coloured bird, best known as a songster. Its upperparts are olive-brown, and underparts buffish-yellow. Often confused with

PLATE 25

Goldcrest (scale 1:2.3)

Firecrest (scale 1:2.3)

*Green Woodpecker
(scale 1:2.3)*

Greenfinch (scale 1:2.3)

FRANCES FRY

the similarly coloured Willow Warbler, but the Chiff-chaff has paler plumage and darker, blackish legs and bill.

SONG/CALL   A 'chiff-chaff-chiff-chaff-chaff' – two oft-repeated notes which give the bird its name. Also a soft 'hweet' note of contact.

RECOGNITION   The Chiff-chaff is one of the first of the summer visitors to arrive in Britain, often being seen in mid-March, well before most of the Warblers. At first glance it is easy to confuse with the Willow Warbler, and the best identification is its distinctive song. It is widely distributed over most of the British Isles, although it is scarcer in the far north. A small population overwinters in southern England. It is more open in its habits than many Warblers, flitting restlessly from branch to branch, and constantly flicking its wings and tail. Much of its insect food is caught on the wing in the manner of Flycatchers, but both Chiff-chaffs and Willow Warblers will sometimes hover momentarily picking insects from the underside of leaves. Mature woodland, hedgerows, parks and heaths are its favourite habitats, and gardens with sufficient shrubs and trees are also visited.

FOOD   Mainly insects, but also moth larvae, spiders and their eggs.

NEST   A domed structure made of dead leaves, plant stems, moss and plant debris, and thickly lined with feathers. The entrance is on the side of the nest. The female builds the nest, which is situated low down in a bush or thick vegetation, or occasionally on the ground in good cover.

EGGS   4–9 glossy white eggs sparsely marked with dark purplish spots or blotches, often concentrated at the larger end. .6 x .45in:15.1 x 12.1mm. Incubation, by the female alone, takes 13–14 days, and fledging 12–15 days.

BREEDING SEASON   From late April onwards. Single-brooded in the north, often double-brooded in the south.

Willow Warbler

SIZE   4¼in:11cm.

DESCRIPTION   A small greenish-yellow Warbler, olive-brown above and yellow-buff below, very similar to the Chiff-chaff but deeper in colour. Unlike the Chiff-chaff the legs and bill are pale brown, and its wings are slightly longer.

SONG/CALL   A quiet 'hooeet' note, rather like the Chiff-chaff, but the song is a musical trill on a descending scale ending with a flourishing 'sooeet-sooeetoo'.

RECOGNITION   The Willow Warbler is the most abundant summer visitor to Britain, widely distributed throughout the country. Often confused with the similarly coloured Chiff-chaff it is most easily distinguished by its song. Its favourite habitat is woodland, heaths and hillsides, but it is less arboreal than the Chiff-chaff and more likely to be seen in open country. Its behaviour is lively and acrobatic, and it seems to imitate perpetual motion feeding amongst vegetation, or catching insects in flight.

FOOD   Insects and larvae, worms and spiders, soft fruits and berries in autumn.

NEST   A domed structure made of leaves, grass, moss and roots, and lined with feathers. Rather similar to the Chiff-chaff's nest, but more loosely built, and more often situated on the ground, although it is sometimes slightly above ground level in bushes or vegetation. The female builds the nest.

EGGS   6–7 usually, sometimes up to 9, glossy white eggs finely speckled with reddish spots or blotches often concentrated at the larger end. .62 x .46in:15.4 x 12.3mm. Incubation, by the female only, takes 13 days, and fledging 13–16 days.

BREEDING SEASON   Mid-April to May. Single-brooded in the north, sometimes double-brooded in the south.

SIZE   4¾in:12cm.

DESCRIPTION   A small greenish yellow finch with bold black markings. The male has green upperparts streaked black, paler greenish-yellow underparts, black crown and bib, yellow rump and yellow wing-bars and tail margins. The female is duller, with no black on the head, and streaked underparts.

SONG/CALL   A 'tsooeet' call, usually given when alarmed, 'tiu-tiu-tiu' and 'chuch-uch-uch' notes. The song is twittering, rather Linnet-like, interspersed with flight call notes. The Siskin is very vocal throughout the year.

RECOGNITION   Most of the Siskins seen in England and Wales are winter visitors from northern Europe, but there is a resident breeding population in northern Scotland and parts of Ireland, and the species is extending its range in pine-afforested areas of England and Wales. Its favourite habitat is coniferous woodland, but alders and birches also provide suitable seed food, and Siskins are often seen amongst these trees with flocks of Redpolls. The Siskin is a very acrobatic bird, and can equal Tits with its ability to balance on the extreme tips of thin branches seeking food. Its agile behaviour and black-streaked green/yellow plumage are the best means of identification. It can be a frequent visitor to birdtables where hanging bags of peanuts put out for Tits have given the Siskin a valuable new source of food.

FOOD   Conifer seeds, particularly spruce, larch and pine, also alder and birch seeds. Peanuts when available.

NEST   Both sexes help build the nest high up in a conifer, at the end of a branch, and usually well hidden. The nest consists of a small cup of twigs, grass, moss and wool, lined with wool, hair or feathers.

EGGS   3–5 usually, sometimes 2–6, very pale blue glossy eggs, finely speckled with pink or lilac and a few spots of darker purplish colour, all markings being more concentrated at the larger end of the egg. .65 x .47in:16.4 x 12.3mm. Incubation, by the female alone, takes 11–14 days and fledging 13–15 days.

BREEDING SEASON   From April or May onwards. Double-brooded.

SIZE 4½in:11.5cm.

DESCRIPTION A small Canary-like finch with green/yellow plumage and short stumpy bill. The male has green upperparts, bright yellow rump and yellow on head and breast and both back and breast are streaked with black. The female is duller with less yellow and more streaking, particularly on the breast.

SONG/CALL A 'tsooeet' call, and 'tirrillillit' flight call; the song is a rapid high pitched jingling.

RECOGNITION Once regarded as a Mediterranean species the Serin has gradually extended its range northwards and is now seen as a summer visitor in southern England. The first British breeding record occured in Dorset in 1967, and it has since bred in other southern counties, but numbers are low. Favoured habitats are orchards and gardens – the Serin is a comparatively tame bird and associates closely with man. At first glance it may be mistaken for the more widely distributed Siskin, but the Serin is yellower overall yet lacks the yellow tail margins of the Siskin.

FOOD Almost entirely weed seeds.

NEST A neat cup made of plant stems, roots, moss and lichens, lined with hair, feathers and plant down. The female builds the nest which is usually situated in a deciduous tree or bush, fairly high up and towards the end of a branch or in a forked branch.

EGGS 4, sometimes 3–5, very light blue eggs spotted or scrawled with reddish-brown or purple, the markings mainly confined to the larger end of the egg. .65 x .43in:16.7 x 11.9mm. Incubation, nearly always by the female alone, takes about 13 days, and fledging 14 days, the young tending to leave the nest early before they can fly properly.

BREEDING SEASON From March to May onwards. Double-brooded.

ICTERINE WARBLER
Rare visitor to Britain from Europe, larger but similar colouring to WILLOW WARBLER. *Not illustrated.*

MELODIOUS WARBLER
Autumn passage migrant from S.W. Europe, larger but also similar in colouring to WILLOW WARBER. *Not illustrated.*

Other green birds which are fully described under different sections.

WOOD WARBLER This member of the Warbler family is described under *YELLOW BIRDS.*

Female CROSSBILL and female SCOTTISH CROSSBILL These birds are fully described under BRIGHT COLOURED BIRDS: RED BIRDS.

Female GOLDEN ORIOLE This bird is described under YELLOW BIRDS.

PLATE 26

Chiff Chaff (scale 1:2.3)

Willow Warbler (scale 1:2.3)

Siskin (scale 1:2.3)

Serin (scale 1:2.3)

FRANCES FRY.

Cirl Bunting

SIZE 6½in:16.5cm

DESCRIPTION An attractive yellow and rufous brown bird of open country. The male has a bold black and yellow head, yellow underparts, rufous back streaked with black, grey-olive rump and dark tail with whiter outer feathers. The female is duller, lacking the black head pattern, with brown upperparts and yellowish underparts streaked with black. The female Cirl Bunting is rather similar in colour to the female Yellow-hammer, but has a grey rump to distinguish her.

SONG/CALL A 'zip' flight call; a jingling song rather similar to the Yellowhammer's but lacking the final 'cheez'; a more monotonous single note – 'che'.

RECOGNITION The Cirl Bunting is resident all year, but is generally found only in sourthern and western areas of England. Female birds are often confused with the more widespread Yellowhammer (for differences see above – under description) but the male is easily recognised by his black and yellow face. It is a rather unobtrusive bird, easily overlooked in spite of its bold head markings, and tends to be only noticeable in spring when the male sings to establish territory. Favoured habitat is woodland edge or parkland, and in winter family parties may visit birdtables and gardens seeking food.

FOOD Weed seeds, cereals, berries, and insects and their larvae for feeding young.

NEST A cup-shaped nest of grass, roots and moss, lined with hair and fine grasses, is built by the female low down in a bush or hedge, or sometimes on the ground in a hollow or depression near the base of a shrub. If disturbed at the nest Cirl (and other) Buntings may feign injury to draw possible predators away from eggs or young.

EGGS 3–4, sometimes 2–5 pale blue or green eggs, speckled and scrawled with black markings. .85 x .63in:20.9 x 15.9mm. Incubation, by the female alone, takes 11–13 days, and fledging 11–13 days also. The female usually has to tend to the young without help from the male.

BREEDING SEASON From mid-May onwards. Double, sometimes treble-brooded.

Yellowhammer

SIZE 6½in:16.5cm

DESCRIPTION Distinctive yellow finch-like bird, although it belongs to the bunting family. The male has yellow head and underparts, chestnut rump, streaked chestnut back and streaked flanks, The female is duller, and more heavily streaked with dark brown. Both sexes have white outer tail feathers, which are conspicious during flight.

SONG/CALL A 'twit-up' or 'chip' call, and a rapid 'chi-chi-choi-chi-choi - - - chwee' song, translated in country-talk as 'a little-bit-of-bread-and-no-cheese.' The song is often delivered from a favourite song-post, or from a roadside hedge.

114

RECOGNITION The general yellow appearance together with chestnut rump and white outer-tail feathers are the Yellowhammer's distinguishing features. It is common throughout the British Isles and resident all year. Favoured habitats are farmland, heaths and commons, away from human settlements, although the Yellowhammer is not a shy bird and may often be seen perched by the roadside singing its well-known song. It rarely visits gardens, preferring to flock with other seed-eating bunting and finches feeding on fields. In spring during courtship the male may strut before the female with wings and tail spread out and crest feathers erected, or pursue her in a rapid twisting flight.

FOOD Largely weed seeds, also grain or wild fruits when available.

NEST A cup-shaped structure of grass, plant stems and moss, lined with hair and fine grass. The female builds the nest, which is situated low down in a bush or brambles, or on the ground under a hedge or in the bank of a ditch. Open woodland or heathland are the most favoured breeding grounds.

EGGS 3–5, sometimes 2–6, glossy white eggs with a bluish or purplish tinge, usually spotted or scrawled with black or purple-brown markings. .85 x .63in:21.6 x 15.3mm. Incubation, usually be the female alone, takes 11–14 days, and fledging 9–14 days.

BREEDING SEASON Begins in late April. Double, sometimes treble-brooded.

Golden Oriole

SIZE 9½in:24cm

DESCRIPTION A striking black and yellow woodland bird. The male has golden-yellow head, back and underparts, with black eye-stripe, black wings and black tail tipped with yellow. The female is a much duller yellow-green, with light yellow underparts streaked with green, and is sometimes mistaken for an immature Green Woodpecker. Both sexes have a red bill and blackish legs.

SONG/CALL A loud whistling 'weela-weeo', or a 'chuck-chuck-wheoo', usually given from a hidden perch high up in a tree. An alarm call of a harsh 'chr-r-r-', or a rather Jay-like screech.

RECOGNITION The thrush-sized Golden Oriole is a regular summer visitor to favoured parts of sourthern England, and small numbers bred most years in East Anglia and southern counties. A few birds stray further north, and nesting has been recorded in Scotland. For such a spectacularly coloured bird it is suprisingly easy to overlook as it is very arboreal in its habits and spends most of its time high up in tree foliage, foraging among the leaves for insects. It is essentially a bird of woodland habitat, preferring broad-leaved trees which give good cover, and in these surroundings the gold and green of its plumage (particularly females and immature birds) blend in with the leaves. The carrying whistling call often reveals a well-hidden bird.

FOOD Insects and their larvae, caterpillars, even bumble-bees sometimes. Fruit when available.

NEST The female builds the nest, a deep cup made of grass, leaf strips and bark, moss sand lichen, and lined with wool or grass. The nest is slung between two horizontal branches with the rim of the cup being woven round the supports, binding them together firmly to withstand the wind. The depth of cup protects eggs and young.

EGGS 3–4, glossy white eggs flushed with pink, sparsely marked with bold dark spots. 1.20 x .75in:30.8 x 18.6mm. Incubation, mainly by the female, takes 14–15 days and fledging the same 14–15 days.

BREEDING SEASON May to June. Usually single-brooded, occasionally double-brooded.

Wood Warbler

SIZE 5in:12.5cm

DESCRIPTION Bright yellow-green warbler, slightly larger than the Chiff-chaff and with longer wings. Yellow-green upperparts, sulphur yellow throat and breast fading to white on the belly, broad yellow eye-stripe. Bill and legs are flesh-coloured.

SONG/CALL A 'pui' and 'whit-whit-white' call, the song consists of a repeated 'pui' or a series of 'strip-stip-stip' notes accelerating to a shivering grasshopper-like thrill. The song is given during flight or when the bird moves amongst tree cover.

RECOGNITION The overall yellow appearance of the Wood Warbler makes it one of the easier Warblers to identify. Its behaviour is similar in many ways to the Chiff-chaff but it is much yellower, and does not flick its wings like the Chiff-chaff. It is a fairly widespread summer visitor in England, Scotland and Wales, but is usually absent from Ireland. It likes woodland habitat, deciduous for preference but conifers or mixed woodland is also used. The male gives an almost butterfly-like display in spring, spiralling down from the tree-tops to the woodland floor with much wing-fluttering.

FOOD Insects and their larvae, and caterpillars of moths.

NEST The Wood Warbler is a ground-nester, hiding its nest in undergrowth if available, otherwise scantily disguised in a hollow or against a mound. The female builds the domed nest of dead leaves, grass, plant stems and bark fibres, with a side entrance, and lines it with fine grass sand hair.

EGGS 6–7 usually, sometimes 4–8, glossy white eggs profusely spotted with dark red-brown or purple-grey markings. .61 x .47in: 15.9 x 12.5mm. Incubation, by the female alone, takes about 13 days, and fledging takes 11–12 days. The young remain dependent on the parent birds for about four weeks after leaving the nest.

BREEDING SEASON From late May onwards. Usually single-brooded, but sometimes double-brooded.

Cirl Bunting (scale 1:2.3)

Yellowhammer (scale 1:2.3)

Golden Oriole (scale 1:2.3)

*Wood Warbler
(scale 1:2.3)*

FRANCES FRY.

Stonechat

SIZE 5in:12.5cm

DESCRIPTION Thick-set, upright-perching chat. The male has black head, dark brown upperparts mottled black, white rump and white on neck, and orangish breast. The female is duller, with brown head and no white collar. Sharp-pointed bill and legs and feet are black.

SONG/CALL A 'weet-stac-stac-' call which sounds like two pebbles knocking together and gives the bird its' name. The song is rather like the Dunnock's – a jingle of repeated double notes.

RECOGNITION The Stonechat is short-tailed and plump, frequenting heaths and commons and coastal regions of Britain. The species is mainly resident although some birds cross the channel in winter seeking a warmer climate. Hard winters take a heavy toll but numbers can recover quite quickly as breeding is fairly prolific. However it is less numerous in Britain than in the past. Stonechats pair off all the year round, and are seen mainly on uncultivated land. In spring the male bird chases the female in courtship display, or 'dances' up and down in the air singing. Sometimes the song is delivered from a songpost on top of a bush or telegraph pole, with repeated call notes and tail flicking.

FOOD Insects and their larvae, worms and spiders, and occasionally seeds.

NEST The female builds the nest, a cup of grass and moss with plant stems or wool occasionally added, and a lining of hair, wool and feathers. The nest is situated on or near the ground, at the base of a bush or a clump of gorse.

EGGS 5–6, sometimes 3–8, very pale blue eggs finely speckled with red-brown. .75 x .58in:18.9 x 14.4mm. Incubation, usually by the female although the male sometimes assists, takes 14–15 days, and fledging 12–13 days.

BREEDING SEASON Late March to June. Double, sometimes treble-brooded.

The Stonechat is also listed under BLACK-HEADED BIRDS.

Whinchat

SIZE 5in:12.5cm

DESCRIPTION Small chat often confused with the Stonechat. The male has mottled brown and black upperparts, a broad white wing-bar, white supercilium and white moustachial stripe, and orange chin and breast fading to buff belly. Sharp-pointed black bill, and black legs and feet. The female is much duller, with less clearly defined supercilium.

SONG/CALL   A harsh 'tic-tic', and a 'tu-tic' and 'tza' The song is a chat-like warble incorporating the calls of other species.

RECOGNITION   The Whinchat is a summer visitor to Britain, arriving from Africa in April and departing back in the autumn. Its habitat is similar to the Stonechats' – heaths and open moorland, but it is also found in lowland pastures, freshwater marshes and more confined areas like railway enbankments. It is often seen perching on top of a bush or on tall plants like thistles, singing its' warbling song. In spring the male sings to the female with lowered wings and quivering, fanned-out tail, with head thrown back, and he also sings while the female is incubating the eggs. Whinchats have declined in numbers in Britain this century, but in recent years there has been signs of a slight recovery, with the species extending its breeding range to conifer plantations.

FOOD   Insects and their larvae, worms and spiders.

NEST   The female builds a cup of grass and moss, lined with finer grass and hair. The nest is usually situated on the ground amongst grass or at the foot of a bush.

EGGS   5–7, sometimes only 4, light blue eggs very finely speckled with red-brown .96 x .73in:19.2 x 14.5mm. Incubation, by the female alone, takes 13–14 days, and fledging 13-14 days also.

BREEDING SEASON   Begins in May or June. Single or double-brooded.

Redstart

SIZE   5½in:14cm

DESCRIPTION   Robin-sized chat. The male has grey crown and back, black face and chin, orange-red breast fading to cream belly, and bright rust-red rump and tail. Sharp-pointed bill, legs and feet are black, The female is duller with brown upperparts and paler orange breast, but has characteristic rust-red tail that is quivered as the bird perches.

SONG/CALL   A 'hweet' call, a louder 'twick', and a 'Hwee-tuc-tuc' alarm call. The song is a varied warbling.

RECOGNITION   The Redstart is a summer visitor to Britain, present from April to September in wooded country, heaths and commons, parks and hedgerows. It is widely distributed throughout Britain except in Ireland where it is a rare visitor, but numbers seem to be declining. It is a very active bird, catching insects on the wing, and quivering its tail when perching. 'The bright tail is also used in courtship display, the male bowing, drooping his wings and splaying the tail to show the bright red feathers, and there is much tail-quivering with both sexes.

FOOD   Mostly insects and their larvae, but also worms and spiders, and some berries in autumn.

NEST The female builds the nest in a natural hole in a tree-stump or wall, or in a hollow in the ground or among tree-roots. The Redstart is not too particular about site so long as a suitable hole is available. The nest consists of a loosely made cup of dead grass, moss and root fibres, lined with hair and feathers.

EGGS 6–7 usually, but numbers can vary from 4–10 sometimes, glossy light blue eggs. .75in x .57in:18.6 x 13.7mm. Incubation, by the female alone, takes 11–14 days, and fledging 14–20 days.

BREEDING SEASON May to June. Double-brooded.

Robin

SIZE 5½in:14cm

DESCRIPTION Britain's best-loved bird, with conspicious orange-red breast and face, olive-brown upperparts and grey-white belly. A line of grey separates the red breast and face from the brown upperparts. Juveniles lack the red breast and have mottled brown plumage.

SONG/CALL A 'tsipp-ip' call, a stronger 'tic', and a rather melancholy warbling song with short separated phrases. The song is heard all year round.

RECOGNITION The familiar red breast, featured on countless Christmas cards, and its confiding habits make the Robin one of the easiest birds to identify. Widely distributed throughout the British Isles, resident, and found in woodland, hedgerows, parks and gardens, and even city centres, the Robin was named as Britain's national bird some years ago. Regular visitors to birdtables, and keen observers of gardening activities, British Robins can become very tame, even feeding from the hand or entering houses, but his confiding behaviour is confined to British birds – continental Robins are shy, retiring birds. The Robin sings to establish territory throughout the year, and can be aggressive towards intruding birds, even its own young. In spring the male will courtship feed the female.

FOOD Insects and their larvae, worms, seeds and autumn soft fruits.

NEST The female builds the nest, often chosing most unusual sites, such as an old discarded kettle or jug, or an old jacket or shoe. More conventional sites are tree-holes, or in a shrub. Nest-boxes are sometimes used. The nest is a bulky cup made of dead leaves, grass or moss, lined with fine grass, roots and hair, rarely with feathers.

EGGS 5–6, sometimes 3–9, non-glossy white eggs speckled with pinkish-brown spots or blotches, sometimes very sparse, sometimes very profuse. .8 x .6in:19.9 x 15.4mm. Incubation, by the female alone, takes 12–15 days, and fledging also about 12–15 days.

BREEDING SEASON From late March to April onwards. Double, sometimes treble-brooded.

PLATE 28

Winchat (scale 1:2.3)

*Stonechat
(scale 1:2.3)*

Redstart (scale 1:2.3)

Robin (scale 1:2.3)

FRANCES FRY

Linnet

SIZE   5¼in:13.5cm

DESCRIPTION   Pretty, small finch, with chestnut brown upperparts, dark brown wings and forked tail edged with white, grey head, and buff underparts streaked black. The breast is pinkish, and in the breeding season the male has a crimson crown and breast which distinguishes him from the female.

SONG/CALL   A 'tsooeet' call, and a constant twittering during flight. The song is also twittering, interspersed with nasal notes, and is usually given from the top of a bush, sometimes in chorus with other Linnets.

RECOGNITION   The Linnet is one of the most common British finches, resident and widely distributed throughout the country with the exception of the Scottish Highlands, but despite its attractive plumage it is often overlooked. Habitat includes heathland, and as habitat has been lost with more mechanized farming methods the species has become more of an urban bird, visiting and nesting in small towns and villages, parks and gardens. Linnets are gregarious birds, forming sizeable flocks on grassland or saltmarshes when searching for food, and breeding together in small colonies. Cock birds sing sweetly in the breeding season, and in Edwardian times Linnets were popular cage birds, prized for their twittering song.

FOOD   Mainly weed seeds, but also caterpillars, insects and their larvae, spiders and some seeds of agricultural crops.

NEST   A bulky cup of grass, plant stems, moss and small twigs, lined with wool and hair, down or feathers. The nest is usually low down in a bush such as gorse or bramble.

EGGS   4–6 usually, rarely 7, slightly or non-glossy, pale blue eggs, finely speckled with purple or pink. .72 x .55in:18.2 x 13.2mm. Incubation, by the female alone, takes 10–14 days, and fledging 11–14 days.

BREEDING SEASON   Begins in mid-April. Double or treble-brooded.

Redpoll

SIZE   5in:13cm

DESCRIPTION   A small brown finch with streaked upperparts, buff underparts with streaked flanks, and pinkish breast and rump. In the breeding season the male has a bright crimson forehead and black bib.

SONG/CALL   A high-pitched metallic flight call; a rapid twittering 'chuch-uch-uch', or 'tui-tui-tui', and a plaintive 'tsooeet' call. The song is a series of brief trills interspersed with flight calls.

RECOGNITION The Redpoll is an acrobatic finch that feeds in the treetops rather like a Tit. Many Redpolls are resident all year round, but large numbers regularly migate to Holland or Germany, and Scandinavian birds arrive in Britain each autumn to overwinter here, so it is difficult to estimate the size of the permanent population. A woodland bird, primarily associated with conifer, the Redpoll also frequents birch and alder woods, and shows signs of extending its range to include farmland and hedgerows. Redpolls are gregarious birds, and often form small flocks when feeding. They are found over most of the British Isles except in outlying Scottish Islands.

FOOD Seeds, mainly of birch or alder, and some insects and their larvae.

NEST A small, untidy cup of grass, fine twigs and plant stems, lined with plant down, feathers and hair. The nest is situated in a tree, shrub or bush at very varying heights – sometimes high up, sometimes almost down to ground level. Pairs often nest near to each other.

EGGS 4–5 usually, sometimes up to 7, glossy light blue eggs with spots, blotches or scrawls or purplish-red. .69 x .56in:16.9 x 12.6mm. Incubation, by the female alone, takes 10-13 days, and fledging 11–14 days.

BREEDING SEASON Begins Late April. Single or double-brooded.

Chaffinch

SIZE 6in:15cm

DESCRIPTION Colourful small finch, with blue-grey head and nape, chestnut back and green rump, and blackish wings with two bold white bars, and black tail edged with white. Cheeks and breast are deep pink, fading to white on the belly. The female is duller, lacking the blue head.

SONG/CALL A distinctive 'pink-pink', and a flight call of 'tsip'. The song consists of a vigorous cascade of about a dozen notes, ending in a flourishing 'choo-ee-o'.

RECOGNITION The Chaffinch is the commonest British finch, resident and widely distributed throughout the country. It has a wide range of habitat, from farmland and wood to parks and gardens. Chaffinches are gregarious birds, and in winter they join other finches, buntings and sparrows in large flocks, searching for food on arable land. Sometimes they form single-specie flocks – all Chaffinches, and usually all of one sex. Chaffinches are regular vistors to gardens and birdtables, and are among Britains most abundant species.

FOOD Insects and their larvae, spiders, seeds, fruit, cereals and beechmast. Birdtable scraps and readily accepted as a supplement diet.

NEST A neat, deep cup made of moss, lichens, grasses and roots, bound together with spiders webs, and decorated with lichen or flakes of bark, with a lining of feather, rootlets, wool and plant down. Both sexes help build the nest, which is usually situated in a tree or shrub, fixed tightly into a fork.

EGGS 4–5 usually sometimes, 2–8, glossy, light blue eggs scrawled with dark chestnut-red blotches. .75 x .58in:18.6 x 14.6mm. Incubation, by the female alone, takes 11–13 days, and fledging 12–15 days.

BREEDING SEASON Begins April or May. Single or double-brooded, according to latitude and climate.

Brambling

SIZE 5¾in:14.5cm

DESCRIPTION Male has orange-buff breast and shoulder patch, black head and upper parts (in breeding plumage), white rump, and white wing bar. In winter upperparts are mottled brown. The female is duller, with brown upperparts, and may be confused with the female Chaffinch, but can be distinguished by paler, buffer plumage, white rump, and dark stripes on crown.

SONG/CALL A metallic-sounding 'tsweep', and a 'tchuc' flight note, repeated rapidly as a flight call. Its song resembles that of the Greenfinch – a repeated 'dzweea' interspersed with a few weak chipping notes.

RECOGNITION The Brambling is a winter visitor to Britain, with several thousands of birds arriving here in October and returning to their Scandinavian breeding grounds in March or April. Bramblings are gregarious birds, forming large flocks with Chaffinches in winter along field margins and hedgerows. Winter habitat includes farmland and woodland, particularly beech woods as beechmast forms a large part of their diet. In summer birchwoods are preferred, or pinewoods. Bramblings may visit gardens, but not so frequently as Chaffinches. The cock birds' striking breeding plumage is usually seen only briefly in Britain in early spring before the birds return to their breeding grounds. There has only been one proven record of Bramblings nesting in Britain (in Sutherland in 1920), although it is thought a few may nest in Scotland.

FOOD Seeds and berries, particularly grass seeds and beechmast, also cereals, and moths and their larvae in summer.

NEST A deep cup of moss, hair and grass, bound with spiders' webs, decorated with bark and lichen, and lined with hair, wool, down and feathers. The female builds the nest, usually in a tree or (rarely) a bush, close to the trunk.

EGGS 5–7, sometimes 4-8, glossy light blue eggs blotched with red or pink markings. .75 x .58in:18.6 x 14.6mm. Incubation, by the female alone, takes 11–12 days, and fledging 11–13 days.

BREEDING SEASON Mid-May to July. Usually single-brooded.

PLATE 29

Redpoll (scale 1:2.3)

Linnet (scale 1:2.3)

Chaffinch (scale 1:2.3)

Brambling (scale 1:2.3)

Other birds with red on head which are fully described under different sections.

GOLDFINCH This mutli-coloured finch is described under BRIGHT COLOURED BIRDS.

SWALLOW This aerial bird is described under DARK BLUE AND WHITE BIRDS.

Other birds with rosy breasts which are fully described under different sections.

BULLFINCH This brightly coloured finch is described under BLACK-HEADED BIRDS.

TURTLE DOVE This attractive dove is described under PINKISH/BROWN BIRDS

ROCK DOVE This dove is described under GREY BIRDS.

WOODPIGEON This large pigeon is described under GREY BIRDS.

RED BACKED SHRIKE This bird is described under BROWN BIRDS.

Great Tit

SIZE   5½in:14cm

DESCRIPTION   The largest British Tit, with glossy blue-black head and neck, white cheeks, and yellow underparts with black band down the centre. Dark green back, black tail and white wing-bars.

SONG/CALL   Many varied calls, including 'tee-choee', a Chaffinch-like 'tsink-tsink', a Blue Tit-like 'chi-chi-chi', a Marsh Tit-like 'tchair-tchair'. The song consists of variations on 'teechew-teechew' calls.

RECOGNITION   The Great Tit is resident and widespread throughout the British Isles. Originally a woodland edge bird its habitat has spread to include farmland, parks and gardens, and it is a frequent visitor to birdtables for peanuts and scraps. It tends to be aggressive towards other smaller species, and will dominate the peanut bags if given the opportunity. In winter Great Tits become more gregarious, and flock together with other Tits seeking food in woods and hedgerows. Like the Blue Tit it may sometimes steal the cream from milk bottles.

FOOD   Insects and their larvae, moths, bees, spiders and worms. Fruit and berries are also taken in winter, and buds in spring, plus food provided by man.

NEST   The Great Tit is a hole-nester, chosing a ready-made site in a tree or wall, or using a nest-box. The female builds the nest – a cup made of grass, moss, roots and lichen, lined with hair, plant down or feather.

EGGS   8–13, sometimes 7–15, slightly glossy white eggs are laid, speckled with purplish red spots or blotches. Markings vary greatly, sometimes profuse, sometimes sparse, but rarely totally absent. .7 x .55in:17.5 x 13.5mm. Incubation, by the female alone, takes 13–14 days, occasionally longer. Fledging 16–22 days.

BREEDING SEASON   Starts in April or May. Usually single-brooded, but sometimes double-brooded.

The Great Tit is also listed under BLACK-HEADED BIRDS and BLUE BIRDS.

Blue Tit

SIZE   4½in:11.5cm

DESCRIPTION   One of the most familiar British birds, associating closely with man. The only Tit with cobalt-blue crown, wings and tail. Green back, white cheeks with black line extending through the eye to around nape and chin, yellow breast, and white wing-bar.

SONG/CALL   A high 'tsee-tsee-tsee' call note, or a scolding 'churr'. The song consists of repeated call notes followed by a long trill.

RECOGNITION   One of the most common resident British birds, easily identified by its blue and yellow plumage. The Bluetit is widespread throughout the British Isles, being found wherever there are trees and bushes, and is a frequent visitor to gardens and bird tables, particularly if tempted by peanuts or a hanging coconut. Agile and acrobatic, the Bluetit is very rescourceful in its association with man, and in addition to the food offered by birdlovers may help itself to the cream of milk by pecking though the foil tops of the bottles left on the step. But few people would grudge this attractive bird its 'perks' as it amply repays the gardener by eating greenfly and other insects pests. In spring the male may be seen courtship feeding the female.

FOOD   Insects and their larvae, particularly aphids, spiders, fruit, berries, seeds and buds, as well as food provided by man.

NEST   The female builds the nest, usually in a hole in a tree or wall, or in a nestbox. The cup-shaped nest is made of moss and lichen, and lined with hair, feathers and down.

EGGS   7–12, sometimes 5–16 eggs are laid, with larger clutches occuring in wild nest-sites, smaller ones in nest-boxes. The eggs are glossy white, variably marked with red or purplish spots or blotches. .58 x 45in:15.6 x 12.0mm. Incubation, by the female only, sometimes begins before the clutch is completed, and takes 12–16 days, and fledging takes 15–23 days.

BREEDING SEASON   Starts in mid-April or May. Single-brooded, sometimes double-brooded.

The Blue Tit is also listed under BLUE BIRDS.

Goldfinch

SIZE   4¾in:12cm

DESCRIPTION   A boldly marked colourful little finch, once known as 'the seven-coloured Linnet' and prized as a cage-bird earlier this century. Scarlet face, black and white head, black and white tail, and striking black and yellow wings, with tawny-brown back and warm buff underparts shading to white. Narrow pointed bill, adapted for feeding on thistle-heads.

SONG/CALL   A 'tswitt-witt-witt' repeated call, and a Canary-like twittering song with variations on the call-notes.

RECOGNITION   Its varied bright colours, particularly the black and crimson head markings and special fondness for thistles make the Goldfinch easy to recognise. It is a common resident in most parts of Britian, except the northern areas of Scotland, although the population is subject to migratory movement with many British birds moving to the continent in autumn and others arriving from further northern regions of Europe. Goldfinches are gregarious birds and often form single-species flocks, called 'charms'. Habitat includes Farmland, hedgerows, parks waste ground and gardens. In

LAND BIRDS

PLATE 30

Blue Tit (scale 1:2.3)

*Great Tit
(scale 1:2.3)*

Goldfinch (scale 1:2.3)

Bluethroat (scale 1:2.3)

FRANCES FRY

spring the Goldfinch gives a courtship display, singing on a branch with wings drooped, swinging slightly from side to side.

FOOD Seeds, especially thistle seeds, knapweed and teasel seeds. Insects and their larvae are also taken to feed their young.

NEST A neat cup made of grass, moss, roots and lichen, lined with plant down and wool, or hair and feathers. The female builds the nest although the male may assist in gathering material, and it is usually situated in a tree or tall shrub, in the twigs towards the end of a branch. A tree with fairly open foliage is preferred.

EGGS 4–6, sometimes 3–7, glossy, very pale blue eggs, finely spotted with purple or red markings. .66 x .5in:17.3 x 14.4mm. Incubation, by the female alone, takes 12–14 days, and fledging 12–15 days.

BREEDING SEASON From late April onwards. Double, sometimes treble-brooded.

Bluethroat

SIZE 5½in:14cm

DESCRIPTION Robin-sized bird, with brown upperparts and white underparts, and bright chestnut base to tail. The male has the bright blue throat-patch that gives the species its name, bordered by black and chestnut bands. The female has a white throat-patch. Juveniles resemble young Robins, but with streaked breast rather than barred.

SONG/CALL A hard 'tac-tac', a soft 'whoeet', and a gutteral 'turruc'. The song is very musical and varied, almost resembling the Nightingale with repeated phrases, but higher in pitch and less rich. Sometimes has a metallic note 'ting-ting-ting'. The song is given from a perch, or during flight.

RECOGNITION The Bluethroat is a migrant bird of passage to most of Britain, with small numbers occurring regularly in spring and autumn, particularly on the east coast. Small numbers stay as summer visitors, and a few have bred in Scotland. Scrub land, heaths and tangled hedges are favoured habitats, or areas of dense vegetation, often close to water. Two distinct sub-species are seen in Britain; central-European birds have a white spot in the centre of the blue throat-patch, and birds from Scandanvia have a red spot. Bluethroats resemble Redstarts in behaviour, with frequent spreading and cocking of the tail.

FOOD Insects and their larvae, worms, and some berries and seeds in winter.

NEST The nest is usually built on the ground, hidden in a hollow, or against a bank, or sometimes at the base of a bush. It is made of plant stems, dead grass, roots and moss, lined with fine grass or hair, rarely feathers.

EGGS 5–7, occasionally up to 9, slightly glossy pale greenish-blue eggs, very finely speckled with light reddish-brown markings which may give a rusty tint to the shell. .70

x 55in:17.8 x 14.1mm. Incubation, by the female alone, takes 14–15 days and fledging about 14 days, with the young leaving the nest before they can fly.

BREEDING SEASON   May or June onwards. Usually single-brooded, but occasionally two broods are raised by the southern sub-species.

 Crossbill

SIZE   6½in:16.5cm

DESCRIPTION   Stockily built bird, slightly larger than a Sparrow, with distinctive crossed bill that gives the species its name. The male bird is crimson, the female yellow-green, both with darker wings and tail.

SONG/CALL   A loud 'chup-chup' call, usually given during flight, and a song consisting of 'chips' and trills warbled together.

RECOGNITION   The crossed bill like a scaled-down version of a Parrot's beak, and bright colour of both sexes make the Crossbill easy to distinguish from all except its close relative, the Scottish Crossbill. These two species are virtually identical at first glance, and where once regarded as one, but the Scottish Crossbill is found only in Scotland, is slightly larger and has a more powerful bill. Habitat is almost exclusively conifer woodlands, and conifer seeds form most of its diet; the cones are held in the feet while the specially adapted bill with the crossed tips extracts the seeds. Some Crossbills are resident all year round in Britain, and breeding colonies are found in East Anglia, the New Forest, Northumberland and Scotland, but numbers swell dramatically every few years when 'irruptions' occur among Continental birds and the overspill comes here. They are gregarious birds, and flock together through the conifers seeking food and shelter.

FOOD   Seeds of pine, larch, spruce and other conifers, sometimes also fruit, weed seeds and insects.

NEST   Crossbills nest high up in pine trees, building a cup of grass, hair and moss, supported on a base of twigs, and lined with feathers.

EGGS   3–4, sometimes 5, glossy very pale blue eggs thinly speckled with purple. .90 x .66in:22.9 x 16.0mm. Incubation, by the female alone, takes 13–16 days, and the young are fledged and ready to nest at 17–22 days.

BREEDING SEASON   Very early, the nest is built in February or March, but bad weather may delay breeding until later. Single-brooded.

 Scottish Crossbill

SIZE   6½in:16.5cm

DESCRIPTION   Male bird crimson, the female yellow-green, both with darker wings and tail. The plumage in indistinguishable from the Crossbill, but the bill is much larger and stronger.

SONG/CALL   A coarse 'tyoop-tyoop' note given during flight, and a song similar to the Crossbill's – a warbled mixture of 'chips' and trills.

RECOGNITION   The Scottish Crossbill is Britain's endemic species, found only in Scotland, where its strong bill enables it to extract the seeds of Scots Pines which the Common Crossbill cannot obtain. The appearance and lifestyle of the two species are so similar that for many years they were regarded as one, but now they are recognised as different and have different names in both English and Latin. Habitat is exclusively pine forests, both old Caledonian and more recent plantations, and the spread of new conifer plantings is enabling the species to extend its range in Scotland. However there is no evidence of it colonising England – birds seen further south are the Common Crossbill.

FOOD   Seeds of Scots pine, also other conifer seeds, berries and rarely other seeds.

NEST   A cup of grasses and moss on a base of twigs, lined with feathers, and built high in a pine tree.

EGGS   3.4 or 5, glossy very pale blue eggs speckled purple, virtually indistinguishable from those of the Crossbill. .90 x 66in:22.9 x 16.0mm. Incubation, by the female alone, takes 13–16 days, and fledging 17–22 days.

BREEDING SEASON   Early, the nest being built in February or March. Single-brooded.

Pheasant

SIZE   Male 30–35in:76–89cm. Female 21–25in:53–63cm: 18in is tail feathers.

DESCRIPTION   Familiar gamebird with long pointed tail, and bright varied plumage. The male is highly coloured, with glossy iridescent green head, red wattles round eyes, and short ear-tufts. frequently a white neck-ring, and very varied plumage – from copper brown to green, or sometimes iridescent black in a melanistic form. The female is much duller, with buff-brown plumage mottled black, and shorter but still lengthy tail.

CALL   A loud 'kork-kok' from the male, often followed by wing-flapping. The female has a thin whistling note.

RECOGNITION   The beautiful Pheasant was said to have been introduced into Britain by the Romans, and it is now a familiar resident gamebird, widely distributed throughout the country, being absent only from the far north of Scotland and its islands. The popularity of pheasant shooting as a field sport is responsible for the continued success of the species, with large numbers of birds reared annually and living protected lives until they face the guns in the autumn. Many birds escape death and return to the wild, frequenting arable land, woods, hedgerows and heaths, and also marshes – their original habitat is Asia where the species originated.

FOOD   The Pheasant has a very varied diet, consisting of seeds and berries, grain, leaves, insects, worms, slugs and other small invertebrates.

Common Crossbill (scale 1:2.3)

(inset) Scottish Crossbill (scale 1:2.3)

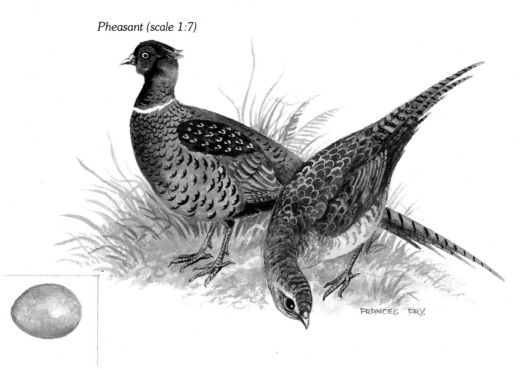

Pheasant (scale 1:7)

FRANCES FRY.

NEST   Male birds are polygamous, and females nest and rear young alone. A shallow hollow, unlined or with sparse vegetation, is used, but very occasionally a flattish, old bird's nest in a tree.

EGGS   7–15, glossy olive brown eggs are laid. 1.85 x 1.45in:45.9 x 36.0mm. Incubation, by the female alone, takes 23–27 days. The young are precocial and ready to leave the nest soon after hatching, and fledge quickly, being able to fly at 12–14 days.

BREEDING SEASON   April to June. Single-brooded.

Rose-Ringed Parakeet

(ring-necked parakeet)

SIZE   16in:40cm

DESCRIPTION   Bright green parakeet, originally brought to Britain as a cage bird. Bright green plumage, long pointed wings and very long tail, red bill. The male has a thin line around the neck, black in front – red on the nape, that gives the species its name.

SONG/CALL   A shrill 'kee-et' call, and a long screech given regularly in flight.

RECOGNITION   The Rose-ringed Parakeet cannot be confused with any other British bird, only perhaps with other escaped parakeets. The species first escaped into the wild in 1969 in London area, and rather surprisingly quickly adapted and established feral breeding populations, first in the suburbs of London, then in Kent, then more of southern England. Despite the setbacks of severe winters the species is now resident in many parts of southern England, especially near the edge of towns, and appears to be steadily increasing. Rose-ringed Parakeets will visit gardens to feed on buds and fruits, and visit birdtables too, and this exotic vistor looks set to become an established breeding species in Britain.

FOOD   Buds and fruit.

NEST   The Rose-ringed Parakeet nests in holes in trees.

EGGS   2–6 eggs are laid, white, very round, smooth, but non glossy. 1.35in x .87in:30.5 x 23.7mm. Incubation, by both sexes, takes 22–24 days, and fledgings 6–7 weeks.

Golden Pheasant

SIZE   23-39½in:87–100cm. The male is larger than the female.

DESCRIPTION   Ornamental gamebird originating to China. The male is a magnificent gaudy bird, with golden cape (that gives the species its name) partly covering the face, yellow back, and bright red underparts and upper tail feathers, the long tail feathers being a mosiac of yellow and black. The female is buff-brown, with barred wings and tail.

SONG/CALL   A high-pitched crowing call, much higher than the common Pheasant.

RECOGNITION The Golden Pheasant was first introduced into Britain in the eighteenth century as an ornamental gamebird. Small numbers were released for shooting, and others escaped, and the species is now established in the wild in the Brecklands of East Anglia, and in Galloway. It was officially added to the British and Irish list in 1971. Despite the bright colours of male birds the species is not easy to observe, being secretive by nature and slipping away agiley through dense vegetation. Main habitat is coniferous woodland. The feral population appears to be increasing steadily, and will doubtless increase its range in time.

FOOD Mainly grain, but seeds, berries and small insects are also taken.

NEST The nesting habits of the Golden Pheasant in the wild are believed to be similar to the common or Ringed-necked Pheasant.

Lady Amherst's Pheasant

SIZE 26½–59in:67–150cm. The largest measurements refer to the male, the smaller to the female.

DESCRIPTION Ornamental pheasant from China. The male is a most beautiful bird, with bottle green-blue chest and back, white underparts, black and silver cape partly covering the the face, yellow and scarlet rump with scarlet feathers extending over very long black and white tail. The female is buff-brown with barred wings and tail, very similar to the female Golden Pheasant.

SONG/CALL A loud crowing 'korrk-kok' call from the male, followed by loud wing-ruslings..

RECOGNITION Lady Amherst's Pheasant was named after the wife of a Governor General of India, and the species originates from the mountains of southwest China and Tibet. It was first introduced into Britain at the beginning of this century, and first ventured into the wild around Woburn, Bedfordshire. A growing feral population now exists in Bedfordshire, and is extending to neighbouring districts. Preferred habitat includes both coniferous and mixed woodland, particularly where the undergrowth is dense enough to provide good cover. Despite the bright plumage of male birds the species is difficult to observe in the wild as they are extremely secretive birds, quick to hide and skulk in vegetation rather than take flight. Lady Amherst's Pheasants will interbreed with Golden Pheasants both in captivity and in the wild, and hybridization is common.

FOOD Similar to common Pheasant – grain, seeds and berries, and insects and invertibrates.

NEST Breeding habits similar to the common Pheasant.

Other bright coloured birds which are fully described under different sections.

GOLDEN ORIOLE This striking black and yellow bird is described under
YELLOW BIRDS.

WAXWING This colourful visitor from Scandinavia is described under
PINKISH/BROWN BIRDS.

PLATE 32

*Rose-ringed Parakeet
(scale 1:4.6)*

Golden Pheasant (scale1:8.2)

Lady Amherst's Pheasant (scale 1:11.7)

FRANCES FRY.

PART TWO:
WATERSIDE BIRDS

Waterside Birds covers birds normally found close to water, both inland and on the coast, but not those normally seen swimming. The largest group of birds covered is the Waders, but smaller birds like some Warblers and Buntings are also included because they are always found in waterside habitats, and this category also includes two Raptors – the Marsh Harrier that lives and hunts in aquatic areas, and the Osprey that is a highly specialized hunter living almost exclusively on fish.

*Ducks and Geese are often seen in semi-domestic waterside surroundings such as parks or towns with riverside garden areas, but these are birds that spend a lot of their lives on water so they will be found in part three – **Water & Sea Birds**. Similarly Swans, Moorhen and Coot are also described in part three – **Water & Sea Birds**.*

Spoonbill

SIZE   34in:86cm

DESCRIPTION   A large, heron-like bird with long spatulate bill. All white plumage, with golden tint on face and lower foreneck in the breeding season when it also has a tufted crest. The long legs are black, and the spoonshaped bill that gives the bird its name is dark horn with a paler tip. Sexes alike, juveniles have black tips on primary wing feathers and pink bill.

CALL   Normally a rather silent bird, but may grunt or rattle its bill, or give a 'huh-huh-huh' sound when at rest.

RECOGNITION   Spoonbills bred in East Anglia until the 17th century, but now they are passage migrants visiting southern and eastern England in spring and autumn, with small numbers overwintering in southern counties, especially in East Anglia and the extreme South West. The nearest nesting colonies are in Holland. They are gregarious birds, usually seen feeding or flying in small parties, in estuaries, marshes or shallow freshwater lagoons, but single wanderers are also sometimes seen. The distinctive spoon-like bill is swept from side to side in the water as the bird scoops up and filters fish, insects and water plants – in olden days when the species was more widespread in Britain it was often known as a 'shovelar' due to its method of feeding. The unique bill provides easy identification at reasonably close viewing, but if seen flying the Spoonbill is sometimes mistaken for a Heron – however a Heron flies with its head drawn back against its body, the Spoonbill flies with its neck fully extended.

FOOD   A varied diet of small fish, insects and their larvae, mollucs, crustaceans, amphibians, worms and water plants – the bill sifting through mud and water and filtering out the food.

The Spoonbill does not breed in Britain or Ireland.

Heron

SIZE   36–39in:90–98cm

DESCRIPTION   Large, elongated bird with long slender bill and long legs, both yellow. Head, neck and underparts are white, grey back, and dark grey flight feathers and tail. A crest of black plumes extends back from the eye, and a broken black stripe decends down the front of the neck to the breast. Sexes alike. During flight the head is drawn back and the legs trail backwards.

SONG/CALL   A loud, far-carrying 'frank' call, often given during flight. When nesting a wide variety of calls are given – mostly raucous and discordant, and bill clapping is frequent.

RECOGNITION   The Heron is easily identified by its large size, and habit of standing hunched and motionless in shallow water waiting patiently for prey which it

Grey Heron (scale 1:7)

Spoonbill (scale 1:7)

FRANCES FRY.

stabs with its sharp bill. Present all year round, Herons are found in all kinds of freshwater habitats, ranging from garden ponds to rivers and even open shores at estuaries. Once seen only in country districts, the Heron has been quick to take advantage of the recent popularity of ornamental garden ponds stocked with fish, and many a suburban garden has been raided for this easy source of food supply.

FOOD Mainly fish, but also small amphibians, small mammals like water voles, beetles insects and occasionally small birds.

NEST Herons nest colonially in tree-top heronries that are used year after year. Courtship starts early in March, with a 'dance' by the male involving neck stretching The nest consists of a bulky platform of twigs, lined with thinner twigs and grass, and sometimes there are several nests close together in one tree.

EGGS 3–5 usually, sometimes 2–7, non-glossy pale greenish-blue eggs are laid at two day intervals. 2.32 x 1.70in:59.9 x 43.2 mm. Incubation takes 23–28 days. Both parents feed the young, which spend 50–55 days in the nest.

BREEDING SEASON Begins February to early March. Usually single-brooded, but very occasionally a second brood is raised.

Dipper

SIZE 7½in:18cm

DESCRIPTION Appears black, with white 'bib' and chestnut belly, but really the upper parts are dark brown, with greyish-black on the back and flanks. Bill and legs are dark blackish-brown.

SONG/CALL A sweet warbling song, and a short 'zit' call.

RECOGNITION Almost Wren-shaped but much larger, the Dipper has a unique life-style. When hunting for food the Dipper wades into water and can walk along the bottom of rivers and streams, head into the current and wings spread. A third eye-lid flicks over the eye protecting it, as the bird seeks out insects from under stones in the river-bed. Always seen by or near to water it often perches on rocks where it bobs up and down. It has a fast, direct flight, and can often be seen skimming low over the water. Resident all year round, and found throughout most of Britain, except the south-east; most common in the north and west.

FOOD Mainly insects, like water-beetles, caddis larvae etc., but also worms and tadpoles, minnows and other small fish.

NEST A substantial domed structure, made of grass, moss and leaves and lined with dead leaves. Both sexes build the nest, which is nearly always on a ledge or in a bankside cavity near to water, sometimes under a bridge or behind a waterfall. The dome canopy overhangs the edge of the cup, forming a downward-facing entrance to the water.

EGGS Usually 5, but sometimes 3–8, smooth but not glossy, white in colour. 1 x ¾in:26.1 x 18.5 mm. Incubation, by the female alone, takes 15–18 days, and fledging 19–25 days. The young can dive and swim before they can fly.

BREEDING SEASON March to April in the south, May to June in the north. Double or sometimes treble-brooded.

Oyster Catcher

SIZE 17in:43cm

DESCRIPTION Large, pied wader with long, stout orange-red bill, and pink legs, and red eyes. Black above, with white underparts and white wing-bar, conspicious in flight. In winter plumage there is a white half-collar on the throat.

SONG/CALL A loud 'kleep-kleep' call, or a piping 'pic-pic-pic', and a song consisting of piping trills.

RECOGNITION The Oystercatcher is a conspicious shore bird, present all year round in coastal areas, particularly estuaries, and widespread inland in Scotland and northern England. In summer its range extends to include river-banks and lakes. Oyster-catchers are gregarious birds, and large flocks can be seen feeding along shorelines and estuaries, feeding mainly on shellfish which they prise open with their strong bills. The population is rising, helped by expansion into new breeding territories inland, spreading from waterside sites to moorland and farmland habitats. In spring and summer Oystercatchers give a 'Piping performance' at their breeding grounds, when groups of birds form circles, running around pointing their bills groundward and giving shrill piping calls.

FOOD Mainly molluscs, especially mussels, also crustaceans like crabs and shrimps, and inland worms and insects.

NEST Both sexes make a shallow scapes in the ground, the female chosing which one shall be the nest site, and sometimes lining it with pebbles, rabbit droppings or plant material.

EGGS Usually 3, sometimes 2–4, oval glossy creamy/stone coloured eggs, boldy blotched with blackish-brown markings. 2.25 x 1.57in:57 x 40mm. Incubation, by both sexes, usually beginning with the last egg, takes 24–27 days. The young are precocial and leave the nest soon after hatching (1 or 3 days). Both parents tend the chicks until they are independent at 34–37 days, and will mob intruders if danger threatens their young.

BREEDING SEASON From mid-April onwards. Single-brooded, but a lost clutch may be replaced.

SIZE 20–23in:51–58cm

DESCRIPTION Spectacular fish-eating bird of prey with dark brown upperparts and white underparts, and brown-flecked white crown. The head is small, and the wings are angled gull-like in flight. Sexes alike.

CALL A shrill creeping cry, rather like the call of a young game-bird.

RECOGNITION The Osprey is one of Britain's rarest breeding birds. The species was hunted to extinction here in 1916, and was only sighted as a rare passage migrant until 1954 when a pair nested at Loch Garten in Inverness-shire. Since then, thanks to special protection from the RSPB, more pairs have bred there and at other Scottish sites. The Osprey is also seen as a passage migrant in other areas, particularly East Anglia, the West Country, and at reservoirs in southern counties of England. The Osprey is also known as the Fish Hawk, and is normally seen near lakes, rivers or coasts. It has a slow, flapping flight, but hovers over water until it sees its prey, then plunges down feet-first into the water, catching the fish in its talons. If the fish is large the Osprey often has difficulty rising from the surface with it, and it has been known for an extra-large fish to turn the tables and kill an Osprey by dragging it down underwater to drown with its talons still locked into the fish. Ospreys are summer visitors, returning to tropical Africa or Southern Asia in winter.

PLATE 34

Dipper (scale 1:3.5)

Osprey (scale 1:5.8)

Oystercatcher (scale 1:5.8)

Avocet (scale 1:5.8)

FRANCES FRY.

FOOD Almost entirely fish – trout, perch, pike, carp or roach etc.

NEST Both sexes build the nest, a massive structure of sticks and branches usually situated on top of a tall tree, but sometimes on a rocky outcrop overlooking water. The female does the actual construction work while the male gathers materials. The same site is often re-used year after year with extra material added each time.

EGGS 3, rarely 2–4, creamy-white eggs blotched with chestnut. 2.46 x 1.83in.:61.6 x 46.4 mm. Incubation, by both sexes with the female taking the greater share, takes 35–38 days. The female broods the young for about 30 days until they feather, the male bringing food. The young vary in size, and the smallest is vulnerable if food is in shorty supply. They do not fly until 51–59 days after hatching, and take a long time to become competent fishermen.

BREEDING SEASON April–May. Single-brooded.

SIZE 17in:43cm

DESCRIPTION A slim black and white bird with long slender legs and long, thin, up-curved bill. Boldly pied plumage, with black on head, nape and wings and white elsewhere, blue/grey legs and black bill. Sexes alike, juveniles browner instead of black.

CALL A loud, flute-like 'kleep' or 'kloo-it'. A loud yelp if disturbed at nest.

RECOGNITION The elegant Avocet was once plentiful in Britain, but fen drainage and persecution from egg collectors and sportsmen led to their extinction as a breeding species here as early as 1825. After World War Two a few breeding pairs returned to Suffolk, and due to excellent protection from the RSPB which secured the breeding sites as reserves the species is now re-established in Britain. This succesful experiment led to the Avocet becoming the symbol of the RSPB. Although numbers are small the Avocet breeds regularly in Suffolk, and overwinters in Cornwall (mainly on the Tamar estuary). Its favourite habitat is brackish lagoons or estuaries. The long bill is swept from side to side in shallow waters, filtering shrimps or insect food from the water. Occasionally Avocets wade through deep water, and will swim or up-end like ducks to obtain food.

FOOD Water insects and their larvae, shrimps, crustaceans and molluses.

NEST Avocets nest in colonies, always near water, on the edge of lagoons, or on sands or mudflats. The nest consists of a shallow scrape with a sparse lining of plant material.

EGGS 4, sometimes 3–5, oval, non-glossy buff eggs spotted and blotched with black. 2 x 1.43in:50.6 x 35.1mm. Incubation, by both sexes, takes 22–24 days. The young are precocial, and able to leave the nest soon after hatching. They are tended by both parents until they are independent at about 6 weeks.

BREEDING SEASON Late April or early May. Single-brooded.

Shore Lark

SIZE   6½in:16.5cm

DESCRIPTION   A very distinctive small bird, with light-brown upperparts and white under-parts, yellow face and throat with black stripe extending through the lores to the cheeks and black break-band. The male has black crown markings which have two tufts which stick up to form 'horns' that are easily recognised. This is the summer, breeding plumage, in winter the breed markings are more obscure, resembling the female's duller plumage.

SONG/CALL   A 'tseep' or a 'tsee-ree', more like double pipit-like calls. The song is given during flight like a Skylark, and is a high-pitched jingling.

RECOGNITION   The Shore Lark is a rare winter visitor to Britain, seen mainly along the East coast of England from Yorkshire to Kent, but also recorded in Scotland and Ireland. A few birds have occasionally stayed on to breed in Scotland. Habitat is usually closely associated with the sea-shore as its name suggests, although in summer it may frequent mountain tops and tundra-like country. It keeps in the open more than the Skylark, perching on rocks or running with a rapid gait, and its flight is more bounding than the Skylark's. In winter birds will form small flocks, sometimes in association with Lapland or Snow Buntings, and these may be seen feeding along the seaweed at tide-mark level. It is quite a tame, confiding bird, but not easy to locate.

FOOD   Weed seeds and insects, and in winter small molluscs and crustaceans.

NEST   The Shore Lark normally nests in tundra, but in Scotland choses barren high ground. The nest is made on the ground, in a hollow sheltered by a plant or rock, and consists of a cup of dried grasses, lined with plants, down or hair.

EGGS   Usually 4, sometimes 2–7, glossy pale greenish eggs speckled with yellow-brown. .93 x .64in:22.7 x 16.3mm. Incubation, by the female alone, takes 10–14 days, and the young are fledged and ready to leave the nest at 9–12 days, although they will not fly yet. If danger threatens the chicks split up and 'freeze' to avoid detection.

BREEDING SEASON   Begins around mid-May. Usually double-brooded.

Little Ringed Plover

SIZE   6in:15cm

DESCRIPTION   Small relation of the Ringed Plover. Upperparts mid-brown, and underparts white, it is distinguished from the Ringer Plover by smaller black collar, absence of white wing-bar, and yellow eye-ring. Legs and feet are flesh-coloured or yellow-green.

SONG/CALL   A whistling 'pee-u' note, and in flight repeated 'gree-a' call.

RECOGNITION The Little Ringed Plover is smaller and rarer than its larger cousin the Ringed Plover, and is more of a freshwater bird, preferring sandy river banks, gravel pits or reservoirs to coasts and estuaries. In the early part of this century it was a rare vagrant bird of passage to Britain, but since 1938 it has become a regular summer visitor, breeding in central and eastern England and parts of southern Scotland. However it remains a rare bird in Wales and Ireland. Its behaviour and feeding habits are basically similar to the Ringed Plover's, although it tends to be rather more excitable and noisy when the breeding season commences.

FOOD Insects and their larvae form a large part of its diet, but small molluscs, spiders and worms are also taken.

NEST The Little Ringed Plover nests on shingle or sand or on dry mud, and occasionally amongst grass. The nest consists of a scrape in the ground, scantily lined with a few pebbles or plant stalks, but sometimes without any lining material.

EGGS Usually 4, rarely 3 or 5, pyriform to oval, non-glossy, stone coloured eggs profuse eggs to blend and merge with the surrounding pebles. I.13 x .88in:27.8 x 22.1mm. Incubation, by both sexes, takes 24–26 days. The young are precocial, ready to leave the nest soon after hatching, and are tended by both parents until they fly at about 24 days.

BREEDING SEASON From late April onwards. Single-brooded in northern areas, often double-brooded in the south.

Ringed Plover

SIZE 7½in:19cm

DESCRIPTION Small, robust plover with prominent black collar and bold black and white markings on side and front of head. Mid-brown upperparts and crown, and white underparts. Superifically resembles the smaller Little Ringed Plover, but is distinguished from it by narrow white wing-bar (most noticeable during flight), orange bill tipped black and orange legs and feet.

SONG/CALL A melodious 'tooi', and a sharper 'klupp' or 'queep'.

RECOGNITION The Ringed Plover is present throughout the year, and is widely distributed along Britain coasts. It frequents shingle and sandy beaches, but is also found inland, at gravel pits, reservoirs and rivers, and sewage-farms. It is more likely to be seen inland during the winter, when substantial flocks form at favoured sites. Like all small plovers it runs about rapidly, pausing every few yards to feed or to bob up and down in a nervous way. Ringed Plovers often associate with flocks of Dunlin and Redshanks. Some birds migrate south in autumn, but other Continental birds arrive to over-winter here.

FOOD Molluses, crustaceans and insects and their larvae, also worms and some vegetable matter. When feeding Ringed Plovers do much rapid foot-plattering, vibrating the wet mud or sand with the feet and thus encouraging prey such as worms to come to the surface.

Little Ringed Plover (scale 2:5.8)

Ringed Plover (scale 2:5.8)

Shore Lark (scale 2:5.8)

Turnstone (scale 2:5.8)

Kentish Plover (scale 2:5.8)

FRANCES FRY

NEST   After courtship display which includes aerial chasing, and bowing with spread tail, the Ringed plover makes a scrape in the ground to serve as a nest. The site is often quite exposed, but sometimes sheltered by a plant tuft. Little or no lining is added – sometimes a few pebbles or plant debris.

EGGS   3–5, most usually 4 pale blueish-grey, pryiform eggs with dark blotchings. 1.5 x 1.0in:35.8 x 25.9mm. Incubation, by both sexes, starts before completion of the clutch and takes 23–26 days. The young are precocial and ready to leave the nest soon after hatching. They are capable of finding their own food, but are guarded and brooded by both parents until they become fully independent at about 25 days.

BREEDING SEASON   Late April onwards. Double-brooded, sometimes treble-brooded.

Turnstone

SIZE   9in:23cm

DESCRIPTION   Chunky, thick-set wader found on sea shore and estuaries. In winter it has brown mottled upperparts and white underparts with smudgy brown breast-band. In summer the back has rich 'tortoiseshell' plumage of black, chestnut and brown, and a bold black breast band and black facial markings complete the transformation. The bill is short and stout, and the legs and feet are orange-yellow.

SONG/CALL   A 'tuk-a-tuk' call , and a twittering, metallic 'kititit' when flushed.

RECOGNITION   The Turnstone is essentially a shore bird, feeding along the tideline turning over stones with its stout bill. The species can be seen along Britain's coasts throughout most of the year, but despite this the Turnstone has never been proved to breed here; most birds are passage migrants in spring and autumn, although many stay to overwinter, and some non-breeding birds are seen in the summer. Turnstones are quite gregarious birds and are often seen in small groups, or in company with Purple Sandpipers or Dunlin. They are very active birds, constantly living up to their name and turning over stones and pebbles in search of food like invertibrates which live beneath the stones; or perching on rocks or man-made objects which protude from the water. Sometimes birds frequent sandy or mud-flats where mussels occur, and more rarely some may be seen inland by reservoirs or rivers, sewage-farms and lagoons.

FOOD   Molluscs, crustaceans and marine insects form a large part of the Turstones' diet, but carrion is also taken occasionally, and in summer a wider rar：? of insects and their larvae.

The Turnstone does not breed in Britain or Ireland.

148

Kentish Plover

SIZE   6¼in:16cm

DESCRIPTION   Typical 'ringed' plover, but smaller and lighter than the more common Ringed Plover. The upperparts are a much paler brown. the underparts white, but the black breast-band is incomplete – just a black line on either side of the breast – and Bill, legs and feet are black. The female is paler than the male, and lacks black eye-stripe and black mark on crown.

SONG/CALL   A 'wit' and a 'chirr', and a melodic 'poo-it' call.

RECOGNITION   Despite the fact that it is named after an English county the Kentish Plover is a rare summer visitor to most of Britain, and an even rarer breeder. Although the species used to breed in Kent it ceased to do so in 1956, and breeding was not restablished there for 20 years. Small numbers do now occasionally breed in Kent and Sussex, but most birds seen are passage migrants. Most likely habitat is shingle or sandy beaches or mudflats. Its behaviour and general habitats are similar to the Ringed Plover, but the Kentish Plover is more active and can move over mudflats with a surprising turn of speed with typical Plover pauses in between its rapid pattering.

FOOD   Insects form a large part of the diet, but molluscs, crustaceans, spiders and worms are also taken.

NEST   The Kentish Plover usually nests on shingle, sometimes on sand or mud. The nest consists of a scrape in the ground, with little or no lining – sometimes fragments of plant debris provide a sparse lining, otherwise the eggs are often partly buried.

EGGS   3, sometimes 2–4, oval to pyriform eggs with very variable ground-colour ranging from stone-buff to oliver and brown tones with fine spotting. 1.30 x .92in: 33.1 x 23.5mm. Incubation, by both sexes, takes about 24 days. The young are precocial and active, ready to leave the nest soon after hatching and finding their own food. Both parents tend them until they reach independence at around 25 days.

BREEDING SEASON   Late April onwards. Single or double-brooded.

Other black, brown and white birds which are fully described under different sections.

REED BUNTING   This Bunting is associated with both waterside locations and dryer areas, and is fully described under LAND BIRDS: BLACK-HEADED BIRDS.

Bearded Tit

SIZE 6½in:16.5cm.

DESCRIPTION A long-tailed tit found only in reed-beds. It has tawny-brown upperparts, and light underparts shading to tawny on the flanks. The male is distinguished by blue-grey head with broad black moustachial stripes. The short, stubby bill is yellow, and the legs and feet are dark. The female is a duller tawny-brown, and lacks the blue-grey head and moustachial stripes. The general impression is of a small rufous bird with a very long graduated tail.

SONG/CALL A distinctive 'ping-ping' call with a vibrant ring to it, and a quieter 'ticc'.

RECOGNITION The Bearded Tit feeds and nests only in reed-beds, and such a restrictive habitat led to the species being confined to East Anglia in the first half of this century. Hard winters added to the reduction in numbers, and by 1947 only a few breeding pairs survived. Fortunately the population started to recover, and 1959 proved such a successful breeding season that the species erupted into new territory and new colonies were established in other reed-growing areas. It is now resident in Essex, Kent, parts of Dorset and Yorkshire as well as East Anglia. The Bearded Tit rarely leaves the shelter of the reeds except for short, rather laboured flights over the reed-tops. Usually it creeps through the ground vegetation, or climbs up and down the reed-stems quite acrobatically. It is gregarious outside the breeding season, and quite tame while nesting.

FOOD Insects and their larvae, and in winter reed seeds.

NEST Both sexes help build the nest among reeds or sedges. The nest consists of a cup of reed leaves, lined with reed-flower heads and occasionally feathers, and is set low among the reed stems.

EGGS 5–7 usually, but sometimes up to 12, glossy, creamy-white eggs sparsely marked with streaks and scrawls of dark brown. .70 x .56in:17.6 x 14.0mm. Incubation, by both sexes, takes 12–13 days, and fledging 9–12 days.

BREEDING SEASON Begins late April. Double, sometimes treble-brooded.

Marsh Warbler

SIZE 5in:13cm.

DESCRIPTION Closely resembles the Reed Warbler, but the plumage has a more olive shade. Olive-brown upperparts with brown or yellowish-brown rump, and buff-white underparts, with pale, flesh-coloured legs and feet. It has a stouter build than the Reed Warbler.

150

SONG/CALL   A strong 'tchic' or 'thuc' call, and churring alarm rattle. A full song, given with great vivacity, with some Canary-like trills, nasal 'za-wee' notes and much mimicry. Sings most often in early Spring, uncommonly at night.

RECOGNITION   The Marsh Warbler is a scarce summer visitor to Britain, arriving late in May, and usually breeding only in south-western England. It is usually found near water frequenting osier beds, low, dense vegetation near water, occasionally hedgerows and cultivated fields. Over-grown areas with nettles and meadowsweet are much favoured. It is not so secretive and skulking in habits as the Reed Warbler, and takes flight more readily. It seems a more excitable bird, and perches higher when singing, often choosing quite exposed branches and bushes as song-posts.

FOOD   Insects and their larvae, particularly marsh-loving insects; also spiders, and in autumn some berries.

NEST   The Marsh Warbler breeds near or over water, making cylindrical cup of grasses and plant stems, lashed by 'handles' to supporting stems of reeds, or meadowsweet or nettles, and lined with an inner cup of fine grasses, roots and hair. Both sexes help build the nest, although the female does most of the work.

EGGS   4–5, sometimes 3–7, glossy, very pale blue-green eggs with irregular blotches of olive-green or grey. .76 x .55in:19.9 x 14.2mm. Incubation, by both sexes, takes 12 days, and fledging takes 10–14 days.

BREEDING SEASON   Begins in May. Single-brooded.

Sedge Warbler

SIZE   5in:13cm.

DESCRIPTION   The most common of the waterside warblers, the Sedge Warbler has rust-brown upperparts streaked black, broad cream supercilium, and buff-cream underparts. Dark legs and feet, and thin, sharp bill. Rust-brown rump, and graduated rounded tail.

SONG/CALL   A harsh 'tuc' call, sometimes repeated quickly to form a 'tuctuctuctuc'. A rich, varied song, consisting of harsh calls, mimicry, chattering and trills.

RECOGNITION   The Sedge Warbler is a summer visitor to Britain, widely distributed throughout the country, though usually absent from very hilly districts and from the Shetlands. Its habitat includes reed beds, sedges and willow scrub, but also dryer areas such as young conifer plantations. Its song is delivered from a perch, or during its short, bouncy display flight. The Sedge Warbler is seldom seen in the open except perching briefly on osiers or tall plants, preferring to creep about in thick cover, clinging to and sidling up reed stems. It flies low, usually for short distances, with its tail spread and depressed.

FOOD   Chiefly insects; also worms, spiders, and in autumn some berries.

NEST   The Sedge Warbler breeds by water, building its nest in rank waterside vegetation, usually within a foot or two of the ground but rarely 6ft above it. Occasionally it builds in hedges or bushes some distance from water. The nest consists of a bulky cup, cylindrical to rounded shape, made of grasses, plant stems, moss, sedges and spiders webs, and lined with fine grasses, hair and plant down. The female does the building, weaving the nest materials around the supporting stems so that the nest is slung between them.

EGGS   5–6 usually, sometimes 3–8, glossy pale green or olive-buff eggs, profusely speckled with olive sometimes obscuring the original ground colour. Often a hair-streak mark. .70 x .52in:17.7 x 13.1mm. Incubation, chiefly by the female, takes 13–14 days, and the young are fledged and ready to fly in 13–14 days, but will leave the nest earlier if disturbed.

BREEDING SEASON   Begins in May. Usually single-brooded, but occasionally two broods are raised.

Reed Warbler

SIZE   5in:13cm.

DESCRIPTION   Slim, round-tailed warbler, with brown upperparts, rufous rump, and light buff underparts shading to white on the throat. Brownish/flesh-coloured legs and feet and sharp, pointed bill.

SONG/CALL   Low 'churr' call note, and low, chirping song consisting of repeated churring notes with odd musical notes in between. It is heard most frequently in early spring.

RECOGNITION   The Reed Warbler is a summer visitor to Britain, arriving in April and leaving in September. It is fairly widely distributed throughout England, scarcer in Wales, and only a vagrant in Scotland and Ireland. As its name implies it is mainly a bird of the reed-beds, although it will also inhabit other waterside areas, hedgerows bordering ditches, and marshy ground, and more rarely dryer ground away from water. It seldom leaves the cover of the reeds, clinging to the stems, sidling up them with a quick, jerky action, or flitting from stem to stem. It only flies short distances, with its tail spread and depressed. It usually sings from the cover of vegetation, and sometimes sings at night.

FOOD   Mainly aquatic insects and their larvae, also spiders and slugs, and in autumn some berries.

NEST   The Reed Warbler usually nests among the reeds, or in rank vegetation bordering water, and although it is not a very gregarious bird shortage of suitable breeding sites often result in almost colonial breeding. The nest is built chiefly by the female, and consists of a deep, cylindrical cup of grass and plant stems woven round the supporting reed-stems. There is an inner cup of finer plant material, hair, wool and feathers.

EGGS   4, sometimes 3–6, glossy, pale green eggs blotched or spotted with olive. .72 x .53in:18.4 x 13.6mm. Incubation, by both sexes, takes 11–12 days, and fledging 11–13 days.

BREEDING SEASON   From May onwards. Single-brooded.

Savi's Warbler

SIZE   5½in:14cm.

DESCRIPTION   Slightly larger than the Reed Warbler, with rufous-brown upperparts, and creamy-buff underparts shading to white at the throat. Faint buff supercilium, and long rounded tail.

SONG/CALL   A quiet 'tswik', and a scolding chatter. Its song is a reeling trill rather like that of the Grasshopper Warbler but slower and shorter. The song is sometimes preceded by low 'ticking' notes, and often seems to come from several directions due to the constant head-turning while the bird is singing.

RECOGNITION   Savi's Warbler is one of Britain's rarer summer visitors, mainly confined to southern England, but its range is steadily increasing, and it has been an established breeding bird since 1960 when it first nested in Kent. Although overall numbers remain small it now breeds in Norfolk, Suffolk and Hampshire as well as Kent, and it is a passage vagrant to other areas of southern Britain. It is less skulking in habit than the Grasshopper Warbler, and sings from a prominent perch like a reed-top. Habitat includes reed-beds, swamps and ditches etc., but always closely associated with water.

FOOD   Aquatic insects and their larvae, dragonflies.

NEST   The female builds the nest, on or near the ground concealed among reeds or sedges. The nest is a loosely built cup of grass stems and dead leaves, often built into the bases of reeds, well concealed and sometimes partly covered. It has an inner cup, woven firmer and lined with finer leaves and fibres.

EGGS   4–5, sometimes 3–6, glossy, white eggs speckled with brown. .78 x .59in:19.7 x 14.5mm. Incubation, by the female alone, takes 12 days, and fledging 12–14 days.

BREEDING SEASON   Begins April. Double-brooded.

Cetti's Warbler

SIZE 5½in:14cm.

DESCRIPTION A small rufous brown bird with secretive habits and a loud voice. Upperparts a dark rufous brown, underparts greyish/white shading to brown on the flanks, with barred undertail coverts. The tail is full and rounded, and often in a cocked position.

SONG/CALL A loud song, given in an explosive burst of sound – a strident 'cheeoo', a 'twic', a 'whuit', and a churring alarm call. The song is usually given from the cover of thick undergrowth.

RECOGNITION Unlike most of the Warbler family Cetti's Warbler is a resident bird. Early in this century it was regarded as a Mediterranean bird, but it has gradually increased its range northwards, and has nested in Britain since the early 1970s, extending from Kent to most of southern and eastern England. It has rather dull plumage and skulking habits, preferring to hide away in dense vegetation on river banks or marshes, and the best means of recognition is its loud explosive song. Numbers are continuing to increase, although hard winters can provide a severe set-back.

FOOD Mainly insects, but earthworms and some vegetable matter when cold weather affects the supply of insect food.

NEST A bulky cup-shaped nest made of leaves, plant stems, roots and fibres, with an inner cup lined with fine grasses, hair, feathers and sometimes reed-flowers. The female bird builds the nest, which is situated low down in a bush or in thick vegetation such as reedbeds.

EGGS 4, sometimes 3–5, smooth, glossy, rust coloured eggs, occasionally with a band of deeper colour at the larger end. .75 x .61in:18.6 x 13.9mm. Incubation, by the female only, takes about 12 days. The young are tended by the parent birds for up to four weeks.

BREEDING SEASON Late April to May. Single-brooded.

AQUATIC WARBLER
Rare visitor with secretive habits. Colour similar to juvenile Sedge Warbler, and voice is also similar. *Not illustrated.*

PLATE 36

*Bearded Tit
(scale 1:2.3)*

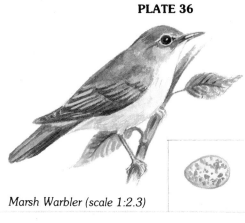

Marsh Warbler (scale 1:2.3)

Sedge Warbler (scale 1:2.3)

Reed Warbler (scale 1:2.3)

Savi's Warbler (scale 1:2.3)

Cetti's Warbler (scale 1:2.3)

FRANCES FRY

Ruff

SIZE   11½in:29cm.

DESCRIPTION   A medium sized wader with brown/black plumage that has considerable colour variations. In spring the male is distinguished by special breeding plumage – bare face wattled red, two plumes on the crown, and an elaborate ruff of feathers round the neck. The ruff may vary in colour from pure white to chestnut, black or buff, or a mixture of these colours. Outside the breeding season Ruffs may be distinguished from other waders by their small head and short, thick bill. The male is much larger than the female.

SONG/CALL   Generally a silent bird, but when flushed it may give a 'teuce' or 'tu-whit'.

RECOGNITION   Although some ruffs overwinter in Britain most are summer visitors and return to Africa in the autumn. With the draining of much of their wetland habitats the species declined and became extinct as British breeders earlier this century, but in 1963 breeding was re-established on the Ouse washes, and small numbers now breed here regularly. Passage migrants are also seen in coastal and wetland areas elsewhere. Male Ruffs arrive at their breeding grounds in March, and females (sometimes called 'Reeves') follow some weeks later. Then both sexes assemble at display areas, known as 'leks', where the males show off the glory of their neck-ruffs, 'freezing' with feathers raised, or fighting mock battles with each other to impress the females.

FOOD   Mainly insects, but also molluscs, crustaceans and worms, and some seeds.

NEST   The Ruff nests in low, marshy areas, making a hollow among grass and lining this with finer grasses. Usually the surrounding herbage conceals the nest well.

EGGS   4, rarely 3, eggs are laid, pyriform shape, and light green or olive in colour with dark blothses and scrawls. 1.70 x 1.22in:43.9 x 30.7mm. The female is left to incubate the eggs and rear the young alone as the male retires to moult his fine nuptial feathers. Incubation takes 20–21 days, and the precocial youngsters leave the nest soon after hatching and become independent after a few days.

BREEDING SEASON   Starts in May. Single-brooded.

Bittern

SIZE   30in:76cm.

DESCRIPTION   A large brown and buff heron with short neck. The overall colour is brown with buff and black striping that provides perfect camouflage in reeds, but closer examination will reveal a black crown and black moustachial streak. The long legs are green, and the sharp bill is yellow. The Bittern usually adopts an upright posture with bill pointing skyward.

156

SONG/CALL   A low, carrying booming note resembling a ship's foghorn, usually repeated 2 or 3 times. Sometimes an 'aark' call.

RECOGNITION   The Bittern is one of Britain's rarest birds. Persecution from egg-collectors and sportsmen, and loss of habitat from land drainage led to the extinction of the species as a breeding bird in Britain in the late 1860s, but nesting began again early this century and continues in the specialised habitat of reed beds. A small number of resident breeding birds exists somewhat precariously in the dense reedbeds of East Anglia, with smaller still numbers in Lancashire and parts of the West Country and Wales, but overall the species continues to decline. The Bittern is a very secretive bird, and is rarely flushed from the cover of reeds, when alarmed it stretches its neck, points its bill to the sky, and sways with the reeds, merging in to near invisibility.

FOOD   Chiefly fish, but also amphibians, aquatic insects and their larvae, small mammals, worms and even young birds are eaten.

NEST   The female builds the nest, a pile of reeds, sedges or similar material in shallow water in reed beds. The actual nesting hollow in the top of the pile is lined with finer grasses.

EGGS   4–6, sometimes 3–7, non-glossy olive-brown eggs are laid at 2–3 day intervals 2.7 x 1.5in:52.6 x 38.5mm. Incubation, by the female alone, begins with the first egg and takes 25–26 days. The female tends the young with no help from the male. They leave the nest at 2–3 weeks, but are not fully independent until 8 weeks.

BREEDING SEASON   March or April. Single-brooded. Males are sometimes polygamous and mate with more than one female.

Marsh Harrier

SIZE   19–22in:48–56cm

DESCRIPTION   Medium-sized, long-winged, long-tailed bird of prey frequenting reed beds and marshy land. Largest of the British Harriers, with broader wings and no white on rump. Plumage tends to be very variable. The male is brown with a pale streaked buff head, nape and breast, and grey tail and secondaries. The female is brown with cream head and shoulders and grey tail. Occasionally all-dark females occur.

SONG/CALL   A rather silent bird except in the breeding season, when a Lapwing-like 'quee-a' is given by the male. The female has a thin whistle.

RECOGNITION   Larger and browner than the other British Harriers, the Marsh Harrier is mainly a summer visitor although some birds do over-winter here, breeding in small numbers in a few reed-beds in eastern England. Drainage of wetlands, and persecution by egg-collectors and sportsmen nearly led to the species becoming extinct in Britain, but now they are protected and hopefully numbers are increasing slowly. It frequents marshy districts, fens and swamps, and hunts by gliding low over

157

reed-beds preying on waterbirds and small amphibians. Its legs often dangle downwards when the bird glides with its wings held in a shallow 'V'.

FOOD Small birds, small mammals and amphibians, also eggs and young of other birds.

NEST The female usually builds the nest unaided, gathering a great mass of reeds and sticks which are sometimes placed on the ground, sometimes in very shallow water amongst dense reeds. The nest is larger than that of the other Harriers, and is lined with grasses.

EGGS 4–5, occasionally 3–8, pale blue-white, non-glossy eggs are laid. 1.93 x 1.50in:50.1 x 38.8mm. Incubation, by the female alone, takes 33–38 days. The female broods the young closely for 7–10 days, but remain dependent for a few more weeks.

BREEDING SEASON April to May. Single-brooded. Males are sometimes polygamous and support two females on their territory.

Snipe

SIZE 10½in:27cm

DESCRIPTION A well camouflaged wader with long straight bill and boldly striped head. Brown upperparts with heavy barring in dark brown and buff, and prominent cream double 'V' on back; underparts buff barred brown with pale flanks. The tail is barred black and tawny with white showing at sides. The long legs are greenish.

SONG/CALL A grating 'scaap' when flushed from cover, and a 'chip-a chipa' song.

RECOGNITION Many Snipe are resident all year round, but numbers increase each autumn as more birds arrive to overwinter in Britain. They are widely distributed throughout the country, and frequent wetland sites, peat-moors, sometimes saltmarshes and on rare occasions the seashore. Snipe are less likely to be seen out in the open than most waders, keeping under cover of vegetation, and are most often seen in flight when disturbed – a rapid erratic zig-sagging flight. During the breeding season both sexes (but especially the male) give a 'drumming' display flight, rising high in the air and diving down with the stiff outertail feathers splayed out the 'bleat' the air, the vibration causing the drumming noise.

FOOD Largely worms, also insects, molluscs, crustaceans and woodlice. Seeds are also taken.

NEST Snipe are ground-nesters, chosing a hollow in the ground and lining it with grass. Near-by vegetation is often pulled over the nest to disguise it.

EGGS 4, sometimes 3, oval to pyriform green or buff toned eggs blotched with dark brown. 1.57 x 1.13in:39.3 x 28.6mm. Incubation, by the female only, takes 18–20 days. The active, precocial young are cared for by both parents until they can fly at

PLATE 37

Ruff (scale 1:4.6)

Bittern (scale 1:7)

Marsh Harrier (scale 1:5.8)

FRANCES
FRY

about 19–20 days. Snipe are thought to carry their chicks away from danger in a similar manner to Woodcock holding the young between the legs in flight.

BREEDING SEASON From April onwards. Usually Single-brooded, but sometimes double-brooded.

Jack Snipe

SIZE 7½in:19cm

DESCRIPTION Small relation of the Common Snipe, with similar plumage – brown upperparts, barred dark brown and buff, and buff underparts. However there are important differences – the flanks are whitish and unmarked by bars, and the back has a metallic green and purple gloss. The bill is much shorter.

SONG/CALL A silent bird for most of the time, even when flushed, but will sometimes give a rather feeble 'skapp', or a deeper 'galloping' note in display.

RECOGNITION The Jack Snipe is a winter visitor to Britain, much rarer than the Common Snipe. It is distributed somewhat irregularly throughout most of the country save the north of Scotland, with the south and east of England being the most favoured areas, and frequents marshes and bogs – similar habitat to the Snipe. It is much less gregarious than the Snipe, and is usually flushed singly, and its flight is less erratic too, lower and more direct. It is crepuscular in habit, and difficult to flush from cover, preferring to 'freeze' until the last possible moment then taking off almost under an intruder's feet. Even when feeding undisturbed in the muddy edges of lakes and rivers it will bob and sway, blending in perfectly with waterside vegetation.

FOOD Largely worms, but molluscs, crustaceans and insects also form part of the diet, and some seeds are taken in winter.

The Jack Snipe does not nest in Britain or Ireland.

Curlew Sandpiper

SIZE 7½in:19cm

DESCRIPTION A passage migrant that resembles the Dunlin in winter plumage, but is distinguished by longer, down-curved bill, longer neck and legs, and slimmer build. Grey-brown mottled upperparts and whitish underparts. Summer breeding plumage is chestnut head and breast, chestnut-brown upperparts boldly mottled black, and white rump.

SONG/CALL A soft 'chirrup', also used as a contact note during flight.

RECOGNITION The Curlew Sandpiper is a passage migrant occuring in fluctuating numbers in spring and autumn. In Britain it is usually scarce in the spring, and is more often seen in late summer or early autumn, in coastal areas or inland

PLATE 38

Jack Snipe (scale 1:3.5)

Common Snipe (scale 1:3.5)

Curlew Sandpiper (scale 1:3.5)

Wimbrel (scale 1:4.6)

FRANCES FRY.

marshes. It occurs most regularly on the south and east coasts of England, but has also been recorded in northwest England, eastern Scotland and southern Ireland. Its habits are similar to the Dunlin, with whom it often associates. It is gregarious and associates with others waders and plovers, feeding on the shore along the tide-line. Much of its food is obtained from recently uncovered flats.

FOOD   Small crusacea, small molluscs, worms, sandhoppers, insects and their larvae, and occasionally some vegetable matter.

The Curlew Sandpiper does not breed in Britain or Ireland.

Whimbrel

SIZE   16in:41cm

DESCRIPTION   Similar to a smaller version of the Curlew, distinguished by shorter bill and striped head. Upperparts brown mottled buff, streaked buff breast with dark brown arrows on flanks, and brown and buff barred tail. In flight a white 'V' is visible up the back.

SONG/CALL   A flight note like a short whistle, repeated several times (usually 7), earning the bird its country name of 'Seven Whistler'. Also a bubbling call similar to the Curlew.

RECOGNITION   The Whimbrel is a summer visitor to Britain, arriving April and departing in October, although a few birds may overwinter in Ireland and the South West of England. It is much rarer than the Curlew, and is usually seen in northern Scotland and its outer Isles, although other areas may be visited by passage migrants, particularly in the autumn. It is a gregarious bird, but is seldom seen in very large flocks. Favoured habitat is open, sandy shores, estuaries and coastal marshes, but it may also frequent dryer moorland areas with heather. It is sometimes called 'the northern Curlew', but is much tamer. It is rarer inland, preferring coasts to moorland except in the breeding season.

FOOD   Worms, molluscs, cruastaceans, and in inland districts insects and some berries.

NEST   The Whimbrel nests on the ground, in dryer, moorland or rough pasture. A shallow hollow, sparsely lined with plant material.

EGGS   Usually 4, sometimes 3–5, oval to pyriform greenish eggs spotted and blotched with brown or olive 2.25 x 1.60in:58.4 x 41.6mm. Incubation, by both sexes, takes 24–28 days. The young are precocial and leave the nest as soon as their down as dried after hatching. Both parents tend the chicks until they achieve full independence at 5–6 weeks.

BREEDING SEASON   From May to June. Single-brooded.

Red-Throated Pipit

SIZE 5¾in:14.5cm

DESCRIPTION An attractive pipit with winter plumage similar to the Tree Pipit, having dark brown upperparts streaked with black and pale, streaked underparts, but the summer breeding plumage is quite distinctive with pale rusty-red throat and breast that gives the species its name.

SONG/CALL A rather abrupt 'choop' note, and a 'psss' or 'skeez' call.

RECOGNITION The Red-throated Pipit is a rare vagrant visitor to Britain, but is recorded almost annually, occurring most often in spring or autumn. It appears fairly regularly in Fair Isle and the Isles of Scilly, and has also been noted on other Scottish islands and in southern Ireland. It frequents damp areas, like grasslands and borders of lakes, rivers and marshes, and is occasionally seen on coastal dunes. Its general behaviour is similar to that of the Tree Pipit, and it perches freely on trees, fences, telegraph wires and even buildings, but it also likes good scrub cover.

FOOD Chiefly insects and their larvae.

The Red-throated Pipit does not breed in Britain or Ireland.

Spotted Crake

SIZE 9½in:23cm

DESCRIPTION Scarce, skulking bird, more often heard than seen, with brown black upper-parts and grey-brown underparts, with fine white spots on back and chest, and barring on flanks. Short, stout yellowish bill with red base, and large legs and feet, olive in colour. Resembles small olive-brown Moorhen, or miniture Corncrake.

SONG/CALL A 'hwhip' or 'quip-quip-quip', repeated for long periods after dark.

RECOGNITION The Spotted Crake is a rather rare summer visitor and passage migrant to Britain, patchily distributed from the Hebrides to the Channel coast. Habitat includes many types of aquatic vegetation with a preference for swampy land, but it does not usually frequent reedbeds. It is a secretive, skulking bird, often most active after dark, and is therefore difficult to observe except on the rare occassions it emerges into open ground. It walks and swims rather like a Moorhen, and is a solitary species. Seen at a distance the plumage looks dark, and the delicate white spotting that gives the species its name is largely lost to view.

FOOD Small molluscs and aquatic insects and their larvae, and seeds and marsh plants.

NEST   The Spotted Crake is thought to nest in Britain, but definite records are difficult to obtain. However for the purposes of this book it is included among the breeding birds of Britain. It builds a bulky cup of leaves and plant material, lined with finer grasses and plant debris, hidden amongst waterside vegetation. The nest is usually just above water level, but sometimes on the ground.

EGGS   8–12, sometimes 6–15, olive-buff eggs spotted red-brown. 1.38 x .98in:33.6 x 24.7mm. Incubation, by both sexes, often begins a little before the clutch is complete and takes 18–21 days. The young are precocial, but hatch over a period of days, and are tended by both parents until they achieve independence.

BREEDING SEASON   May–July. Double-brooded.

Rock Pipit

SIZE   6½in:16.5cm

DESCRIPTION   Largest of the British pipits, with grey-brown upperparts streaked black and pale greyish underparts streaked black, and dark brown legs, feet and bill.

SONG/CALL   A 'tsip' or 'tsup', and a trilling song resembling the Meadow Pipits but fuller and more melodic with the terminal trill more pronounced.

RECOGNITION   The Rock Pipit is present throughout the year, and is distributed along Britains coastline, and inland in summer at reservoirs, sewage-farms and other waterside areas. It is essentially a coastal bird in winter. Outside the breeding season it is gregarious and often found in flocks. Its general behaviour resembles the Tree Pipit, but it is rather more active and restless, and less likely to perch on trees. The display flight, given in spring, is similar to the Meadow Pipit's.

FOOD   Chiefly insects, but also sandhoppers, small crustacea, and some seeds, and spiders.

NEST   The Rock Pipit usually breeds near to the sea, hiding the nest in a crevice of rock, or hole in a cliff, or occasionally a grassy bank. The nest consists of a cup built into the hollow, made of grasses and plant stems and moss, and lined with finer grasses, fibre or hair.

EGGS   4–6, glossy, greyish-white eggs spotted brown and pale grey with an occasional dark hairstreak. .83 x 65in:21.4 x 15.6mm. Incubation, by the female alone, takes about 14 days, and the young are fledged at around 16 days.

BREEDING SEASON   Starts late April or May. Usually double-breeded.

Water Rail

SIZE   11in:28cm

DESCRIPTION   Secretive, marsh-dwelling bird that is more often heard than seen. Outline resembles a small Moorhen with long, thin, red bill. Upperparts brown heavily streaked with black, underparts grey with bold black and white barring on flanks and undertail converts. Long legs and big feet which dangle down during flight.

SONG/CALL   A sharp 'Kik-kik-kik', sometimes followed by a trill, repeated insistently in spring at dusk and during the night. Also grunting and squeling noises reminiscent of pigs.

RECOGNITION   The Water Rail is resident throughout the year, and widespread throughout most of the British Isles except northern and eastern Scotland, but the overall population is thought to be under 4,000 pairs, and it is not easy to observe, preferring to keep well under cover in reeds and waterside vegetation. Reedbeds, marshes and swampy land are its favourite habitat, and river margins and gravel pits or sewage-farms are also visited outside the breeding season. Its skulking habits and retiring nature makes observation difficult, but it is occasionally seen out in the open, particularly in winter when severe weather may force it out of its normal habitat. In general behaviour it resembles the Moorhen, with a deliberate high-stepping walk with spasmodic tail-jerking. Its slim build enabled it to slip away quickly and quietly through the reeds, and it can swim readily with Moorhen-like action.

FOOD   Insects and their larvae, spiders, small crustacea, worms and small fish, some vegetable matter like roots, seeds and berries, is also taken.

NEST   The Water Rail builds a bulky cup of dead leaves and reeds, concealed in waterside vegetation or reeds, low down just above the water level.

EGGS   6–10, cream-buff eggs with sparse red-brown markings. 1.46 x 1.05in:35.9 x 26.0mm. Incubation, by both sexes but mainly by the female, takes 19–20 days. The young are precocial, but remain in the nest for a few days after hatching, brooded by one parent while the other brings food. They achieve independence at 7–8 weeks.

BREEDING SEASON   April–June. Double-brooded.

Water Pipit

SIZE   6½in:16.5cm

DESCRIPTION   Close relation of the Rock Pipit, with similar plumage of grey-brown upperparts and paler underparts streaked black, but always lighter in colour. In summer breeding plumage it has a distinctive pink flush on the breast, a broad white eye-stripe, and greyer upperparts.

SONG/CALL   A thin 'tsip' or 'tseep-eep', and trilling song.

RECOGNITION   The Water Pipit is a regular winter visitor, chiefly seen in S.E. England, but also the Midlands, parts of Wales and Ireland, and the Shetlands. It is occasionally seen in summer, but more usually from September to April, when it is easily mistaken for the closely related Rock Pipit. It is always associated with water, and frequents lowland freshwater habitats, but in its native breeding area which stretches from the Mediterranean northwards to Germany it prefers mountainous terrain with quick-flowing streams. Its general behaviour resembles that of the Tree Pipit and Rock Pipit.

FOOD   Insects and their larvae, and animal and vegetable matter picked up on the shore.

The Water Pipit does not breed in Britain or Ireland.

Tawny Pipit

SIZE   6½in:16.5cm

DESCRIPTION   Pale-coloured Pipit with long legs and upright stance, and slim outline. Sandy-buff upperparts, and pale buff underparts with extremely pale steaking, with light eye-stripe and light outer-tail feathers. The most 'wagtail-like' of the pipits.

SONG/CALL   A Sparrow-like 'chirrup' flight note, and a 'tzic', a 'sweep' and a 'tzuuc'.

RECOGNITION   The Tawny Pipit is a vagrant visitor to Britain, seen mainly in spring and autumn along the south coast of England and in East Anglia,, and in southern Ireland. It is recorded almost every year, and occasionally a few non-breeding birds are seen in the summer. In the breeding season it frequents dry areas such as sand dunes and heaths, and arid pasture land, but at other seasons it prefers damper ground such as the banks of rivers and reservoirs. On the ground it walks and runs with a good turn of speed, moving its tail up and down like a wagtail. Its flight is also wagtail-like, with long undulations. It will often perch on rocks, bushes, telegraph wires or fences.

FOOD   Mainly insects and their larvae

The Tawny Pipit does not normally breed in Britain or Ireland.

Dunlin

SIZE   6½–7½in:17–19cm

DESCRIPTION   Small, rather dumpy wader with grey-brown upperparts edged buff, and greyish underparts, and white wing-bar that is noticeable during flight. In summer breeding plumage the back is chestnut and black, and there is a striking black patch low on the breast. The bill has a slight downward curve.

SONG/CALL   A nasal 'Dzeep' in flight, and a trilling song of varying length given from the ground or during display flight.

WATERSIDE BIRDS

Spotted Crake (scale 1:3.5)

Red-throated Pipit (scale 1:2.3)

Rock Pipit (scale 1:2.3)

Water Rail (scale 1:3.5)

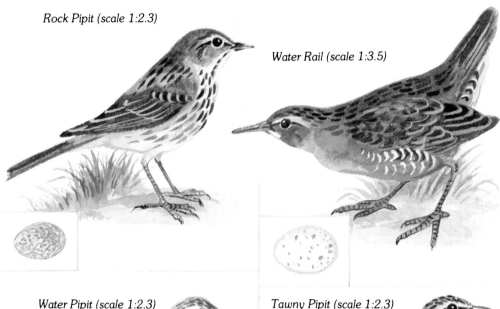

Water Pipit (scale 1:2.3)

Tawny Pipit (scale 1:2.3)

FRANCES FRY

RECOGNITION The Dunlin is one of the most commom waders, present throughout the year, and widely distributed along the coastline of the British isles. It is also found inland on grassy moors or freshwater marshes, sewage-farms, reservoirs and lakes. It is extremely gregarious, and can be found in small groups or large flocks, often in association with other species like Ringed Plover or Redshank. It feeds along the shoreline between the tides, and will wade or swim in the water if necessary. Individual birds or small parties are often quite tame, but larger flocks are difficult to approach, and are quick to take flight. As with Starlings the large flock can wheel and turn in the air in perfect unison.

FOOD Insects and their larvae, worms, crustacea and small molluscs.

NEST The Dunlin nests on the ground, almost always close to water, often in semi-colonial conditions with several pairs nesting together in close proximity. The nest consists of a cup-shaped hollow in a grass tussock, lined with leaves or grass.

EGGS 4, occasionally 2–6, oval to pyriform greenish eggs with very variable dark brown markings. 1.38 x .95in:34.8 x 24.8mm. Incubation, by both sexes, takes 21–22 days. The active, precocial young leave the nest soon after hatching, and are brooded by the female for a few days, then tended by both parents, with the male leaving before they achieve full independence at about 25 days.

BREEDING SEASON Starts in mid-May. Single-brooded.

Knot

SIZE 10in:25cm

DESCRIPTION Gregarious wader with grey upperparts edged white giving a 'scaly' effect, and white underparts barred grey, with white wing-bar, and lightly barred rump and tail. In summer breeding plumage the head and underparts become rich chestnut, and the back chestnut with black mottling. Rather 'dumpy' outline.

SONG/CALL A 'knut', and a more mellow, whistling 'quick-ick'.

RECOGNITION The Knot is a passage migrant to Britain, seen in large numbers in spring and autumn with many birds staying on to winter along the coasts on estuaries and mudflats. It is rarely seen inland. It is a very gregarious bird, and can often be identified by its habit of feeding in large, dense flocks (sometimes over two thousand strong) along the shoreline. Its general habits are similar to the Dunlin, with most of its food being obtained from freshly uncovered mudflats or wading into the water. If disturbed the flock will take off and sweep along the shore in perfect unison. As feeding depends so much upon the tides birds feed by day or night and rest when the tide is high.

FOOD Insects, molluscs, crustacea and worms.

The Knot does not breed in Britain or Ireland, but some non-breeding birds are occasionally seen on shore in summer.

Black-Tailed Godwit

SIZE 16in:41cm

DESCRIPTION Large wader with very long bill and legs. In winter it is a grey bird, dark above and lighter below. In summer breeding plumage it has a bright chestnut head, neck and breast, brown upperparts mottled with black and buff white wing bar and white tail with broad black terminal band that gives the species its name. The long bill is pinkish-red shading to black at the tip, and the legs are greenish-black.

SONG/CALL A 'wicka-wicka-wicka' flight call, a 'pee-oo-ee' heard in the breeding season and a 'wotta-we-do' song with emphasis on the last syllable.

RECOGNITION The Black-tailed Godwit a regular passage migrant to Britain, seen mainly in coastal areas and occasionally inland waters, but a small number of birds are residental all year round since the establishment of a breeding colony in East Anglia. Successful breeding has also been recorded in Kent and Somerset, Orkney and Shetland, and other parts of Scotland. It is an elegant bird, easy to distinguish with its very long legs and bill. It frequents flooded grassland, marshes and bogs, and in winter estuaries and open shores. It is a tall, graceful bird, often seen perching on fences or trees in the breeding season, or wading deep into the water. It is a gregarious bird, and is generally seen in small parties or larger flocks.

FOOD Insects and their larvae, small crustacea, molluscs and worms.

NEST The Black-tailed Godwit nests on the ground, using a hollow lined with grass, hidden amongst vegetation near water.

EGGS 4, sometimes 3–5, oval to pyriform eggs, varying in colour from pale greenish-blue to olive with brown markings. 2.12 x 1.50in:54.7 x 37.3mm. Incubation, by both birds, takes 22–24 days. The young are precocial, leaving the nest as soon as they are dry, and are tended by both parents until they can fly at about 4 weeks.

BREEDING SEASON From late April onwards. Single-brooded.

Bar-tailed Godwit

SIZE 15in:38cm.

DESCRIPTION Arctic relation of the Black-tailed Godwit, distinguished from it by shorter legs and lack of white wing-bar. In winter it is grey/brown above and lighter below. In summer breeding plumage (not often seen in Britain) it has chestnut head and underparts, and rufous streaked upperparts. The female is somewhat duller and browner. At all seasons it has the distinctive barred tail that gives the species its name.

SONG/CALL A 'kirrick' flight note, and a 'keu-oo' in the breeding season.

RECOGNITION   The Bar-tailed Godwit is a passage migrant and winter visitor to Britain, generally distributed around all coasts but scarce in the Orkneys and Shetlands. Large numbers may overwinter at favoured estuaries, and some non-breeding birds are seen in the summer. It is a gregarious bird, and is usually seen in large flocks, either feeding at estuaries or flying in rather loose straggling formations. When seen in flight the bird looks stocky in build, but it can perform intricate movements in the air, plunging, diving and twisting in flight. It often associates with other species like Oystercatchers or Redshank, feeding along the tide-line of the shore. Although it has long legs they are considerably shorter than the Black-tailed Godwit's, and the overall impression is of a plumper, stockier bird.

FOOD   Insects and their larvae, crustacea, molluscs and worms. Food is obtained by probing in the mud with the bill, and the female has a longer bill than the male.

The Bar-tailed Godwit does not breed in Britain or Ireland.

Other brown birds with barred or speckled plumage which are fully described under different sections.

CURLEW   This large wader is equally at home in wetland or dry moorland habitat, and is fully described in the LAND BIRD section, under BROWN BIRDS WITH SPECKLED PLUMAGE.

STONE CURLEW   Although similar in appearance to waders, the Stone Curlew belongs to a different family – the Thick-knees – and is often found in dryer, moorland habitat. It is described in the LAND BIRD section, under BROWN BIRDS WITH SPECKLED PLUMAGE.

DOTTEREL   This rather scarce wader is usually associated with mountainous habitat, and is fully described in the LAND BIRD section, under BROWN BIRDS.

Dunlin (scale 2:5.8)

Knot (scale 1:3.5)

Black-tailed Godwit (scale 1:5.8)

Bar-tailed Godwit (scale 1:5.8)

Common Sandpiper

SIZE   7¾in:20cm.

DESCRIPTION   Small wader with brown upperparts, brown streaked breast, and pure white belly. It has a well-defined white wing-bar, and dark rump. Bill dark, legs and feet greenish.

SONG/CALL   A 'twee-wee-wee' when flushed, and a song, usually given during flight but sometimes from the ground, is a repeated 'kitti-weewit'.

RECOGNITION   The Common Sandpiper is a summer visitor to Britain, scarce in southern counties of England but fairly well distributed throughout Scotland and Wales, and western Ireland. It frequents hilly country with streams and rivers, and will perch on mid-stream rocks like a Dipper. On passage it frequents lowland streams and reservoirs, marshes and sometimes estuaries. It is a rather solitary bird, and is rarely seen in large flocks. It is best distinguished by its habit of 'bobbing' like a Wagtail. Its flight too is different from most waders, with rapid, shallow wing-beats that produce a fluttering effect low over water. It can swim and dive well.

FOOD   Insects and their larvae, molluscs, crustacea and worms, and also some vegetable matter.

NEST   The Common Sandpiper nests on the ground, in a hollow scrape lined with grass or plant material. The nest is often situated in shingle or hidden in waterside vegetation.

EGGS   4 usually, sometimes 3–5, oval to pyriform pale buff eggs speckled with reddish brown markings and some larger blotches. 1.45 x 1.0in:36.4 x 26.3mm. Incubation, by both sexes, begins with the last egg and takes 20–23 days. The young are precocial and active, leaving the nest soon after hatching, and are tended by both parents for about 4 weeks until they achieve full independence.

BREEDING SEASON   Starts in May. Single-brooded.

Purple Sandpiper

SIZE   8¼in:21cm.

DESCRIPTION   A plump, dark-coloured wader, with grey-brown upperparts with a purplish tinge that gives the species its name, and mottled grey breast and flanks shading to white undertail coverts. Pale eye-ring and chin, and yellowish legs, feet and bill. In breeding plumage the back feathers have a rufous edging that gives the bird an altogether browner appearance. White wing-bar on secondaries is noticeable during flight.

SONG/CALL   Rather a silent species, but may give a 'weet-wit' or 'Tritt' flight note.

RECOGNITION   The Purple Sandpiper is a winter visitor to Britain, found mainly on western and northern coasts from October to April. It is essentially a coastal species outside the breeding season, frequenting rocky or boulder-strewn shores, feeding amongst intertidal pools. It is often seen in association with Turnstones. It is an agile forager amongst the seaweed, dodging waves but swimming easily if swept off its feet by the tide. It is quite tame, and seldom flies far if disturbed. Its flight is swift and more direct than most sandpipers. It may occasionally be seen on muddy shores with stoney patches, but will rarely stay long in such surroundings, preferring rocky coasts with flat rocks projecting into the sea. On such shores it will wander quite happily around piers groynes and similar seaside masonry.

FOOD   Small fish, worms, molluscs, crustacea and insects, with some vegetable matter and some seeds.

The Purple Sandpiper does not usually breed in Britain or Ireland. One breeding pair was recorded in Scotland in 1978, and a few birds are occasionally seen in the summer in far northern locations like the Farne Islands and Shetland, but these seem isolated occurences.

Green Sandpiper

SIZE   9in:23cm.

DESCRIPTION   Medium-sized wader with dark plumage that can look black and white in flight. Upperparts dark grey-green spotted with white, underparts white streaked black on breast, and with some lighter barring on the flanks. Long, thin bill, and long legs blackish in colour. Black-barred tail and white rump.

SONG/CALL   A 'tweet-weet-weet' alarm and flight call, and a trilling 'titti-looidee' song.

RECOGNITION   The Green Sandpiper is a rather scarce passage migrant to Britain, seen mainly in autumn in small numbers in England and Wales, with a few birds wintering in Southern England. It is a very rare breeder in Scotland. It frequents freshwater habitats, and prefers plenty of tree cover. On passage it may visit a wider range of lakes, streams or sewage-farms etc, but it is rarely seen on the open shore. It is a shy bird, and is usually seen singly or in couples, and seldom associates with other species. When flushed it flies high, and goes right out of sight with an erratic, wheeling flight and jerky wing-beats.

FOOD   Insects and their larvae, worms, crustacea, molluscs, and some vegetable matter.

NEST   The Green Sandpiper usually nests in a tree in the discarded nest of another species, especially thrushes. Sometimes larger nests are utilised, like a Woodpigeon's platform, or an old Squirrel's drey. Little or no extra material is added to the old nest.

EGGS   4, sometimes 2–3, pyriform eggs, greenish-buff with dark purplish-brown markings. 1.57 x 1.10in:39.1 x 28mm. Incubation, by both birds but mainly by the female, takes 20–23 days. The young are precocial and active, leaving the nest soon after hatching, and are tended by both parents at first, later by the male alone, until they can fly at about 4 weeks.

BREEDING SEASON   From mid-April to June. Single-brooded.

Wood Sandpiper

SIZE   8in:20cm.

DESCRIPTION   Elegant wader with brown upperparts and white underparts, with brown streaking on neck and breast. The back is spotted with white, and it has a white rump, and barred tail. The long legs are pale yellowish-green, and project beyond the tail in flight.

SONG/CALL   A 'chip-yip-yip' flight note, a 'chew-ew', and a trilling song, usually given in flight, of 'tleea-tleea-tleea'.

RECOGNITION   The Wood Sandpiper is mainly a passage migrant to Britain, more frequent in autumn than spring, and seen mainly on the south and east coasts of England; but small numbers breed in Scotland. It is usually found in freshwater habitats, and prefers some tree cover; occasionally it will visit salt-marshes, but it is rarely seen on the open shore. Its general behaviour is similar to the Green Sandpiper, but is is less shy and rather more gregarious, and is often seen in small flocks. If disturbed it will fly and wheel round with noisy cries.

FOOD   Insects and their larvae, worms, small molluscs, some vegetable matter, and occasionally small fish.

NEST   The Wood Sandpiper usually nests on open ground, using a shallow hollow lined with grass and leaves, in a sheltered site in cover of vegetation. Occasionally it nests above ground, using the old nest of a Thrush or Shrike, without extra material added.

EGGS   4, sometimes 3, pyriform, pale green eggs with dark blackish-brown markings. 1.50 x 1.10in:38.3 x 26.4mm. Incubation, by both birds but mainly by the female, takes 22–23 days. The active precocial young leave the nest as soon as they are dry, and are tended by both parents to begin with, later by the male alone.

BREEDING SEASON   Late May or June. Single-brooded.

Red-necked Phalarope

SIZE   7in:18cm.

DESCRIPTION   Small wader that is most often seen swimming. In winter it is difficult to distinguish from the Grey Phalarope, having grey upperparts and white underparts, but it has a longer bill, and the back tends to be streaked with white. In

PLATE 41

Common Sandpiper (scale 1:3.5)

Purple Sandpiper (scale 1:3.5)

Green Sandpiper (scale 1:3.5)   *Wood Sandpiper (scale 1:3.5)*

FRANCES FRY

summer it has slate-grey head and upperparts, white throat and underparts, and orange-red patch on side of neck that gives the species it's name. The female is brighter than the male.

SONG/CALL   A 'whit-whit-whit' in flight, lower pitched than the Grey Phalarope.

RECOGNITION   The Red-necked Phalarope is a summer visitor to Britain, breeding in very small numbers in Shetland, Orkney and the Outer Hebrides. Elsewhere it is mainly seen as a passage migrant in autumn. It winters at sea. Inland habitat includes freshwater marshes or lakes with some vegetation cover nearby. It is a very tame bird. Like the Grey Phalarope it is most frequently seen swimming, and will often spin round on the water to bring food to the surface. Large flocks are sometimes seen offshore, swimming on the sea.

FOOD   Insects and their larvae, small molluscs and worms, and plankton in winter.

NEST   The Red-necked Phalarope practices role reversal (like the Dotteral) with the female taking the initiative in courtship and breeding. Once the eggs are laid she loses all interest, and the male is left to incubate the eggs and rear the young. The nest is built by both sexes, and consists of a hollow built into a grass tussock, with a grass lining.

EGGS   Usually 4, sometimes 3, oval to pyriform eggs, olive blotched with blackish-purple markings. 1.15 x .82in:29.9 x 21.0mm. The eggs are laid at 1–2 day intervals. Incubation, by the male alone, takes 18–20 days. The young are precocial and active, and are tended by the male for 18–22 days until fully fledged and able to fly.

BREEDING SEASON   Begins in late May. Single-brooded.

Sanderling

SIZE   8in:20cm.

DESCRIPTION   Small, plump wader with pale grey upperparts and white underparts with black at the bend of the wing. White wing-bar, prominent in flight and white-edged tail. In summer breeding plumage the back and chest are warm brown marbled buff with dark speckling. Black bill, legs and feet.

SONG/CALL   A 'twick' contact note in flight.

RECOGNITION   The Sanderling is a passage migrant or winter visitor to Britain, fairly well distributed along the coasts with the exception of Scotland. Small numbers of birds overwinter here, and a few non-breeding birds are seen in summer, but most birds are seen in autumn along the seashore. Sanderlings are very active, and seem to dart across the sands at great speed, resembling a clockwork toy, and feeding at the water's edge. It is quite a tame bird, preferring to run from observers rather than take flight. It is gregarious, and often forms small flocks, sometimes in association with other waders like Turnstones, Dunlin, Knot or Purple Sandpipers, but it is always easily distinguished from these by it's frantic activity.

FOOD   Small crustacea, worms, molluscs, and in summer insects and some vegetable matter.

The Sanderling does not breed in Britain or Ireland.

Little Stint

SIZE   5¼in:13cm.

DESCRIPTION   Smallest of the waders, with superficial resemblence to the Dunlin, but distinguished by it's diminutive size, shorter straight bill, and white breast. Grey upperparts with darker markings and white underparts with dusky streaking on sides of breast. In breeding plumage the upperparts are rufous mottled black and the breast is buff. Black legs, feet and bill. Distinctive light 'V' on back.

SONG/CALL   A 'chit' or 'tit', repeated about three times.

RECOGNITION   The Little Stint is a passage migrant to Britain, more plentiful in autumn than spring, but rather a rare bird, occuring mostly on the east and west coasts of Scotland and parts of Ireland. It frequents estuaries, shorelines, and coastal and sometimes inland marshes. It is often found in company with Dunlin, but is a livelier bird with quicker movements, and feeds by vigorously probing the sand or mud with its bill instead of picking food from the surface. It is generally a tame bird. Small flocks are often seen in coastal areas in autumn, but if seen inland it occurs singly or in very small groups.

FOOD   Worms, crustacea, small molluscs, also insects and their larvae, and some seeds in summer and autumn.

The Little Stint does not breed in Britain or Ireland.

Grey Phalarope

SIZE   8in:20cm.

DESCRIPTION   Small wader, often seen swimming, with grey upperparts and white underparts. White cheeks and dark patch extending from eye over cheeks, and 'long-bodied' appearance. In summer breeding plumage it could well be called the 'red' phalarope, as the chin and underparts become bright chestnut-red, while the upperparts are scalloped black and buff. In contrast to most birds the female is the most colourful, the male being much duller, especially on the head.

SONG/CALL   A whistling 'twit'.

RECOGNITION   The Grey Phalarope is a passage migrant that spends most of the winter at sea. It is usually only seen in ones and twos in Britain, but occasionally stormy weather will blow hundreds ashore. Most birds are seen in the autumn, and usually in southwest England. Phalaropes are the only small waders that habitually swim, and are more usually seen on water than ashore, and 'spin' in the water to stir up food from below, or 'up-end' like a duck. It will bob like a Moorhen, and dab from side to side picking insects off the water. It is often quite a tame bird, and reluctant to take wing.

FOOD   Insects and their larvae, crustacea and molluscs, worms and some vegetable matter also.

The Grey Phalarope does not breed in Britain or Ireland.

Temminck's Stint

SIZE   5½in:14cm.

DESCRIPTION   Small wader rather like a miniature Common Sandpiper. Grey upperparts with dark markings, and greyish-white underparts fading to white undertail coverts. In summer breeding plumage the back is browner and the belly whiter. Dark bill, but legs and feet vary in colour from brown to green to yellow, but never black as in Little Stint.

SONG/CALL   A 'ptirr' contact note, and a high-pitched trilling titter when flushed.

RECOGNITION   Temminck's Stint is a scarce summer visitor and passage migrant to Britain seen chiefly in the autumn in East Anglia and Kent. It has made several attempts to breed in Scotland, and was successful in Easter Ross in 1971, and a small colony now exists there. It is primarily a fresh-water bird, preferring marshes, sewage-farms lakes and reservoirs to seashore. It is usually seen singly or in small groups, and unlike most waders does not readily consort with other species. It picks its food delicately from the water's edge, and moves quickly with lively movements. It may perch freely on fences, bushes or rocks, and is usually quite tame.

FOOD   Insects and their larvae, also worms.

NEST   Temminck's Stint nests on the ground, amongst low herbage. The nest consists of a shallow hollow lined with plant material, leaves and grass.

EGGS   Usually 4, sometimes 3, oval to pyriform olive-green eggs with blotching and spotting in brown. 1.12 x .78in:28.0 x 20.4mm. Incubation, by both sexes but mainly the male, takes 21–22 days. The young are precocial and leave the nest soon after hatching. Both parents tend the chicks until they achieve independence at 15–18 days.

BREEDING SEASON   Temminck's Stints are late breeders, with the first eggs being laid in mid June. Usually single-brooded, but a lost clutch may be replaced, and sometimes a second brood is raised.

PLATE 42

Sanderling (scale 1:3.5)

Red necked Phalarope
(scale 2:5.8)

Grey Phalarope (scale 2:5.8)

Little Stint (scale 2:5.8)

Temminck's Stint
(scale 2:5.8)

FRANCES FRY.

Grey Plover

SIZE 11in:28cm.

DESCRIPTION Plump plover with close resemblance to the Golden Plover, but distinguished by larger, stouter build, stronger bill, and in summer plumage by silvery-grey spangling on back instead of gold. In summer the face and upperparts are black bordered by white, with white rump and barred tail. In winter the upperparts are mottled brown-grey, the breast grey-streaked and the belly white.

SONG/CALL A long, thin, whistled flight-note 'tlee-oo-ee', with three distinct syllables.

RECOGNITION The Grey Plover is mainly a winter visitor and passage migrant, seen at various British and Irish estuaries, mostly in autumn. It is rarely seen inland. A few birds are occasionally seen in summer. Unlike the Golden Plover it rarely forms large flocks, and is usually seen in groups of two or three, often in association with other shore birds. Generally it is shy and wary. Habitat includes seashore, mudflats and estuaries. It finds most of it's food in wet mud or sand, picking it off the surface with it's short, stout bill.

FOOD Worms, molluscs and crustaceans, with some insects and some vegetable matter also.

The Grey Plover does not breed in Britain or Ireland.

Redshank

SIZE 11in:28cm.

DESCRIPTION Medium-sized wader with orange-red legs and feet and red base to bill. Upperparts brown with slightly greyish tint, underparts grey-white with darker streaks. In summer breeding plumage the back is a warmer brown streaked with black. In flight it shows a broad white tailing edge to the wing and a white rump extending up the back to form a 'V'. These markings produce three distinctive white triangles in flight.

SONG/CALL A repeated 'tu-hu-hu', and a 'tuu' or 'teuk' alarm call. The song consists of a repeated yodelled 'tu-udle', and may be given on the ground or during display flight.

RECOGNITION The Redshank is widely distributed throughout the British Isles, both inland and along the coast, and frequents marshy land and lowland moors, sewage-farms, reservoirs, and coastal areas like estuaries. Most birds are resident all year round, but some migrate south for the winter, and Continental birds visit as passage migrants. It is a shy bird, restless and noisy, and quick to take alarm and cry out to warn other birds of approaching danger. Inland it is usually seen in small groups, but on the coast it may form large flocks, and it often associates with other waders. In the breeding season it tends to move inland, and may be seen perching on trees or fences, but many birds return to the shore to feed. It swims readily. When alighting it often holds it wings raised above its back for a few moments.

FOOD   Insects, molluscs, crustacea, worms, spiders, sometimes small fish, and also some vegetable matter such as seeds and berries.

NEST   The Redshank nests on the ground, lining a hollow with nearby plant material. The nest is usually well concealed by herbage or tussocks of grass. The female prepares the nest.

EGGS   4, sometimes 3–5, pyriform buff eggs with brown markings. 1.75 x 1.25in:45.3 x 31.6mm. Incubation, by both sexes, takes 23–24 days. The young are precocial and leave the nest soon after hatching, and are tended by both parents until they are independent at about 30 days.

BREEDING SEASON   Starts in April. Single-brooded.

Greenshank

SIZE   12in:30cm.

DESCRIPTION   Large, elegant wader with long, slightly up-turned bill, and long greenish legs. Upperparts slate-grey/brown and underparts white with slight streaking on the breast. In summer breeding plumage the back becomes darker greenish-grey with black markings. A white rump extends up the back to form a 'V' that is distinctive in flight. The tail is narrowly barred.

SONG/CALL   A 'tew-tew-tew' when flushed, and a 'ru-tu, ru-tu, ru-tu' song often given during flight.

RECOGNITION   The Greenshank is a summer visitor and passage migrant to Britain. A few birds overwinter in southwest England and Ireland, and small numbers breed in Scotland. Breeding has also been recorded in Ireland in recent years. It is sparsely distributed along Britains coasts, but is most often seen in northern Scotland and the outlying Islands. Habitat includes open moorland (in the breeding season), lakes and marshes, and in winter estuaries and coastal marshes. It has similar habits to the Redshank, like 'bobbing' when uneasy, and perches freely on trees and fences. The long upcurved bill probes for food in wet areas and is also swept from side to side when searching for food in shallow water.

FOOD   Insects and their larvae, crustacea, molluscs, worms and small fish.

NEST   The Greenshank nests on the ground, usually close to a mark such as a log or rock or dead branch. The actual nest is a hollow lined with vegetation, and is very difficult to locate.

EGGS   Usually 4, sometimes 3–5, pyriform creamy eggs blotched and speckled with dark brown. 2.0 x 1.42in:51.4 x 34.8mm. Incubation, by both sexes but mainly the female, takes 24–25 days. The young are precocial and leave the nest the day after hatching, and are tended by both parents until they are independent at 28–30 days.

BREEDING SEASON   From early May onwards. Single-brooded.

Spotted Redshank

SIZE   12in:30cm.

DESCRIPTION   Scarce relation of the Redshank, with grey upperparts spotted and barred with white, white underparts speckled and barred with grey, and white lower back. Legs, feet and bill are reddish as with Redshank, but are longer. Summer breeding plumage is rarely seen in Britain, but is very distinctive, being jet black spotted with white on the back.

SONG/CALL   A flight-note of 'tchueet', and a 'chick-a-chick-a-chick'. A 'noo-too, noo-too' song.

RECOGNITION   The Spotted Redshank is a passage migrant to Britain, and a scarce winter visitor to coastal marshes, mainly along the southern shores of England and southwest Ireland. Its habitat is similar to the Redshanks', and it often associates with Redshank and Greenshank, although in winter it prefers brackish waters to estuaries and seashore. It is usually seen in small parties or singly, and is rather a shy bird. Never a plentiful visitor, most birds are seen in autumn, but as well as the small numbers of winter residents a few birds are seen in summer in beautiful black breeding plumage.

FOOD   Insects and their larvae, crustacea, molluscs, worms, and sometimes small fishes and frogs are also taken.

The Spotted Redshank does not breed in Britain or Ireland.

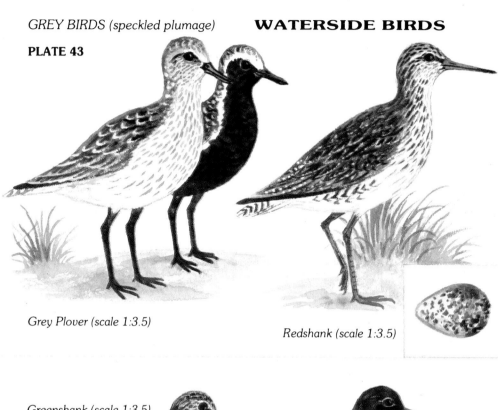

Grey Plover (scale 1:3.5)

Redshank (scale 1:3.5)

Greenshank (scale 1:3.5)

FRANCES FRY.

Spotted Redshank (scale 1:3.5)

Kingfisher

SIZE   6½in:16.5cm.

DESCRIPTION   One of the most brilliant coloured British birds, with iridescent blue-green upperparts barred with black on crown and wings, white throat and bright chestnut-orange underparts. Long, dagger-like bill, and short red legs and feet. It is often seen as a streak of bright cobalt blue flying fast over water.

SONG/CALL   A loud 'chee' or 'chee-kee' usually given in flight.

RECOGNITION   The brilliant Kingfisher is resident and widely distributed in England, Wales and Ireland, but scarce in Scotland. It is found near all types of fresh water, from ponds and canals to rivers, marshes and even the seashore in hard weather, although it prefers to hunt in slow-flowing waters. Most often seen as a swift-moving dash of bright colour over water, it usually hunts from the vantage point of a branch overhanging water, then diving on its prey of small fish. Sometimes it will hover over the water before plunging in to catch its fish which is beaten against a branch or post to kill it, then swallowed head first. In severe winters when frozen water cuts off the food supply Kingfishers can starve to death, and numbers fall drastically.

FOOD   Small fish, especially minnows, crustaceans and worms, water-beetles, water insects and their larvae.

NEST   Kingfishers excavate their nest by boring a tunnel in a river bank, or sand bank. Both sexes help make the tunnel, which is about 1–3ft long, rising slightly at the end to a rounded nest-chamber. No nest material is used, but the chamber quickly becomes lined with fish-bones.

EGGS   6–7, sometimes 4–8, glossy white eggs are laid, very round in shape. .88 x .75in:22.6 x 18.6mm. Incubation, by both sexes, takes 19–21 days, and fledging 23–27 days.

BREEDING SEASON   Begins late April and continues into August. Double-brooded, with the same nest-hole often being used again.

Grey Wagtail

SIZE   7in:18cm.

DESCRIPTION   A slim bird with very long tail. Blue-grey head and back, and yellow underparts. The head has a white supercilium and moustachial streak, and in summer the male has a black throat. The female is duller, with a white chin. In winter the male resembles the female. Despite its name it is a bright coloured bird.

SONG/CALL   A sharp 'zit' or 'titse' call, and a seldom heard 'tsee-see-see' song.

RECOGNITION   The Grey Wagtail is resident and widely distributed throughout the British Isles. It is always found in habitats close to water, and prefers fast-flowing streams and rivers. Grey Wagtails tend to be solitary birds, and do not form large flocks like other wagtails, but in hilly districts it is sometimes seen in company with Dippers. They usually breed beside fast-flowing rivers, but in winter move to lowland streams, cress beds or sewage farms. Grey Wagtails suffer in severe winter weather, and many northern birds move further south for the winter, with some leaving Britain for the warmer climate of Europe.

FOOD Mostly insects, also water-beetles, dragonfly nymphs and other aquatic larvae, small fish and molluscs.

NEST The female builds the cup-shaped nest of twigs, roots, grasses and moss, lined with hair or feathers. The nest is usually in a hole or hollow in a bank or cliff close to running water. Sometimes the old nest of another species (such as a Dipper) is used.

EGGS 4–6, rarely 3–7, glossy, greyish-buff eggs mottled brown. .75 x .61in:18.6 x 14.3mm. Incubation is mainly by the female but the male may assist sometimes. It takes 11–14 days for the eggs to hatch, and 11–16 days for the young to fledge.

BREEDING SEASON April–May onwards. Usually single-brooded, but occasionally two broods are raised.

Yellow Wagtail

SIZE 6½in:16.5cm.

DESCRIPTION A slim, elegant bird with long tail and predominently yellow plumage. Green-brown upperparts and yellow underparts with yellow supercilium on male. The female is duller with paler underparts.

SONG/CALL A 'tsweep' call note, and a brief warbling song.

RECOGNITION The Yellow Wagtail lives up to its name, with bright yellow plumage and long wagging tail, but it may sometimes be mistaken for the female Grey Wagtail despite its browner mantle and shorter tail. The Yellow Wagtail is a summer visitor to Britain, well distributed throughout England and Wales, but scarce in Scotland and very irregular in Ireland. It frequents lowland pastures, arable land and marshes, usually near water, and perches freely on fences, bushes or trees, and is often seen feeding amongst cattle. It is a gregarious species outside the breeding season. Unlike the Grey Wagtail it prefers shallow slow-moving water. The Yellow Wagtail is closely related to the Blue-headed Wagtail which sometimes occurs in Britain as a passage migrant, and is distinguished by its grey/blue head. There are many sub-species of these wagtails, but the Yellow Wagtail is the one most usually seen in Britain.

FOOD Mainly insects and caterpillars, also worms and spiders.

NEST   Courtship display of hovering, chest-puffing and tail-spreading. The nest is a cup made of grasses, plant stems and roots, thickly lined with hair or wool, and placed in a hollow in the ground, or in thick herbage or hidden under the leaves of a low-growing plant.

EGGS   5–6 usually, rarely 7, glossy buff or greyish eggs finely speckled with yellow or buff-brown spots, and often showing a hair-streak mark. .75 x .55in:18.6 x 14.1mm. Incubation, mainly by the female but with some assistance from the male, begins with the last egg and takes 12–14 days. Fledging takes about 17 days, with the young leaving the nest shortly before they can fly (10–13 days).

BREEDING SEASON   Begins around mid-May. Single- or double-brooded.

BLUE HEADED WAGTAIL
Occasional summer visitor from central Europe, very similar to Yellow Wagtail except for blueish crown. It is thought to interbreed with the Yellow Wagtail.

Illustrated in inset of Yellow Wagtail painting.

Other bright coloured birds which are fully described under different sections.

THE RUFF   The male of this wader species has spectacular breeding plumage, often with brightly coloured ear-coverts and neck-ruff, but its winter plumage resembles the duller brown tones of the female. Therefore this bird is fully described under BROWN BIRDS (speckled plumage).

Kingfisher (scale 1:2.3)

Grey Wagtail (scale 1:2.3)

Yellow Wagtail (scale 1:2.3)

FRANCES FRY

PART THREE:
WATER & SEA BIRDS

Water & Sea Birds is a wide-ranging category, covering those birds usually seen on the water or flying over it as well as those species that are essentially marine in life-style.

This section could really be sub-divided into two separate parts:-

Water Birds: comprising of those species that live on or around inland waters, including many birds that have a lifestyle more waterside than water living, like Swans, Geese and Dabbling Ducks.

Sea Birds: comprising Diving Ducks, Gulls, Terns, Cormorants and Gannets, Skuas and Auks, Divers and Grebes, Petrels and Shearwaters, and Sea Ducks.

As always the birds do not stick to rigid categories, and there is often overlapping of territory and habitat. Indeed, many species classified as seabirds spend at least part of their lives inland. A classic example is the Black-headed Gull, which is now found inland almost more than at sea. Species such as Divers and Grebes are found in both inland and coastal waters.

For the purposes of this book (i.e. to keep identification as simple as possible) both types are included together in this third and final section.

Many species are difficult to place in specific colours, as they could fit several different colour groupings, but cross-references should help overcome the problem.

189

Black Guillemot

SIZE   13½in:34cm.

DESCRIPTION   Member of the auk family, with all black plumage save for broad white wing-patch. Red legs and feet, and slim black bill. In winter plumage the head and underparts are greyish-white, and the back is barred black and white.

CALL   A thin, whistling 'peeeee', sometimes repeated to sound like twittering.

RECOGNITION   The Black Guillemot is resident all year round, but is scarcer than other auks of similar size, and is found mainly along the western coasts of Scotland and northern England, and most of Ireland. It is sometimes still called by its old Viking name of 'tystie'. It is very much a marine bird, but may occasionally venture inland on sea lochs; but its favourite habitat is rocky coasts and cliffs. It is an expert diver and fisherman, and has a display in spring that involves diving, chasing and calling with open bill to show bright red gape of the mouth. It is gregarious, usually forming single-species flocks or small parties at the foot of cliffs, but sometimes it is seen singly or in pairs.

FOOD   Fish, crustacea and molluscs, seized from the bottom of fairly shallow water. The Black Guillemot plunge-dives for its food, and can remain submerged for up to a minute. Worms and seaweed are also taken sometimes.

NEST   The Black Guillemot nests on sea coasts, in a hole or crevice in cliffs, in hollows among boulders, or even in holes in masonry. The nest sites tend to be more dispersed than most auks, and colonies consist of loosely scattered pairs.

EGGS   Usually 2, sometimes 1 or 3, white eggs with grey or reddish-brown markings, and a green inside to the shell. 2.25 x 1.55in:58.1 x 39.5mm. Incubation, by both sexes, takes 21–25 days. The altricial young are tended by both parents until they are fully fledged at 34–40 days.

BREEDING SEASON   Begins in May. Single-brooded.

Shag

SIZE   30in:76cm.

DESCRIPTION   Large black seabird, similar in outline to the cormorant, but smaller, and with no white markings. The all-black plumage has a green sheen, and there is a bare patch of Yellow skin at the gape of the bill. In the breeding season it has a recurved crest. The long neck and slim build gives the Shag a serpentine look.

CALL   A loud 'Kroak-kraik' or 'ar-ar', with brief clicking notes inbetween.

RECOGNITION   The Shag is resident all year round, and is well distributed around the coastline of Britain. Unlike the larger Cormorant it is exclusively a marine bird, found only on rocky coasts, and is very rarely seen inland. It is at home in rough or smooth waters, and swims sitting low in the water. Perching on rocks it has an upright

PLATE 45

Black Guillemot (scale 1:5.2)

Cormorant (scale 1:8.7)

Shag (scale 1:8.7)

FRANCES FRY

stance, although less so than the Cormorant, and it shares the same habit of spreading its wings out to dry. It is a gregarious bird, and may form large colonies in favoured habitats. When flying flocks will form a 'V' formation like geese.

FOOD   The Shag is an expert fisherman, diving from the sea or air to catch the fish which form the main part of its diet. Crustacae, molluscs and algae are also taken occasionally.

NEST   The Shag breeds colonially, in colonies of varying sizes on cliff-ledges or among rocky boulders. Both sexes help build a nest of decayed seaweed and whatever other plant material that is available. The male usually collects the material, and the female does the construction work.

EGGS   Usually 3, sometimes 2–6, light blue, very elongated eggs are laid. 2.48 x 1.50in:62.9 x 38.4mm. Incubation by both sexes starts with the first egg laid, and takes 30–31 days. The altricial young are brooded for the first 2 weeks, then fed by both parents until they achieve independence at around 76 days.

BREEDING SEASON   Starts in March. Single-brooded, but if an early clutch is lost it may be replaced.

Cormorant

SIZE   36in:90cm.

DESCRIPTION   Large black seabird with long, serpentine shape, and long bill, an almost primeaval appearance shared only by the Shag. On closer inspection the Black plumage has a metallic green sheen on the back, and the wings are very dark brown, and the border of black to the feathers produce a scaly effect. The bill is yellow, the feet palmated and black. In summer there is a white patch on the face, and on the flank.

CALL   Normally a silent bird, but in the breeding season it has some deep, raucus calls of the 'karrk' or 'kworrk' variety.

RECOGNITION   The Cormorant is present throughout the year, and found around most of the British coastline, frequenting estaries and tidal rivers as well as rocky shores. It is also often found inland around reservoirs and rivers, and may even breed at freshwater sites in favoured areas. It is an expert fisherman and diver, and on return to shore may be seen perching on rocks with an upright stance with its wings held spread-out to dry, an almost heraldic pose. When swimming it sits low in the water, and if alarmed will practically submerge, leaving only its head and neck visible above the surface. Cormorants are gregarious birds, often forming small flocks, and nesting in colonies, but sometimes birds are seen singly.

FOOD   Fish forms almost all of the diet, and is obtained by diving. The prey is brought back to the surface, and sometimes thrown in the air before being swallowed whole. Crustacea and algae are also taken occasionally.

NEST   The Cormorant nests colonially upon seacoasts or islands, using a heap of seaweed or sticks, but at inland sites the nest is a more substantial structure of sticks, lined with leaves, grasses and water plants. The male brings most of the material and the female does the construction work.

EGGS 3–4, rarely 5–6, elongated pale blue eggs are laid at 2 day intervals. 2.57 x 1.60in:65.8 x 40.7mm. Incubation, by both sexes, takes 28–29 days. The altricial young are tended by both parents, and remain in the nest for about 5 weeks. They are fledged at 50–60 days, but do not become fully independent until 11–12 weeks.

BREEDING SEASON Starts in early April. Single-brooded.

Common Scoter

SIZE 19in:48cm.

DESCRIPTION All-black sea-duck, with patch of yellow-orange on bill. The female is brown, with buff barring on the flanks, and pale sides to the face. Short pointed tail held in an elevated position during swimming.

CALL The most vocal of the scoters, with a plaintive piping call from the male, and harsh growling from the female – a 'kr-r-r' resembling other diving ducks.

RECOGNITION The Common Scoter is usually seen in flocks offshore along British and Irish coasts during winter months, although it is present throughout the year. A small resident population is maintained in northern Scotland, parts of western Scotland and western Ireland, and breeding is regular in these areas, but elsewhere it is a winter-visitor, generally shy, and most often seen during bad weather when rough seas force it towards the shore. In winter it is essentially a marine bird, but in the breeding season it frequents lochs in moorland country, or the tundra-like vegetation of the northern Isles. It is a heavily-built bird, often riding low in the water, and sometimes has difficulty in rising from the water. It is gregarious, and large 'rafts' of birds may be seen offshore in winter.

FOOD Molluscs form a large part of the diet, usually obtained by diving; also small crustacea and worms, and in summer some insects.

NEST The Common Scoter usually nests in heather or other suitable vegetatation within a few yards of water. A hollow lined with a little plant material or down and feathers serves as the nest-site.

EGGS 6–9 eggs are laid (occasionally 5–10) pale creamy-buff in colour. 2.57 x 1.78in:65.4 x 44.9mm. Incubation, by the female alone and beginning on completion of the clutch, takes 27–31 days. The young are precocial and take to water quickly, but are tended by the female for 6–7 weeks until they can fly.

BREEDING SEASON Begins in May. Single-Brooded.

Velvet Scoter

SIZE 22in:56cm.

DESCRIPTION All-black sea-duck, resembling the Common Scoter but larger and distinguished by white wing-patch. There are other, smaller differences too, like the small white patch beneath the eye, larger bill with slight knob, and reddish legs and feet. The female is brown, with two whitish patches on the face (in front of and behind the eye), with blackish bill and duller legs.

CALL   A silent bird normally, but may occasionally give a croak or a growl or a whistle.

RECOGNITION   The Velvet Scoter winters along the east coasts of Scotland and England, and is a passage migrant or winter visitor elsewhere, rather scarce, but sometimes seen in company with Common Scoters or Eiders. Largest numbers are usually seen in January, and most birds have gone in March, although the odd few may stay the summer. It is less gregarious than the Common Scoter, seldom appearing in large flocks, and rarely comes to land. In behaviour it is very like the Common Scoter.

FOOD   Main molluscs and crustacea.

The Velvet Scoter has been suspected of breeding in Scotland but this is not proven, so the species is regarded officially as not breeding in Britain or Ireland.

Coot

SIZE   16in:41cm.

DESCRIPTION   All black water bird, round in shape, with white frontal shield and bill. Very large feet, semi-palmated and silvery-grey in colour.

CALL   A loud 'Kewk' or 'Kowk', varying in pitch.

RECOGNITION   The Coot is resident all year round, and is found throughout most of the British Isles except the hilly areas of Scotland and the outer Isles. It is a freshwater bird, but prefers larger waters than the Moorhen, like lakes, reservoirs and marsh, but may sometimes be found at estuaries in winter. It is more gregarious than the Moorhen, and is seen in sizeble flocks, or in association with ducks. Like the Moorhen it rises from the water with difficulty, and has to patter along the surface for some distance before achieving lift-off, and the flight is rather laboured. It is a rather quarrelsome, aggressive bird.

FOOD   Mostly aquatic vegetation, taken by up-ending, or by diving. Grass is also eaten, and some animal food, like worms, molluscs and insects.

NEST   The Coot often nests in company with its own kind, among trees or growing vegetation in or by water, or occasionally on fallen trees. Both sexes help build the nest, which consists of a bulky cup of dead leaves and water plants, and resembles a mound of debris when completed.

EGGS   6–9, sometimes 5–15, buffish eggs speckled with dark brown or black. 2.7 X 1.44:52.6 x 36.2mm. Eggs are laid consecutively. Incubation, by both sexes, begins early and takes 21–24 days. The young are precocial, and leave the nest a few days after hatching, but return to it, or to specially built brooding platforms. They are independent at about 8 weeks.

Velvet Scoter (scale 1:6.4)

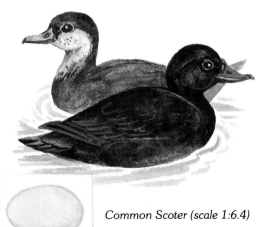

Common Scoter (scale 1:6.4)

Coot (scale 1:5.2)

Moorhen (scale 1:5.2)

BREEDING SEASON Begins in March. Double, sometimes treble-brooded.

Moorhen

SIZE 13in:33cm.

DESCRIPTION Brown/black water-bird with white stripes on its flanks, and conspicuous white under-tail coverts divided by a central black line. Red eye, and red base to yellow bill. Large feet, and legs are green with red 'garter' at the thigh.

CALL A 'Kr-r-rok' alarm call, and a 'kittick' with variations.

RECOGNITION The Moorhen is a familiar water bird, present all year round, and frequenting a wide range of freshwater sites, from rivers and marshes to village ponds and even city-centre ornamental waters. It is less common in moorland or mountainous regions. It is easily identified by its habit of cocking its white tail as it swims or walks. Its flight appears laboured and weak, with dangling legs, and it flies for short distances only, preferring to run for cover whenever possible, or dive below water. It is not generally very gregarious, but may sometimes be seen in loose flocks where nest sites are scarce, or in winter.

FOOD Mainly vegetable matter, including seeds, fruit and leaves, and some animal food such as insects and their larvae, worms and snails, tadpoles and fish.

NEST Both sexes help build the nest, which consists of a platform of vegetation usually situated at the water's edge, or amongst aquatic plants. Additional nests are sometimes constructed on the same territory, and are used for brooding young.

EGGS 5–11, but numbers vary considerably. 2–22 have been recorded, but it is suspected that very large clutches may be laid by two females. The eggs are glossy, and range from grey-white to green with red-brown spots and blotches. 1.77 x 1.24in:44.5 x 31.4mm. Incubation, by both sexes, may begin before completion of the clutch and takes 19–22 days. The young are precocial and leave the nest a few days after hatching, and can fly in 6–7 weeks, but tend to remain in the family group for some time afterwards.

BREEDING SEASON Begins in March or April. Double, sometimes treble-brooded.

Other black birds which are fully described under different sections.

STORM PETREL This small black seabird is fully described under BLACK/ WHITE:BROWN/WHITE birds.
SOOTY SHEARWATER Is fully described under BLACK/WHITE: BROWN/ WHITE birds
SOOTY TERN Is fully described under GREY/WHITE birds as this describes its winter plumage.

Mute Swan

SIZE   60in:152cm.

DESCRIPTION   Very large all-white water bird with long, gracefully curving neck, and bright orange-red bill. The male has a much larger knob on bill than the female. Juveniles have brown-grey plumage, and take several years to become pure white.

CALL   Contrary to its name the Mute Swan is not totally silent, and has a variety of hisses and snorts when defending its territory.

RECOGNITION   The Mute Swan is Britains largest resident water bird, easily identified by its size, colour and aggressive behaviour. It could only be confused with the swans that are winter visitors – the Whooper and Bewick's – and these are distinguished by a yellow base to their bills. It is widely distributed throughout the British Isles except very hilly districts, frequenting rivers and tidal estuaries, reservoirs and ponds, marshes, or more domesticated surroundings like town parks, but in recent years has shown a decline in numbers largely due to lead poisoning caused by careless abandoning of lead weights by fishermen. In favoured areas Mute Swans may form large colonies, but in the breeding season small territories of water are defended against intruders by vigorous threat displays with wings arched back.

FOOD   Mainly aquatic vegetation, often taken by up-ending with the long neck reaching deep underwater to pull up weeds and plant material. Some animal matter, like small frogs, worms or molluscs are also taken.

NEST   The Mute Swan usually nests at the water's edge, building a large mound of plant material with a raised hollow at the centre that is lined with a little down. In wild surroundings pairs usually nest alone in aggressive solitude, but in semi-domestic terrain birds may nest colonially in close proximity to each other.

EGGS   5–7, sometimes 4–12 blueish/white, elliptical eggs are laid on alternate days 4.50 x 2.29in:115 x 74.2mm. Incubation, beginning when the clutch is nearing completion, is mainly by the female with the male relieving her occasionally, and takes 34–38 days. The young are precocial, staying in the nest for only a day or two before following their parents on the water. Both parents tend them until independence at about 4 months, and when danger threatens may carry the young cygnets on their backs.

BREEDING SEASON   Mid-April to May. Single-brooded.

Bewick's Swan

SIZE   48in:122cm.

DESCRIPTION   Smallest of the swans to visit Britain, with all-white plumage, and yellow patch on black bill. The size and shape of this yellow patch can vary considerably between individual swans, and can serve to identify regular visitors to popular wintering grounds like the Wildfowl Trust's refuge at Slimbridge.

CALL   A loud honking flight call, and a quiet babble when feeding or a musical 'hoo'.

RECOGNITION   The Bewick's Swan is a winter visitor to Britain, occuring regularly in Ireland and England, particularly East Anglia. Smaller and more 'Goose-shaped' than other swans, the Bewick's Swan is very gregarious, and gathers together in large flocks at favoured feeding grounds. Its habitat and behaviour is similar to the Whooper Swan, and it is very vocal, particularly during flight. When swimming it sits with its tail-end high out of the water, whereas the Whooper swims with tail down. It breeds in the Arctic, but begins its noisy, elaborate courtship display with attendant fights while still in its winter quarters, and family parties tend to stay together through the winter.

FOOD   Aquatic vegetation obtained by 'up-ending', and roots and leaves, or cereals if available.

The Bewick's Swan does not breed in Britain or Ireland.

SIZE   60in:152cm.

DESCRIPTION   Large white swan, distinguished from the similar-sized Mute Swan by yellow bill tipped black with no basal knob. Its neck is equally long, but is held more vertically. Juveniles have grey-buff plumage.

CALL   Much more vocal than the Mute Swan, with loud trumpeting flight calls, and a 'hoop-hoop-hoop' with the whoop sound that gives the species its name.

RECOGNITION   The Whooper Swan is a winter visitor to Britain, most numerous in Scotland and Ireland. A few birds stay the summer, and breeding sometimes occurs in Scotland. In the breeding season it frequents moorland lochs or pools, but in winter it prefers the sea coast or inland rivers and reservoirs, or flooded grassland. Its general behaviour is similar in many respects to the Mute Swan, but it does not arch its wings in aggression, and it walks better on land. The long neck is held less curved than that of the Mute Swan, and looks more slender. Outside the breeding season it is very gregarious and often forms large flocks, but when nesting it becomes solitary.

FOOD   Aquatic vegetarian obtained by 'up-ending', and worms, molluscs and aquatic insects are also taken. In winter it may feed on farmland, taking grass or waste cereals.

NEST   The Whooper Swan builds a large mound of vegetation with a lining of down and feathers, placed near the water's edge, usually on an islet or swamp bank.

EGGS   5–6, sometimes 4–8, long eliptical creamy-white eggs are laid, on alternate days 4.45 x 2.80in: 113.4 x 72.2mm. Incubation, by the female alone with the

PLATE 47

Mute Swan (scale 1:14)

Bewicks Swan (scale 1:14)

Whooper Swan (scale 1:14)

FRANCES FRY.

usually standing guard nearby, takes 35–42 days. The young are precocial and active, leaving the nest soon after hatching, and are cared for by both parents. The family remains together for the rest of the year, even during migration.

BREEDING SEASON Early May to June depending on the weather. Single-brooded.

Other white birds which are fully described under different sections.

ICELAND GULL, GLAUCOUS GULL   The above birds have very light grey and white plumage, although the overall appearance may often seem white. They are fully described under GREY AND WHITE BIRDS.

Black-Throated Diver

SIZE 23–27in:58–68cm.

DESCRIPTION Typical diver with long tapering bill, and predominantly black and white plumage. In breeding plumage the head and back of neck are grey with a bold black patch in front of the throat that gives the species its name. The back is black, with patterned white bands on the scapulars and shoulders, and the underparts are white. Black and white streaks mark the side of the neck and breast. In winter upperparts are dark grey/black and underparts pale, rather similar to the Great Northern Diver.

CALL A deep 'kwow', and a high-pitched wailing song.

RECOGNITION The Black-Throated Diver is present throughout the year, breeding in small numbers in northern Scotland and the Northern Isles, and elsewhere a winter visitor in small numbers, being found mainly along the coasts of Scotland and south eastern England. It is essentially an aquatic bird, and confined to coastal waters except in the breeding season when it may visit large lochs. It is an expert swimmer and diver, as its name implies, and catches most of its food underwater. It also flies powerfully, and can rise from even small areas of water quite easily, unlike the Great Northern Diver that needs a long run for take-off. It is not noticeably gregarious, and is usually seen singly or in pairs.

FOOD Mainly fish, but also crustacea, molluscs, worms and some algae.

NEST The Black-throated Diver nests besides the water, usually on an island site. The nest ranges from a simple scrape lined with scant vegetation to a large heap of vegetable matter.

EGGS Normally 2, but sometimes 3, or if the first clutch is lost 1 replacement is laid. The eggs are long oval or subelliptical, green or olive brown in colour, spotted black. 3.25 x 2.05in:83.7 x 52.6mm. Incubation, by both sexes, begins with the first egg and takes 28–29 days. The precocial, active young leave the nest soon after hatching, and are tended by both parents until they can fly at 8 weeks.

BREEDING SEASON Begins in May. Single-brooded, although if a clutch is lost it may be replaced (see above under eggs).

Red-Throated Diver

SIZE 21–23in:53–58cm.

DESCRIPTION Smallest British Diver, with dark grey/brown upperparts, white underparts, grey head and neck, and distinguishing red throat patch that gives the species its name. (The overall effect is of dark plumage on the back, and for this reason this species is included in the black/white section with the other divers. In winter the back is covered with fine white spots).

CALL A duck-like 'kwuk-kwuk', and a wailing song.

RECOGNITION The Red-throated Diver is present all year, breeding in north-west Scotland, and a regular winter visitor to all British coasts. Outside the breeding season it is a marine bird found only on coasts and estuaries, but it comes inland to nest on lochs. Like all divers, it is an expert swimmer and diver, and a good flyer too, taking off easily from small areas of water. Ashore it is awkward and clumsy. It is more sociable than other divers, occasionally breeding in small colonies, and often forming small groups of about 10–12 birds. When alarmed it submerges completely, leaving only its bill showing above water.

FOOD Mainly fish, but molluscs, crustacea, and some vegetable matter are also taken.

NEST The Red-throated Diver nests close to the water. Usually on the shore of a loch. The nest consists of a scrape in the ground with a variable amount of vegetation used as nesting material – sometimes very little, sometimes enough to form a sizeable mound.

EGGS 2 usually, occasionally 1 or 3, long eggs, olive-buff to green, marked with black spots and blotches. 2.80 x 1.83in:74.9 x 48.3mm. Incubation, by both sexes, but mainly by the female takes 24–29 days. The young are precocial and active, and leave the nest soon after hatching, and are tended by both parents until they are fully fledged and able to fly at about 6 weeks.

BREEDING SEASON May or June. Single-brooded.

Great Northern Diver

SIZE 27–32in:68–81cm.

DESCRIPTION The largest diver, with predominently black and white plumage. In breeding plumage the head and neck are green/black with a purple sheen, with a collar of black and white stripes on the neck, and the dark slate-grey/black upperparts are covered with large square spots forming a regular pattern of oblique bars. The underparts are white with black streaks at the side of the breast. In winter it is a slate-grey above, and pale below. Long black bill.

CALL Generally silent in winter, but in summer it gives loud wailing cries and 'chuckles'.

RECOGNITION The Great Northern Diver is a winter visitor to Britain, found mainly along the coasts of Scotland and Ireland, and southern England. It is marine in habit in winter, but in summer may visit lakes and rivers inland. Non-breeding birds are sometimes seen on sea-coasts in summer, particularly in Shetland. An expert swimmer, it will sink low in the water if alarmed, practically submerging the whole body with only the head showing above water. It is rather reluctant to take wing, and flies laboriously at first until it attains height, and it requires a long stretch of water for take-off. It is inquisitive, and may sometimes express equal curiosity to an observer. It is usually seen singly or in pairs, but sometimes forms small groups, and at migration time may be seen at sea in parties. Sometimes it shows aggressive behaviour towards other birds.

The Great Northern Diver does not normally breed in Britain or Ireland, although some birds do spend the summer in Scotland. There is one record of successful breeding, in the Inner Hebrides in 1970.

PLATE 48

Black-throated Diver (scale 1:7)

Red-throated Diver (scale 1:7)

Great Northern Diver (scale 1:7)

FRANCES FRY.

Little Auk

SIZE 8in:20cm.

DESCRIPTION Smallest of the auk family, with black and white plumage, and dumpy appearance. Upperparts black, with white streaked scapulars and white tips to secondaries, and white underparts. In summer the chin, throat and breast are black. The bill is short and stubby.

CALL A quiet 'wow', or on breeding territories a noisy 'kaak-aak-ak-ak-ak'.

RECOGNITION The Little Auk is a prolific species in its native territory of the Arctic, but it is a rather scarce winter visitor to Britain, regular only in Shetland and parts of northern Scotland. Most birds are seen during stormy weather when strong winds drive them near the coast or occasionally inland to seek refuge on lakes and reservoirs. Usually though the Little Auk is essentially a marine species, and apart from the breeding season it remains constantly at sea. Its small size (comparable to a Starling) and squat shape distinguish this species from the other auks, but sometimes cause it to be mistaken for a young Puffin. Normally it is a very gregarious bird, forming sizeable flocks swimming on or flying low over the water with rapid, whirring wings that give an illusion of great speed; but in Britain stragglers are usually seen singly close to shore.

FOOD Plankton and crustacea form the bulk of the diet. The Little Auk dives for its food and uses its wings underwater to 'fly', staying submerged for half a minute or more.

The Little Auk does not breed in Britain or Ireland.

Puffin

SIZE 12in:30cm.

DESCRIPTION Small auk, readily distinguished by its Parrot-like bill coloured red, orange and yellow, and orange-red legs and feet. Crown and upperparts black, cheeks and underparts white with black collar around neck. The bright triangular bill, eye-ring, and bold face markings combine to give the bird an almost 'clown-like' appearance, and the short, dumpy outline with large head adds to this illusion.

CALL The Puffin has only one note, a growling 'arr', sometimes uttered singly, but more often given in threes, with the first note higher than the second and the third lower still.

RECOGNITION The Puffin is present all year round, but is very localised in distribution and generally scarce along southern and eastern coasts between Dorset and Lincolnshire and Shetlands. It frequents inshore and offshore waters, sometimes deep waters, but in the breeding season it prefers grassy clifftops or turfy islands. On the ground it may assume an upright stance, or rest with body prone on the ground. Puffins are very gregarious, and are often seen in large flocks, or smaller parties perched on the clifftops.

FOOD Small fish and sand-eels taken by diving from the surface. Also molluscs and other marine organisms, and some algae.

NEST The Puffins nest colonially on turf slopes on cliff-tops or islands, usually nesting in a burrow vacated by a Rabbit or Shearwater, or one excavated by themselves. Sometimes a hole among boulders or a natural crevice may be used. Nesting colonies on favourite islands may be very large, and breeding birds may be quite tame.

EGGS 1, sometimes 2, eggs are laid, white in colour, shortish and rather round in shape. 2.37 x 1.69in:60.8 x 42.3mm. Incubation, usually by the female although the male may occasionally assist, takes 40–43 days. The young are altricial, and are tended by both parents for about 40 days, then deserted. The chick (or chicks) then finds its way to the sea under cover of darkness.

BREEDING SEASON Positions in the breeding colony may be occupied as early as March, but the eggs are laid in May. Single-brooded.

Razorbill

SIZE 16in:41cm.

DESCRIPTION Typical auk, with black upperparts and white underparts. It is much the same size as the Guillemot, but is distinguished from it by black upperparts not brown, and deep bill with transverse white bar that gives the Razorbill its name. In the breeding season a white line runs from the base of the bill to the eye. In winter the chin, throat and cheeks are white.

CALL A growling 'caarrrr' sound, and a tremulous whirring sound.

RECOGNITION The Razorbill is present throughout the year, and is fairly widely distributed along the British coastline with the exception of southeast and eastern England. At a distance it may be confused with the more abundant Guillemot, but it is a plumper, more compact bird, with thicker neck and deeper bill, and sits higher in the water. On land it is ungainly, walking with a waddling gait, and its flight is marked by rapid whirring of its wings. It frequents both inshore and off-shore waters, and outside the breeding season may be found well out from coasts. In the breeding season it resorts to cliffs and boulder-strewn shores, where it may associate with guillemots. It is an expert diver, and can swim faster underwater than on the surface. Razorbills are usually very gregarious, and are often seen in small parties and groups at all seasons.

FOOD Fish form a large part of the diet, obtained by plunge-diving from the surface and underwater pursuit. Crustacea, worms and molluscs are also taken.

NEST The Razorbill nests colonially on cliffs or among boulders and rocks along the shore. No actual nest material is used, the eggs being laid in a crevice or hole beneath a boulder.

EGGS 1, sometimes 2, eggs are laid, oval in shape, and very variable in colour, ranging from white to green, spotted with brown or black. 2.90 x 1.80in:73.1 x

45.9mm. Incubation, by both sexes, takes 25–35 days. The young are tended by both parents, and leave the nest at 12–14 days, when they go to sea in the company of an adult.

BREEDING SEASON   May or June. Single-brooded.

Guillemot

SIZE   16½in:42cm.

DESCRIPTION   Slim, elegant seabird with dark brown and white plumage, the brown so deep that the general appearance is of a black and white bird. Dark brown upperparts, head and throat, white underparts, and slender, pointed bill. In winter the throat is white. A sub-species, known as the 'Bridled' or 'Bridled' guillemot has a white line around the eye and a white line extending from it to the side of the head, but this is a relatively scarce bird except in the Shetlands.

CALL   A growling 'arrr' with considerable variations of pitch.

RECOGNITION   The Guillemot is resident throughout the year, patchily distributed along the coastline, being most plentiful in Scotland and very scarce along the east coast of England. It is essentially a marine bird, coming ashore only to breed on suitable cliffs. When on land it stands upright. It is very gregarious, forming large flocks, often in association with Razorbills. It is an expert swimmer and diver, and may decend about 28 feet in search of food, and stay underwater for over a minute.

FOOD   Fish, crustacea, molluscs and algae.

NEST   The Guillemot nests colonially, sometimes in company with Razorbills, on cliffs or rock stacks.

EGGS   Only 1 egg is laid, on a bare rock ledge, the pyriform shape preventing it rolling off into the sea below. The colour is very variable, ranging from white or buff to green or blue, with varying blotches and spots of dark hues. The egg is very large – 3.20 x 1.95in:81.5 x 49.9mm. Both sexes help incubate the egg, resting on the webs of the feet as they squat over it, and hatching takes 28–35 days. The young chick is tended by both parents, and is able to leave its ledge for the sea at 18–25 days, although it cannot fly for another 3 weeks.

BREEDING SEASON   Begins in May in the south , June in the north.

The Guillemot is also listed under BROWN AND WHITE BIRDS.

PLATE 49

Little Auk (scale 1:4.6)

Puffin (scale 1:4.6)

Razorbill (scale 1:4.6)

Guillemot (scale 1:4.6)

Brent Goose

SIZE   22–24in:56–61cm.

DESCRIPTION   The smallest and darkest of the 'black' geese, with two distinct sub-species – the dark-breasted and the light-breasted. The head, neck and upper breast are black, with white flash on upper neck and the upperparts are dark grey/brown with light edges to the feathers. Upper and undertail coverts are white, and the tail is white with broad black terminal band. The dark-beasted race has dark breast nearly as dark as the upperparts, but the light-breasted species has a pale breast shading to white. Bill, legs and feet are black.

CALL   A rather croaking 'krrowk' call.

RECOGNITION   The Brent Goose is a winter visitor to Britain, found around the coasts of England, Wales and Ireland, but scarce in Scotland. Numbers were decreasing rapidly due to hunting, but the population is now recovering due to protective legislation. It is marine in habit and habitat, and is seldom seen inland, preferring to frequent estuaries and tidal flats, resting on the water at high tide, and retiring to the sea at night or when disturbed. It is gregarious, and often forms large flocks. Its flight is swift, like most geese, but it does not fly in regular formation like the distinct 'V's of other geese, but in wavy lines.

FOOD   Mainly marine vegetation, although in summer it will also take grasses and salting plants, and has recently taken to grazing on farmland.

The Brent Goose does not breed in Britain or Ireland.

Eider Duck

SIZE   23in:58cm.

DESCRIPTION   Large, heavily built sea duck with elongated head of triangular shape. The male is predominently black and white, and is the only duck with a black belly and white back. The breast is white tinged with pink, and the head is white with black crown and light green nape. The female is brown, closely barred with black. Both sexes have large triangular bill extending upwards towards the eye in a point.

CALL   The male makes a loud 'coo-ing', the female has a rather grating 'cor-r-r'.

RECOGNITION   The Eider is often thought of as a sub-Arctic bird, associated with cold northern breeding grounds such as Iceland or Scandinavia, but many birds are native to these shores also and are found along the coasts of Scotland and Northern Ireland, and parts of England and Wales too. Essentially marine birds, they are often seen close inshore at all seasons. They are gregarious birds, and form sizeable flocks. In spring their noisy courtship calls call attention to them.

FOOD   Molluscs and crustacea obtained by diving, or pulled off rocks by the powerful bill.

NEST   The Eider breeds an exposed sites such as rocks or islands, or inshore on lakes or rivers close to the sea. The female choses a hollow which is lined with vegetation and the famous Eider down, a thick mass of soft down that is 'farmed' commerically in Iceland where the first lining is taken leaving the female to pluck another from her breast to replace it. Sociable, often nesting in colonies.

EGGS   4–6, sometimes 3–10, pale grey/green eggs are laid. 3.0 x 2.0in:76.7 x 51.4mm. Incubation, by the female alone, takes 27–28 days. The female sits tightly on her eggs, covering the eggs with the thick down lining when leaving the nest to prevent them chilling. The active, precocial chicks leave the nest soon after hatching and take to the water or sea. Several broods sometimes join together and form one large group. They are fully dependent at 8–10 weeks.

BREEDING SEASON   May to mid-June. Single-brooded.

Barnacle Goose

SIZE   27–23in:69–58cm.

DESCRIPTION   Small, so-called 'black' goose, with conspicious white face and forehead, black neck and breast, with blue/grey upperparts edged with white tips to the feathers, greyish underparts, white rump and black tail. Small black bill, black legs and feet. Sexes alike.

CALL   A barking 'gnuk'. A distant flock can sound like yapping dogs.

RECOGNITION   The Barnacle Goose is a winter visitor to Britain, found mainly along the western coasts of Scotland and Ireland. Two separate populations visit here – Greenland birds frequent western Scotland and Ireland, and Spitsbergen birds visit the Solway Firth. Birds seen in other localities are usually escapees from wildfowl collections. It is a gregarious species and very large flocks occur in favoured areas, where they may be seen feeding along the shoreline of estuaries, or saltings or grassy islands. They are seldom seen far inland.

FOOD   Mainly grass, but also seeds of salting plants and some clovers.

The Barnacle Goose does not breed in Britain or Ireland.

Canada Goose

SIZE   35–30in:89–76cm.

DESCRIPTION   Largest of the 'black' geese, in reality more brown than black. It has a black head with white patch on throat and cheek and a long black neck, but the upperparts are brown barred buff, and the underparts buff barred brown, with white

WATER & SEA BIRDS

PLATE 50

Brent Goose
(scale 1:8.2)

Eider Duck (scale 1:8.2)

Barnacle Goose (scale 1:8.2)

Canada Goose (scale 1:8.2)

FRANCES FRY

under the tail and a broad black terminal band on the white tail. It is the largest European goose. Sexes alike.

CALL   A carrying 'aa-honk' during flight, and a swan-like hiss at intruders.

RECOGNITION   The Canada Goose is resident throughout the year in Britain, although birds located in southern areas migrate to more northerly regions to moult. Easily identified by its large size, and tends to be tamer than most other species of geese. It is highly gregarious except during the breeding season, and frequents lakes, ponds or marshy land with surrounding woodland, or flooded grasslands. Normally a diurnal feeder it can often be seen grazing like the 'grey' geese, and has become unpopular with some farmers because of crop damage.

FOOD   Grass or aquatic vegetation.

NEST   The Canada Goose usually nests near to water, on an islet or in woody vegetation. On larger waterways it may nest colonially, but individual territories are defended vigorously. The nest consists of a hollow lined with plant debris with an inner lining of down and feathers.

EGGS   5–6, sometimes 2–11, large creamy-white eggs are laid. 3.38 x 2.30in:85.7 x 58.2mm. Incubation, by the female alone with the male standing guard over her, takes 28–30 days. The young are precocial and active, flying at around 9 weeks, but usually stay with their parents until the next spring.

BREEDING SEASON   Late March or April. Single-brooded.

Other black and white birds which are fully described under different sections.

TUFTED DUCK   This blue, black and white bird is described under the heading *BLUE, BLACK AND WHITE BIRDS.*

SLAVONIAN GREBE   This bird is fully described under *WATER & SEA BIRDS: BRIGHT COLOURED BIRDS. In winter plumage it is predominantly black and white.*

THE SMEW: This black and white bird is fully described under BROWN/ BLACK/WHITE BIRDS.

Bean Goose

SIZE   28–35in:71–89cm.

DESCRIPTION   The brownest of the 'grey' geese, often very dark, with a long, slim appearance, and noticeably long neck. Head, neck and back are dark brown, and chest is paler, with a light edging to the feathers. Legs and feet are orange-yellow, and the stout bill is orange-yellow and black.

CALL   Quieter than the other grey geese, with a deep 'ung-unk' call.

RECOGNITION   The Bean Goose is a winter visitor to Britain from northern Europe and Russia. Once large numbers used to arrive each October and stay until April, but in recent years there has been a drastic decline, and it is now usually seen only in Scotland at Dumfries, and on the Yare marshes near Yarmouth. Elsewhere it is a scarce visitor to farmland. In habit and habitat it is similar to the Greylag, but it seldom feeds on stubble. It is gregarious, and often forms large flocks, but these are rarely seen in Britain. Although it may associate with other species along the coast, it nearly always roosts inland.

FOOD   Grasses form the main part of its diet, but it will also graze on cereal crops, or clover.

The Bean Goose does not breed in Britain or Ireland.

Pink-footed Goose

SIZE   24–30in:61–76cm.

DESCRIPTION   Smallest of the 'grey' geese, with small bill, and small dark head that contrasts with the paler grey/brown body. Overall the winter plumage is greyer than the summer, which is browner in tone. The bill is black with a pink band, and the legs and feet are pink as the name implies.

CALL   A variety of calls 'ung-unk', 'wink-wink-wink' amongst them.

RECOGNITION   The Pink-footed Goose is a winter visitor to Britain, arriving from Iceland or Greenland in large numbers in October and leaving in April. It is mainly seen in Scotland and eastern England, but in favoured areas, such as Loch Leven and the Solway, huge flocks may occur. Its habits are similar to the other 'grey' geese, and it frequents similar habitat of rivers and marshes, and sometimes estuaries. It is extremely gregarious.

FOOD   Vegetable matter, including grasses and cereal crops. Increased barley growing in Scotland has provided the Pink-footed Goose with a tempting food source, and this is thought to be the main reason for greater numbers visiting Scotland and a corresponding decrease in England. It has also led to a conflict of interest between farmers and conservationists in some areas.

The Pink-footed Goose does not breed in Britain or Ireland.

Greylag Goose

SIZE   35–30in:89–76cm.

DESCRIPTION   Largest of the 'grey' geese, and the only native breeding species, it is the ancestor of most domestic geese. Paler grey in colour than other 'grey' geese with grey plumage overall except for white undertail coverts and white uppertail edged with broad grey band. Large orange coloured bill, and pink legs and feet. Sexes alike. The name 'Greylag' is said to derive from the pale grey forewing, or lingering behind in spring.

CALL   Typical domestic goose call 'aahng-ung-ung'.

RECOGNITION   The Greylag Goose is a widely distributed species, coming further south than most other geese. Truly native British birds are found only in the Outer Hebrides but feral populations are found in many parts of Britain and Ireland, and are joined by thousands more in winter with many birds coming from Iceland. It is found on grassland, estuaries and lakes, and is gregarious by nature, forming small flocks in inland waters. Its plump build resembles domestic geese, but its behaviour is typically wild. Paired birds usually stay together for life, and family units remain together for a whole year.

FOOD   Primarily a grassland grazer, but a wide variety of aquatic plants are also taken and in Scotland barley stubble and potatoes also form part of the diet.

NEST   The Greylag Goose nests close to water, on offshore islands, marshes, by lakes or rivers. Not quite a colonial nester, but several nests may occur in the same locality, and domestic and feral birds may share the same territory for breeding. The nest is a scrape in the ground, with a scanty lining of vegetation, and some down.

EGGS   4–6, sometimes 3–8, oval creamish eggs with fine granular texture to the shell. 3.40 x 2.35in:85.3 x 58mm. Incubation, by the female alone but with the male attending close by, takes 27–28 days. The young are precocial and active, but remain with their parents even after they achieve full independence at about 8 weeks.

BREEDING SEASON   Late March to late April. Single-brooded.

White-fronted Goose

SIZE   26–30in:66–76cm.

DESCRIPTION   A dark 'grey' goose with dark brown plumage on head, back and wings, and greyish breast with black barring. White undertail coverts, and prominent white patch at base of bill that gives the species its name. Legs and feet are orange, but the bill colour varies – orange for the Greenland race, and pink for the Siberian race.

CALL   A high-pitched 'kow-yow' call.

RECOGNITION   The White-fronted Goose is a winter visitor to Britain, arriving in October, and departing in March or April. Both the Greenland and Siberian races visit, with Greenland White-fronts being found in Scotland, Ireland and west Wales, and Siberian birds going to south Wales and southern England. It frequents salt-marshes and rivers, and flooded grassland, and is also seen in fields of young grain. It is very gregarious, and often forms large flocks made up of family units. Like most grey geese the White-front is a bird of open country, essentially a land-feeder although it will sometimes feed in shallow water. It is often diurnal in habit, feeding in early morning or at night if too much disturbed during the day. The flocks tend to be very wary and suspicious, and are difficult to approach.

FOOD   Mainly grasses from pasture land, but can sometimes cause a problem for farmers by feeding on young grain.

The White-fronted Goose does not breed in Britain or Ireland, but returns to its homelands of Greenland or Russia.

Other brown/grey birds which are fully described under different sections

RED-THROATED DIVER   *This bird is fully described under BLACK/WHITE BIRDS.*

PLATE 51

Bean Goose (scale 1:9.3)

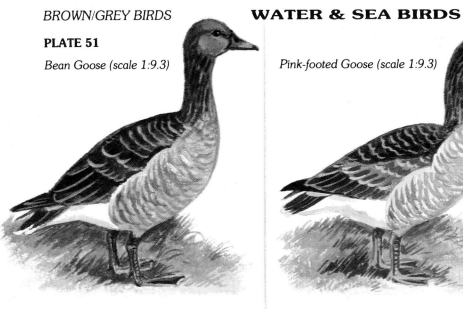

Pink-footed Goose (scale 1:9.3)

Greylag Goose (scale 1:9.3)

White-fronted Goose (scale 1:9.3)

FRANCES FRY

Leach's Petrel

SIZE   8in:20cm.

DESCRIPTION   Starling-sized black seabird with forked tail, which serves to distinguish it from the smaller but similarly coloured Storm Petrel. All black plumage except for white rump, and light bar on wing. Slightly more brown/black than Storm Petrel.

CALL   A purring 'r-r-r' note, and a crowing 'her-kitti-werke' heard at breeding grounds.

RECOGNITION   The Leach's Petrel is a summer visitor to Britain, much rarer than the Storm Petrel, but occuring regularly off the coasts of northern Scotland and parts of western Ireland. Essentially a marine bird it is rarely seen close to shore, but occasionally bad weather may drive it inland. Its flight is more buoyant and erratic than the Storm Petrel's, and unlike that species it is seen singly or in small parties, and does not follow ships in hope of food. Nest sites are generally only visited after darkness has fallen, and although there are a few nesting colonies in Britain and Ireland it is a difficult bird to observe.

FOOD   Small fish, molluscs and crustacea are sometimes taken, but plankton forms the bulk of the diet.

NEST   Leach's Petrel nests on offshore islands with turf or rocky slopes, and excavates a burrow in soft soil, or under rocks, or in banks. It is a colonial nester, and in favoured breeding sites several pairs may share a communal entrance to a large burrow with several nesting chambers. A little plant debris is used to line the nest.

EGGS   A single white egg, often with a ring of fine red markings at the larger end. 1.25 x 0.95in:32.8 x 23.8mm. Incubation, by both sexes with each bird sitting for an unbroken spell of 5–6 days, takes 41–42 days. The young is altrical, covered with fine down, and is brooded for the first 5 days, then fed every night by the parents. It is fully fledged at 63–70 days when it leaves the nest under cover of darkness and goes to the sea. Opinion is divided as to whether the chick is deserted first when it is about 40 days old.

BREEDING SEASON   Late May to October. Single-brooded.

Leach's Petrel is also listed under BROWN BIRDS, as the plumage is a brownish-black.

Manx Shearwater

SIZE   14in:35cm.

DESCRIPTION   Distinguished from other shearwaters by black upperparts and white underparts, the black extending well below the eye. Typical shearwater flight showing first dark upperparts then white underparts in sharp contrast.

CALL   A silent bird while at sea, but in breeding grounds has a variety of cries, screams and wails. These cries are usually given at night, and the eerie sounds may have given rise to many a ghost story.

RECOGNITION   The Manx Shearwater takes its name from the Isle of Man which has long been one of its breeding strongholds. It is a spring and summer visitor to Britain, arriving as early as February and leaving for South America in autumn. It is essentially a marine bird, like all shearwaters, and is most likely to be seen off Scottish and Irish coasts, although it is also seen off Wales and the West Country. Clumsy and vulnerable on land the birds spend most daylight hours at sea, coming ashore at night to the breeding grounds. Once on land it often has difficulty taking off again, and may need an elevated place to aid launching into flight.

FOOD   Mostly small fish, but squid, molluscs and crustaceans are also taken.

NEST   The Manx Shearwater nests in colonies in burrows, on offshore islands or cliff-tops. Both sexes help excavate the burrow, which is about 3ft long. The nest chamber at the end contains a little nest material such as plants or feathers.

EGGS   Only 1 egg is laid, white and non-glossy. 2½ x 1.60in:60.9 x 41.9mm. Incubation by both sexes, takes 52–54 days. Each bird sits 4–5 days, the sitter being fed by its mate at night. The young is altrical and downy, and is brooded for a week, then fed nightly until it is fledged at about 60 days. The parents then desert the chick, which usually remains in the burrow without food for up to a fortnight, then it emerges and makes its way to the sea under cover of darkness. It will not breed until 5–6 years.

BREEDING SEASON   Usually May to September. Single-brooded.

Storm Petrel

SIZE   6in:15cm.

DESCRIPTION   Black, sparrow-sized seabird, with weak-looking fluttering flight that flies low over the water. The plumage is all black save for bold white rump, and pale bar on underwing. Square tail. Legs dangle down when the bird feeds at sea, pecking food from the surface of the water.

CALL   Silent except during the breeding season, when it has a purring 'arr-rr-r', a rapid 'wick-wick-wick', and a 'Chikka' call.

RECOGNITION   The tiny Storm Petrel is mainly a summer visitor to Britain, seen mostly off Scottish and Irish shores from April to November. In rough weather birds are sometimes blown inland which probably accounts for the name 'storm' petrel, but usually it is only seen at sea. It often follows vessels hoping for food scraps, and hovers close to the waves with almost bat-like flight, or patters the water with dangling feet. It usually approaches land only after darkness has fallen and most activity at breeding sites also takes place at dusk or in darkness.

FOOD   Fish and plankton, or floating offal.

NEST The Storm Petrel is a tunnel nesting bird, breeding on offshore islands with turf or rocky slopes. It nests colonially, but numbers vary – sometimes a few scattered pairs, sometimes a large scattered group. The tunnel is excavated in soft soil, with a nest-chamber lined with scanty nest material. Occasionally a cavity in a wall or boulders serves for a nest site.

EGGS 1 single egg only, white and non-glossy, sometimes with a zone of fine reddish spots at the larger end. 1.12in x 0.80in:28 x 21.2mm. Incubation, by both sexes takes 38–40 days, with each bird sitting for 2–3 days at a time. The young is altrical, fed by both parents usually at night but sometimes with 2–3 day intervals. The chick can fly at 60–66 days.

BREEDING SEASON Late May to July. Single-brooded.

Sooty Shearwater

SIZE 16in:41cm.

DESCRIPTION Dark brown shearwater with pale whitish wing linings. At a distance may appear black, hence the name 'sooty' shearwater. Somewhat similar is size and flight to the Great Shearwater, but the body looks heavier, the wings are narrower and more angled during flight. May be confused with dark Skua.

CALL Rather silent except at breeding grounds, when it has gull-like cries.

RECOGNITION The Sooty Shearwater is an autumn visitor to Britain, seen off coasts in August and September. It is one of the great travellers of the bird world, ranging from its breeding colonies in the South Atlantic to Northern Hemispheres. Essentially marine in habit, and seldom seen near to land, it is most usually seen near the horizon skimming close to the sea. Off British coasts it is usually seen in twos or threes, but where numbers are more plentiful it is gregarious and will form flocks at sea.

FOOD Fish, squid and crustaceans, taken by diving.

The Sooty Shearwater does not breed in Britain or Ireland – its main breeding grounds are in New Zealand and the South Atlantic.

Great Shearwater

SIZE 18in:46cm.

DESCRIPTION Large shearwater with brown upperparts and white underparts, with white collar separating dark chocolate brown cap, and dark brown tail. Sexes alike. Flies with stiff wings, turning from side to side showing first upperparts then underparts, swooping low over the water.

CALL Typical gull-like cries.

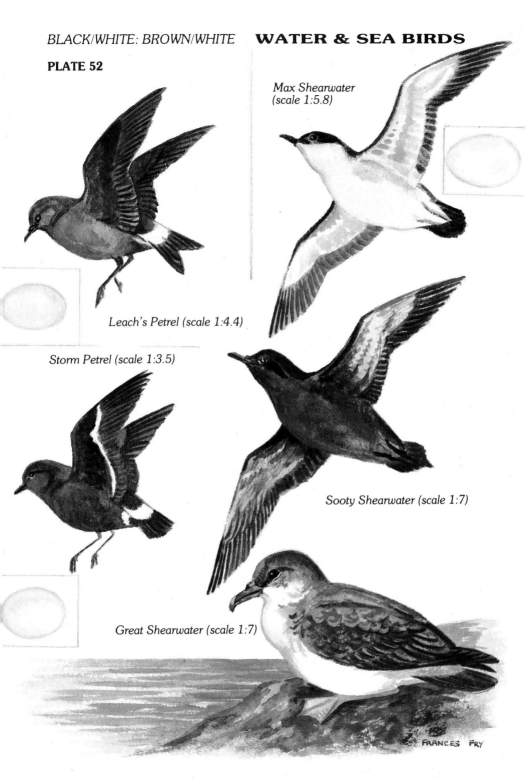

Max Shearwater (scale 1:5.8)

Leach's Petrel (scale 1:4.4)

Storm Petrel (scale 1:3.5)

Sooty Shearwater (scale 1:7)

Great Shearwater (scale 1:7)

FRANCES FRY

RECOGNITION The Great Shearwater is mainly a summer or autumn visitor to Britain, seen most frequently off the coasts of southern and western Ireland, and western England. It is essentially a marine bird and seldom occurs very close to land. They are gregarious birds and flocks often follow whales and porpoises. There are a few recorded sightings in winter and spring, but most birds are usually seen off Britain in late summer.

FOOD Fish and squid, obtained by diving, or fish waste from fishing boats.

The Great Shearwater does not breed in Britain or Ireland. The main breeding grounds are in Tristan da Cunha.

Long-tailed Skua

SIZE 20–22in:51–56cm.

DESCRIPTION Smallest of the skuas, with distinctive long tail streamers that give the species its name. Brown upperparts, yellowish-grey underparts, with blackish crown, and blue-grey legs and feet. Slender wings, and graceful tern-like flights.

CALL A silent bird except at its breeding grounds.

RECOGNITION The Long-tailed Skua is a passage migrant to Britain, occuring mostly in the autumn, but sometimes in the spring and summer. It is seen mainly on the east coast of England, occasionally on the east coast of Scotland, and rarely elsewhere, and numbers are small. It is essentially a marine bird, and spends all its life at sea except for the breeding season, swimming buoyantly with its long tail pointing upward. It is a skilled, graceful flier, and may sometimes harry other birds in flight. It can also hover like a Kestrel, and perform acrobatics with other birds.

FOOD Fish and offal, and sometimes terns and gulls and their eggs.

The Long-tailed Skua does not breed in Britain or Ireland.

Pomarine Skua

SIZE 20in:51cm.

DESCRIPTION Typical skua, more heavily built than the Arctic Skua, with dark brown upperparts and white underparts in the light phase of its plumage, light brown underparts in the dark phase. Most distinguishing features are elongated central tail feathers that are broad and twisted with a blunt end, and a dusky breast band. Young birds lack the twisted tail feathers.

CALL Gull-like calls, and a 'which-yew' note.

RECOGNITION The Pomarine Skua is mostly an autumn visitor to Britain, seen off North Sea coasts, with a few spring migrants appearing in the Channel and along western coasts. It is a difficult bird to observe as it usually keeps well out to sea, only coming inshore in stormy weather. In flight it looks heavier than the Arctic Skua, and it tends to be more solitary in habits. Like all skuas it harries other smaller birds to make them disgorge food.

FOOD Fish, usually obtained from other birds, eggs and young of other species, carrion and offal if available.

The Pomarine Skua does not nest in Britain or Ireland – its main breeding grounds are in the Arctic.

Great Skua (Bonxie)

SIZE   23in:58cm.

DESCRIPTION   Large gull-like brown seabird, with very aggressive habits. Its plumage is brown flecked with lighter markings, with a white flash on the wings visible during flight. A rather squared-off tail with two small notches in the centre.

CALL   A 'tuk-tuk', a 'skerr', and a loud 'hah-hah-hah' note used in display.

RECOGNITION   The Great Skua is mainly a summer visitor to Britain's coasts, seen mostly off northern Scotland and S.W. Ireland. A maritime species, it is seldom seen inshore except during the breeding season. Most plentiful in the Shetland Isles, where it is often known by the alternative name of 'bonxie' harking back to Viking times. It is much given to piracy, harrying smaller gulls and terns to snatch their food, and defending its breeding territory fiercely against all intruders – animal or human. Despite this aggressive streak it is a gregarious species, feeding in loose flocks and breeding colonially.

FOOD   Mainly fish, usually obtained by forcing other birds to disgorge their catches. Birds may also be taken, and stranded fish or offal if available.

NEST   The Great Skua nests in heather or rough pasture, usually in colonies but with the nests well spaced out. The nest consists of a shallow scrape without a lining.

EGGS   2, sometimes only 1, olive-green eggs to brown marked with blotches and spots of browns and purple-grey. More rarely eggs may be unmarked and a pale blue hue. 2.75 x 2in:70.6 x 49.1mm. Incubation, by both sexes, takes 28–30 days. The young are altrical and downy, and are tended by both parents. At first the female broods while the male brings food. The young fledge quickly, about 30 days, but the family unit remains intact until they are fully independent at 6-7 weeks.

BREEDING SEASON   Late May to June. Single-brooded.

Arctic Skua

SIZE   18in:46cm.

DESCRIPTION   Graceful skua with brown and white plumage and elongated central tail feathers in the breeding season, black cap, and long pointed wings reminiscent of a Peregrine Falcon. The upperparts are dark brown, the underparts white in light phase, light brown in dark phase. The plumage varies from pale to dark, with an intermediate phase often seen in Britain.

CALL   A wailing miaow-like 'ka-aaow' and a 'tuk-tuk' note.

RECOGNITION   The Arctic Skua is a summer visitor to British coasts, breeding in the northern Isles of Scotland, and is seen as a passage migrant in other coastal

PLATE 53

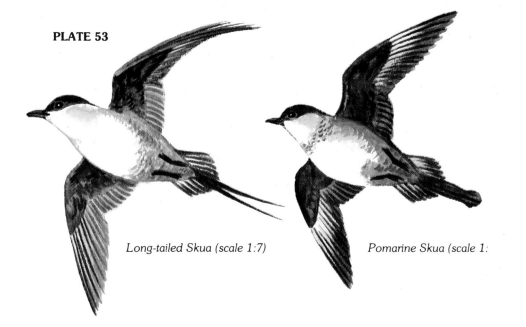

Long-tailed Skua (scale 1:7)

Pomarine Skua (scale 1:

Great Skua (scale 1:7)

Arctic Skua (scale 1:7)

FRANCES FRY.

regions. Maritime in habits, except during the breeding season, although it may take refuge inland in stormy weather during migration. It is a skilled and graceful flyer, resembling the hawks in its glides and swoops. Like all the skuas it lives mainly by piracy, harassing terns and small gulls in the air to make them drop their food. It is also very aggressive at the breeding grounds, and will attack all intruders viciously, even man.

FOOD   Mostly fish which other birds have been forced to disgorge, but birds and eggs are also taken, as is offal or stranded fish if available.

NEST   The Arctic Skua nests in heather or rough ground, or sometimes in marshy areas. Usually nests in colonies, but occasionally as scattered pairs. The nest is a scrape or hollow with little or no lining, sometimes some grass or heather.

EGGS   2, occasionally 1, olive eggs blotched and spotted with brown and grey. The markings are very variable, and often sparse. 2.05 x 1.56in:57.2 x 40.1mm. Incubation, by both sexes, takes 24–28 days. The young are altricial and downy, and are cared for by both parents. They may leave the nest after a few days, remaining nearby, and can fly at about 30 days. Full independence comes at 7–8 weeks.

BREEDING SEASON   Late May to June. Single-brooded.

Other brown birds which are fully described under different sections.

LITTLE GREBE (DABCHICK) This small grebe is fully described under WATER & SEA BIRDS: BRIGHT COLOURED BIRDS.
Most female ducks come under the description of brown birds, but will be found under the headings best describing the plumage of the male birds.
Similarly many juvenile gulls have predominantly brown speckled plumage, and can be difficult for the amateur birdwatcher to distinguish. Size, bill and leg colouring, and colour of eye will show some characteristics as mature birds, and may aid identification.

Long-Tailed Duck

SIZE   21–16in:53–41cm.

DESCRIPTION   Long-tailed sea duck with round head and short bill. It is the only sea duck with white on body and dark wings. In winter the male is dark brown and white, in summer he is black and white. The long pointed tail-feathers give a similarity in outline to the larger, darker Pintail, but the Long-tailed duck is essentially a marine bird, whilst the Pintail is found on inland waters. The female lacks the long tail-feathers, appearing more 'chunky' than the male, and is brown and white.

CALL   Noisy Goose-like call by the male, consisting of high nasal notes, and a barking call from the female.

RECOGNITION   The Long-tailed Duck is a scarce winter visitor to Britain, seen mainly along northern coasts. It rarely comes ashore except during the breeding season, prefering to feed in shallow seas. Although gregarious large flocks are seldom seen off British coasts. Courting begins early in spring before the flocks leave their winter feeding grounds, with drakes raising their long tails in display, and much vigorous calling. This courtship calling has been compared to distant bagpipes or a hound pack baying; and in North America it is thought to resemble the chanting of Red Indians and has given the species the alternative name of Old Squaw.

FOOD   Crustacea and molluscs, obtained by diving, form the major part of the diet, but plant material and some berries are also taken in summer.

NEST   The Long-tailed Duck nests in tundra or arctic scrub, or on islets in lake or sea, and although breeding has been suspected in Britain it has not been confirmed.

Smew

SIZE   16in:41cm.

DESCRIPTION   Smallest of the sawbill ducks, sometimes called 'White Nuns' because of the beautiful black and white plumage of the male. At rest or on land the male appears as pure white with a few black markings (black patch or lores, behind eye and on back) but in flight it shows much more black on the wings. Females and juveniles have chestnut red head with white throat and cheeks, with grey upperparts and paler underparts.

CALL   The Smew is a very silent bird except during the breeding season when it may give a hoarse grunting or rattling call.

RECOGNITION   The Snew is a winter visitor to Britain, present from November to April, and is found mostly in southern England, in particular reservoirs. Elsewhere it is a rather rare visitor to our coasts. However it is traditional in its choice of winter haunts, and once it has visited a particular area may return year after year. It is gregarious and often forms small flocks, but is shy and easily disturbed. When alarmed it sinks its body low in the water, and it is an expert diver.

225

PLATE 54

Long-tailed Duck (scale 1:8.2)   *Smew (scale 1:8.2)*

Pintail (scale 1:8.2)   *Scaup (scale 1:8.2)*

FRANCES FRY

FOOD   Animal matter, particularly fish obtained by diving from the surface, also insects and their larvae in summer, and some vegetable matter.

The Smew does not breed in Britain or Ireland.

The Smew is also listed under Black and White birds.

Pintail

SIZE   22in:56cm.

DESCRIPTION   Elegant, long-tailed duck with narrow, pointed wings. The male has a dark brown head and neck with a white band extending down the side of the neck to join the white breast, and vermiculated grey flanks and back, with black undertail coverts with white patch. The female has similar colouring to the female mallard, but is slightly greyer, with slender neck and pointed tail. The most distinctive feature of both sexes is the central tail feathers that extend to a point, and give the species its name.

CALL   The male has a low whistle, the female a rather subdued 'quack'.

RECOGNITION   The Pintail is largely a winter visitor to Britain, although some birds are resident here throughout the year. It is found on lakes, marshes or moorland pools in locally around Britains coasts, with largest numbers in the Fen country. Naturally shy and suspicious, it is difficult to approach closely, but it is gregarious and often forms large flocks in winter, sometimes with other species like Teal or Mallard. A strong, fast flyer. It also walks well on land. On water the long tail is held well up, and during the breeding season it is held right back over the head in display.

FOOD   Largely vegetable matter obtained by 'up-ending', but some animal matter too, like insects, worms, frogs and molluscs.

NEST   The Pintail is one of Britain's rarer breeding birds, but small numbers are recorded annually in Scotland, northern England and the Fens. Where numbers are sufficient it often nests semi-colonially, usually in low vegetation like heather or grasses near water or on island sites. The nest is a hollow, lined with plant material, down and feathers.

EGGS   7–9, sometimes 6–12, rather longish eggs, cream or greenish-blue in colour. 2.10 x 1.79in:54.2 x 37.5mm Incubation, by the female alone, begins on completion of the clutch and takes 21–23 days. The active, precocial young take to the water soon after hatching. Although the male is usually present the female seems to tend the ducklings on her own until they are fully fledged at about 7 weeks.

BREEDING SEASON   Starts in mid-April. Single-brooded.

Scaup

SIZE 19in:48cm.

DESCRIPTION The marine equivalent of the Tufted Duck, with superficially similar colouring, but lacking crest and greener on head. The male is predominently black and white, but has grey back, and the brown female is distinguished by bold white patch around bill and broader outline. Both sexes have a prominent white wing-bar visible during flight.

CALL A quiet species; the female has a harsh 'karr-karr', the male a soft coo used as a courtship note.

RECOGNITION The Scaup is a winter visitor to Britain, found around the coasts, particularly in sheltered bays where its favourite food of mussels are found. It is a gregarious bird, and may form large flocks both at sea and in flight. It is an expert swimmer and diver, even in rough seas, and in essentially maritime in habits, rarely venturing inland except during the breeding season.

FOOD Mussels and other molluscs form a major part of the diet, with other crustacea.

NEST The Scaup does not usually nest in Britain, although there have been isolated reports that is has done so. Most birds return in the spring to the tundra breeding grounds in Scandinavia, Iceland and Russia.

Other birds which are fully described under different sections.

THE GUILLEMOT This dark brown and white seabird appears black and white and is fully described under BLACK AND WHITE BIRDS.

THE CANADA GOOSE Is fully described under BLACK AND WHITE BIRDS.

Lesser Black-backed Gull

SIZE   22–21in:56–53cm.

DESCRIPTION   Medium sized gull, similar in colour to the Great Black-backed Gull, with black/slate grey and wings and white head and underparts, and yellow bill with red spot on lower mandible. Legs and feet are usually yellow, but sometimes pink. Smaller size is best distinguishing features from Great Black-backed Gull.

CALL   A 'kyow' and a variety of barking calls.

RECOGNITION   The Lesser Black-backed Gull used to be mainly a summer visitor to Britain, but increasing numbers are now resident all year round. It is found along most of the coastline except the east coast of England, and breeds inland in hilly districts of England and Wales. On coast and sea it occupies similar habitat to the Herring Gull, and like that species is found on reservoirs and playing fields. Its behaviour resembles that of the Herring Gull rather than the Great Black-backed Gull, and it is not so aggressive as its larger namesake. It is gregarious and those birds that migrate to warmer climes in winter do so in flocks, often in company with other species of gulls.

FOOD   Fish, crustacea, worms and molluscs, also insects, mice and voles, eggs and carrion if available. It is less likely to feed off rubbish tips than Herring or Great Black-backed Gulls.

NEST   The Lesser Black-backed Gull breeds colonially, on level tops of cliffs or islands, shingle beaches, or moorland, or more rarely on roofs in coastal areas. The nest is a shallow hollow in the ground well lined with plant material or seaweed.

EGGS   3 usually, sometimes 1 or 2, non-glossy olive-green eggs with brown spots and blotches, laid on alternate days. 2.62 x 1.88in;67.6 x 47mm. Incubation, by both sexes takes 25–29 days. The young are semi-precocial and downy, and are tended by both parents for about 7 weeks, until they can fly.

BREEDING SEASON   Late April to May. Single-brooded.

Black-headed Gull

SIZE   14½in:36cm.

DESCRIPTION   Common British gull, which despite its name has dark chocolate brown head, not black although it may appear so from a distance. In winter the head becomes white with just a dark smudge behind the eyes. Upperparts dove-grey, with dark-tipped primaries on wings and white forewing; underparts white. Legs, feet and bill are red.

CALL   A harsh 'kwaar' call.

229

RECOGNITION   The Black-headed Gull is one of the most common British gulls, resident all year round, and as plentiful inland as on the coast. Many Continental birds also visit our shores in winter. The species has greatly increased in numbers this century, and has been quick to adapt to new environments, and to associate with man. It is very gregarious and large flocks are found on reservoirs, at sewage farms, rubbish tips, and at roosts. It has an aggressive nature, and will harry other species, such as grebes, to steal their food.

FOOD   Very varied, ranging from fish and crustacea to offal and carrion, debris and waste from tips.

NEST   The Black-headed Gull nests colonially, on sites varying from estuaries and dunes to marshes and inland lakes and pools, or more rarely on buildings. The nest is a hollow scrape lined with a variable amount of vegetative material. Both sexes help with the construction, with the male adding most material.

EGGS   3, sometimes 2, more occasionally 5 or 6, light olive eggs blotched and spotted with dark blackish markings. 2 x 1.53in;51.9 x 37.2mm. Incubation, by both sexes, begins with the first egg and takes 21–27 days. The young are precocial and downy, and are tended by both parents. They often leave the nest a few days after hatching, but remain close by. They can fly at about 5–6 weeks.

BREEDING SEASON   Mid April to late May. Single-brooded.

The Black-headed Gull is also listed under GREY/WHITE birds on account of its winter plumage.

Mediterranean Gull

SIZE   15in:38cm.

DESCRIPTION   Small black-headed gull, rather similar to the Black-headed Gull in size, but more heavily built, and lacking dark wing-tips. It has a black head, light grey back and wings, and white underparts, with red legs, feet and bill. In winter the black head becomes white, with dark smudge behind the eye. There is an incomplete white eye-ring.

CALL   A 'Kow-kow-kow' call.

RECOGNITION   The Mediterranean Gull is a passage migrant and winter visitor to Britain, seen mainly on the south and east coasts of England. Although overall numbers are small the species is extending its range in sourthern Britain since the 1950s, and may occasionally breed here. It is usually seen in coastal areas, rarely inland except during the breeding season. Its behaviour and habits are similar to the Black-headed Gulls.

FOOD   Small fish, molluscs and insects.

NEST   The Mediterranean Gull breeds on islands in shallow lakes or lagoons, or on

PLATE 55

Black-headed Gull
(scale 1:7)

Mediterranean Gull (scale 1:7)

Lesser Black-backed Gull
(scale 1:7)

Great Black-backed Gull (scale 1:8.2)

Little Gull (scale 1:7)

FRANCES FRY.

marshy areas with herbage near to shores in colonies, sometimes in association with other species. The nest consists of a shallow hollow lined with plant stems, grass and some feathers.

EGGS 3, sometimes 2, smooth, non-glossy pale creamy-yellow eggs, marked with speckles, spots and scrawls of dark brown-black. 2.10 x 1.50in:53.7 x 38.1mm. Incubation is thought to be around 21–27 days, but as breeding numbers are small in Britain at the present time information has not yet been collated. The young are precocial and downy.

BREEDING SEASON Begins late May. Single-brooded.

The Mediterranean Gull is also listed under WHITE/GREY birds on account of its winter plumage.

Great Black-backed Gull

SIZE 31–25in:79–64cm.

DESCRIPTION Large, powerful gull with black back and wings, and white head and underparts, large head with thick, strong yellow bill with red spot near the tip of the lower mandible. The legs and feet are flesh coloured.

CALL An 'uk-uk-uk' call, and a short 'owk'.

RECOGNITION The Black-backed Gull is resident all year round, and is found along most of Britains coastline, and often inland as well. Its lifestyle is generally more marine than many gulls and it is often found far out at sea, but in recent years increased numbers gather to roost at reservoirs and inland lakes. It is an aggressive bird, and preys on other seabirds such as Puffins and Shearwaters. Not so tame as the Herring Gull, but will follow boats or hang around fishing ports hoping for fish waste and scraps. Its flight looks slow and ponderous, the broad body seeming to weight the bird down. Often gregarious, it is also seen singly or in couples, alone or in flocks of other species of gulls.

FOOD Very varied: fish, crustacea, molluscs and worms; small animals like mice and voles, also garbage and carrion, and in summer nestlings and eggs of other seabirds, Occasionally larger prey such as rabbits or a weakly lamb may be taken.

NEST The Great Black-backed Gull nests colonially or singly according to sites available. Large colonies are found on estuaries and coasts, or smaller numbers on cliff ledges sand banks by shallow inland waters, or more rarely on shingle or salt-marsh, or moorland. Both birds help build the nest, which is made of a large amount of sticks, heather, seaweed or grass, with some feathers.

EGGS 2–3 olive-green eggs are laid on alternate days, spotted with dark brown or grey markings. Occasionally the ground shade may vary and be blueish or pink. 3 x 2.10in:76.6 x 53.9mm. Incubation, by both sexes begins before completion of the clutch and takes 26–30 days. The young are semi-precocial and downy, and are tended by both parents for about 50 days until they are fully fledged and can fly.

BREEDING SEASON Mid April to May. Single-brooded.

Little Gull

SIZE 11n:28cm.

DESCRIPTION Small, rather tern-like gull, with black head, grey back and wings, and white underparts. The legs and feet are red, but the bill changes colour, being red in summer, black in winter. Best identification is small size, and dark underwing. In winter the black cap is replaced by a single dark smudge behind the eye.

CALL A 'kek-eke-kek' call.

RECOGNITION The Little Gull is a passage and winter visitor to Britain, seen most often in the autumn when sizeable flocks may appear along the north, east and south coasts of Scotland and England. Numbers visiting British shores are increasing. In the breeding season it frequents marshes and lakes, but it is more usually seen at sea or along the shore. It is gregarious, and even where numbers are small is usually seen in small flocks rather than singly.

FOOD Small fish, crustcea, worms, molluscs and insects, and a little vegetable matter. Food is often obtained by picking objects from the water's surface in the manner of a marsh tern.

The Little Gull has not so far bred successfully in Britain or Ireland, although it first attempted to nest (at the Ouse Washes) in 1975. Further efforts in 1978 also failed, but hopefully in time it may become a Britain breeding bird.

Other black-headed birds which are fully described under different sections.

COMMON TERN, LITTLE TERN, ARCTIC TERN, ROSEATE TERN, SANDWICH TERN **All these birds are fully described under WATER & SEA BIRDS: GREY AND WHITE BIRDS.**

BLACK TERN **(winter plumage) This species is fully described under WATER & SEA BIRDS: GREY/WHITE BIRDS.**

GREAT SHEARWATER **This species is fully described under WATER & SEA BIRDS: BROWN AND WHITE BIRDS.**

Iceland Gull

SIZE   26–22in:66–56cm.

DESCRIPTION   Pale gull, resembling the Glaucous Gull, but usually considerably smaller in size, with shorter and less heavy bill. Light grey back and wings, and white head and underparts, with flesh-coloured legs and feet, and yellow bill with red tip.

CALL   Shriller than Herring Gull, with a 'ack-ack-ack' alarm call.

RECOGNITION   The Iceland Gull is a scarce winter visitor to Britain, seen mainly along the east coasts, in similar habitat to the Glaucous Gull. Its general behaviour is similar to the Herring Gull's. Usually seen from mid-October to May, but irregular, and numbers are small.

FOOD   Small fish, molluscs and crustacea, offal and garbage if available.

The Iceland Gull does not breed in Britain or Ireland; and despite its name the only known breeding grounds are in Greenland.

Glaucous Gull

SIZE   32–25in:81–64cm.

DESCRIPTION   Large gull, with pale grey back and wings, and white head and underparts, flesh-coloured legs and feet, and yellow bill with red spot near tip of lower mandible. Similar in size and build to the Herring Gull, but distinguished from it by much lighter plumage and no black wing-tips.

CALL   Very similar to the Herring Gull, but shriller.

RECOGNITION   The Glaucous Gull is a winter visitor to Britain, seen mainly on eastern coasts, and rather rare elsewhere although it has been recorded on reservoirs in the London area. Numbers tend to be small in Britain, but a severe winter may bring an increase in birds visiting our shores. Its behaviour is somewhat similar to the Black-headed Gull, although it is less aggressive. More solitary in habit than most gulls.

FOOD   Fish, crustacea, molluscs, worms and seaweed, also carrion, small birds etc.

The Glaucous Gull does not nest in Britain or Ireland.

The Glaucous Gull is also listed under WHITE BIRDS, taking into account the very light grey of the back plumage.

Gannet

SIZE   36in:90cm.

DESCRIPTION   Large white 'Goose-like' bird (sometimes called the Solan Goose) with long narrow black-tipped wings, and pointed tail and stout pointed bill that combine to give a 'cigar-shape' to the body, particularly noticeable during flight. The head is shaded with yellow, and the stout bill is steel-grey. Juveniles start life black speckled with white, and become progressively whiter with age, achieving full adult plumage when 4 or 5 years old.

CALL A hoarse 'urrah' at breeding grounds or occasionally on takeoff from the sea, also an 'oo-ah' and a rasping 'crok-crok'.

RECOGNITION The Gannet is resident all year round, and is widely distributed around the coasts of Britain and Ireland, with particularly large numbers in the Northern Isles. The remote island of St Kilda off the Scottish coast has a huge population, about 40% of the British total, and the British Isles has about 70% of the world total of the species. The Gannet is an essentially marine bird, and stays at sea except for the breeding season, when it frequents cliffs and uninhabited islands as nest-sites. Sometimes seen singly, it is gregarious and is often seen in small parties, but large numbers may follow fishing fleets hoping for discarded fish. It is an expert swimmer and diver, plunge diving vertically from the air, closing its wings just before it enters the water.

FOOD Almost entirely fish.

NEST The Gannet has a ritual courtship consisting of bowing, preening and head-pointing, and nests in large colonies on cliff ledges or cliff tops. The nest is a round mound of seaweed and dropping, with additional plant debris sometimes added.

EGGS Usually only 1 egg is laid, long elliptical, with chalky white outer-layer and blueish shell beneath. 2.55 x 1.95in:78.1 x 49.1mm. Incubation, by both sexes, takes 43–45 days. The Gannet has no brood patch, and covers the egg with the web of the foot and rests on top of it. The chick is fed on regurgitated food until it is fledged at 84–97 days, then neglected to encourage it to go to sea and fend for itself.

BREEDING SEASON April or May. Single-brooded.

PLATE 56

Iceland Gull (scale 1:8.2)

Glaucous Gull (scale 1:8.2)

Cannet (scale 1:8.2)

FRANCES FRY.

Common Tern

SIZE   14in:35cm.

DESCRIPTION   Most widespread British tern, as the name implies. Pale grey upperparts, white underparts, with black cap and long slim wings and forked tail common to all terns. The bill is red tipped black, and the legs red also.

CALL   A rather grating 'kree-err', and a 'kikikik' note.

RECOGNITION   The Common Tern is a summer visitor to Britain, seen around most coasts but rather scarce in Wales and western England. Like all terns an expert flyer, with graceful long wings and forked tail that gives the alternative name for the tern family – 'sea swallows'. Most often seen near the coast, but will also frequent rivers and lakes inland on migration. It is a gregarious bird, and will often be seen in large colonies at breeding grounds or good fishing areas.

FOOD   Mostly small fish, obtained by diving headfirst into shallow waters, but worms, crustacea, molluscs and insects are also taken.

NEST   The Common Tern nests in colonies, on shingle banks, sand-dunes, salt-marshes or rocky islets, occasionally by freshwater lakes and rivers. The nest is a hollow in the ground, sometimes unlined but more often lined with a little plant material and a few feathers.

EGGS   Usually 3, sometimes 2–4, non-glossy eggs of cream or yellowish hue blotched with grey or brown spots and squiggles. 1.59 x 1.18in:41.3 x 30.5mm. Incubation, by both sexes, takes 28–30 days. The young are altricial and downy, and are tended by both sexes with female taking the major share, takes 20–23 days. The young are semi-precocial and downy, and may leave the nest after about 3 days, returning to be brooded. Both parents tend the chicks, which can swim at an early age, and can fly at about 28 days.

BREEDING SEASON   Late May to early July. Usually Single-brooded, but occasionally a second brood may be raised. Most birds do not breed until 3 or 4 years old .

Little Tern

SIZE   9½in:24cm.

DESCRIPTION   Smallest British tern, as the name denotes. Upperparts grey with dark wing-tips, underparts white, with deeply-forked tail but no streamers. Black cap but white forehead, and yellow bill, red legs. Fast wing-beats during flight, and much hovering before diving for food also help distinguish from other terns.

CALL   A loud 'kik-kik', and a 'kirri-kirri-kirr-'.

RECOGNITION   The Little Tern is a summer visitor to Britain, widespread around most coasts except in N.W. Scotland, but overall numbers seem to be declining. It may occur inland on passage, but in the breeding season it is found only on seashores and islands with sand or shingle beaches. Unfortunately this brings it into conflict with holiday-makers, and many pairs fail to breed successfully due to human disturbance. Fencing of colonies and strict protection has helped, and in some areas birds have taken to nesting on flat roofs instead of beaches.

FOOD   Fish, crustacea and molluscs, and also insects caught on the wing.

NEST   The Little Tern is a colonial nester on sand or shingle beaches (see above) but colonies tend to be more straggly and spread out than other tern species. The nest is a shallow hollow with little or no lining, but sometimes a few pebbles or some plant material added.

EGGS   2–3, rarely 4, non-glossy pale olive/stone coloured eggs are laid, blotched with dark brown or grey markings, often concentrated at the larger end. 1.25 x 0.94in:32.1 x 23.5mm. Incubation, by both sexes, begins with the second egg and takes 19–22 days. The young are semi-precocial and downy, and may leave the nest the day after hatching but remain nearby. Both parents tend the chicks, which may fly at 15–17 days.

BREEDING SEASON   Mid-May to June. Single-brooded, but a lost clutch may be replaced.

Arctic Tern

SIZE   14in:35cm.

DESCRIPTION   Long-winged tern that has fantastic migratory flight from Arctic to Antartic and back. Very similar to the Common Tern, with grey upperparts, black cap and white underparts, but is distinguished by longer tail streamers, white and semi-transparent flight feathers, and red bill darker in hue and with no black tip.

CALL   Rather similar to the Common Tern, a harsh 'kee-yar'.

RECOGNITION   The Arctic Tern is a summer visitor to Britain, rather scarce in England and Wales, but plentiful in Ireland and Scotland. Most maritime in habits of all the terns, and seldom seen inland except on passage. Very gregarious, and aggressive on breeding territories, driving away intruders by swooping at them and pecking.

FOOD   Small fish, particularly sand-eels, crustacea and squid, molluscs and insects. most food is obtained by diving. In the breeding season the male presents fish to the female as part of his courtship display.

NEST   The Arctic Tern nests colonially, often in association with Common Terns, on rocky islets, shingle or sand banks and dunes. The nest is a shallow hollow scaped in the ground by the female, unlined or with a sparse lining of plant material and debris.

EGGS   2, sometimes 1–3, eggs are laid, non-glossy and buff to pale green in colour, with variable dark brownish markings and scrawls. 1.55 x 1.1in:40.2 x 29.4mm. Incubation, by both sexes, takes 20–22 days. The young are semi-precocial and downy, and may leave the nest soon after hatching, remaining nearby. Both parents tend the young, until they fly at about 28 days, and may continue to feed them for a longer period.

BREEDING SEASON   Late May to June. Single-brooded.

Sandwich Tern

SIZE   16in:41cm.

DESCRIPTION   Largest British tern, taking its name from Sandwich Bay in Kent where the species was first identified and named. Pale grey upperparts and white below, with black cap that forms an untidy looking crest, and black bill tipped with yellow. The legs are short and black. The tail has a pronounced 'V' fork. In winter the forehead becomes white, and this change is sometimes noticeable during the summer.

CALL   A harsh 'kirrik' call.

RECOGNITION   The Sandwich Tern is a regular summer visitor to British coasts, and is seen in many areas of England and Ireland, north Wales and southern Scotland. It is scarce in the western isles, and is not found in Shetland. Its stronghold is in Norfolk, and sadly it no longer breeds in Sandwich. Heavier looking than other terns, it has the species maritime habits, and is usually found near to coasts on sandy or shingle bars and islands, although it may visit inland waters on passage. Very gregarious, and less aggressive than the Common Tern or the Arctic Tern.

FOOD   Predominently fish, with sand-eels, worms and molluscs supplementing the diet.

NEST   The Sandwich Tern is a colonial nester, breeding near or on coasts, on shingle banks or sand dunes. Often forms large breeding colonies, but is very sensitive to disturbance, and will quickly desert even long-established colonies if alarmed. Sometimes nests near to Black-headed Gulls. The nest consists of a shallow hollow, with a sparse lining of plant material, or no lining.

EGGS   2 usually, 1–3 occasionally, pale yellowish-buff eggs blotched with brown. 2 x 1.47in:51.5 x 36mm. Incubation, by both sexes, takes 20–24 days. The young are semi-precocial and downy, and are tended by both parents. After about 10 days the chicks leave the nest, and assemble in creche colonies with other youngsters, although the parents continue to feed their own young.

BREEDING SEASON   Late April to May. Single-brooded.

PLATE 57

Common Tern (scale 1:3.5)   *Little Tern (scale 1:3.5)*

Sandwich Tern (scale 1:3.5)

Arctic Tern (scale 1:3.5)

Black Tern (scale 1:3.5)

Roaeate Tern (scale 1:3.5)

FRANCES FRY

Roseate Tern

SIZE   15in:38cm.

DESCRIPTION   Pale, almost white tern, with longer tail streamers than other terns, and more boyant flight. Very pale grey upperparts, appearing almost white, black cap, and white breast that has a rosy flush to the feathers in the breeding season (hence the name 'roseate'.) The red legs are slightly longer than the other species of terns, and the bill is black with red base in the breeding season. In wintertime the forehead becomes white.

CALL   A rasping 'aach-aach' alarm call, a 'chuvick', and a chattering 'kekekekekekek'.

RECOGNITION   The Roseate Tern is a summer visitor to Britain and is one of our rarer seabirds, with only about 6 regular breeding sites. The largest of these is at Tern Island in Co. Wexford, with others at Anglesey, on islands in the Firth of Forth, and on the Farne islands. Odd pairs may nest in colonies of other terns, but it is rarely seen away from breeding areas, and is seldom found inland.

FOOD   Small fish caught at sea, and sand eels. May sometimes rob other terns.

NEST   The Roseate Tern is a colonial nester, sometimes in colonies of other terns, on rocky islets or shingle or sand banks. The nest is a shallow hollow, usually unlined.

EGGS   1–2,occasionally 3 eggs are laid at 2–3 day intervals, buff coloured with brownish markings. 1.74 x 1.15in:1.15in: 44.1 x 30.1mm. Incubation, by both sexes but mainly the female begins early in laying of clutch and takes 21–26 days. The young are semi-precocial and downy, and are tended by both parents.

BREEDING SEASON   June. Single-brooded.

The Roseate Tern is also listed under WHITE BIRDS, as the light grey back may appear white from a distance.

Black Tern

SIZE   9½in:24cm.

DESCRIPTION   Unmistakeable in breeding plumage, with back, tail and wings slate-grey, and black head and underparts, and white undertail coverts, with black bill and dark red legs. The overall effect is black, and the outline is typical of all terns with long wings, short legs and forked tail, In winter (and autumn) the plumage changes to resemble other terns, with grey upperparts and white underparts, with black hind-crown and dark smudge on bend of wing.

CALL   Rather quiet, with a monosyllabic 'kik kik' or 'krew' at breeding grounds.

RECOGNITION   The Black Tern is a regular bird of passage to Britain, seen mostly in spring and autumn, mainly in southern and eastern England but occuring on other coasts also. In the last century it was a regular breeding bird in eastern England, but then breeding ceased, to be resumed in 1966 in the Ouse Washes after an absence of about 100 years. Intermittant breeding at this and other sites has continued, and it bred in Ireland in 1967, but it remains one of our rarest breeding birds. Although a coastal bird on passage, it is a marsh tern rather than a seabird, and is found in marshy habitats, lowland lakes and reservoirs.

FOOD   Aquatic insects and their larvae, picked from the waters surface in flight, and small frogs and tadpoles, spiders and leeches also.

NEST   The Black Tern is a colonial nester where numbers permit, but not in Britain where numbers are small. It breeds on shallow, still waters, fresh or brackish, where there is reedy vegetation, or marshes and fens. The nest is a heap of floating vegetation such as reeds and waterplants, anchored to growing plants; or on firm ground amongst marshy herbage the nest may be a scrape with a sparse lining of plant material .

EGGS   1.32 X 1in:34.8 x 25.2mm. Incubation, by both sexes but with the female taking the major share of the sitting, takes 14–17 days. The young are semi-precocial and and downy, and although active remain at the nest for about 2 weeks. Both parents tend the chicks until they fly at about 4 weeks.

BREEDING SEASON   Mid to late May. Single-brooded.

The Black Tern is also listed under GREY AND WHITE BIRDS, representing its winter plumage.

Common Gull

SIZE 16in:41cm.

DESCRIPTION Medium sized gull, with grey back and wings, white head and underparts, black wing tips with white 'mirrors', and yellow-green legs and bill. A smallish head and dark eye give it a gentle look. Immature birds are brown-backed fading to grey with age. The bill is smaller than most gulls, and is a good distinguishing feature.

CALL A high-pitched 'kee-ya', and a 'kak-kak-kak' call.

RECOGNITION The Common Gull is widespread throughout the British Isles in winter, but many of these birds are Continental visitors. Many thousands are resident all year round, but most breeding birds are found in Scotland and Northern Ireland. On coasts it frequents similar territory to the Herring Gull, but it is more of an inland bird than that species, and is often found in urban areas, or on moorland, grassland, lakes and reservoirs. It is gregarious at all seasons, and may associate with other species like Black-headed Gulls or Herring Gulls.

FOOD Marine invertibrates, fish and molluscs on the coast; insects, earthworms and seeds inland, and also carrion, small birds and eggs. It may feed on rubbish tips inland. Overall a very varied diet.

NEST The Common Gull breeds colonially, on islands in lakes, on moorland, or on shingle near a river, or more rarely in trees and bushes. It often nests in colonies with Herring Gulls. The female does most of the nest building, which consists of an accumulation of plant material in a hollow scrape.

EGGS 3, sometimes 1–4, light olive eggs, marked with black or brown blotches and scrawls. 2.25 x 1.60in:57.6 x 41.4. Incubation, by both sexes, begins with the last egg and takes 22–27 days. The young are semi-precocial and downy, and leave the nest within a day or two of hatching, but remain close by, tended by both parents. They can fly at about 4–5 weeks.

BREEDING SEASON Begins in May. Single-brooded.

Kittiwake

SIZE 31–25in:79–64cm.

DESCRIPTION Long-winged gull with truly maritime lifestyle. Somewhat resembles the Common Gull, with white head and underparts, grey back, yellow bill and dark eyes, but is distinguished by jet black wing-tips, yellow legs and slightly forked tail. Immature birds have black mark behind eye, black half-collar, black band on tail and black pattern on wings.

CALL 'Kitti-wark', that gives the bird its name.

243

RECOGNITION   The Kittiwake is present throughout the year, and is widespread around the coasts of Britain with the greatest concentration of numbers in the north and west where large cliffs are found. Its habitat is more strictly marine than most gulls, and it is usually seen at sea or along cliffs, although it may bathe in freshwater near to the shore. Its flight is swift and graceful, and it habitually follows ships for food. It is a great wanderer, and transatlantic crossings are often made, with young birds crossing and remaining on the other side of the Atlantic for a year or two before returning to the colony where they were born. Breeding does not take place until 4 years. A long-lived species – up to 20 years has been recorded. Very gregarious by nature.

FOOD   Small fish, molluscs and crustacea, taken from the surface in flight or by tern-like diving. Insects, seeds, grass etc . . . are also taken.

NEST   The Kittiwake nests colonially, usually on ledges on steep cliffs, but greatly increased numbers in recent years have encouraged new nest sites such as buildings. In some seaside towns roofs, chimneys and even windowsills are used for nesting. Unlike most gulls a proper nest is constructed, made of grass, mud, moss and seaweed, the material being well tramped down to help it cling to precarious sites.

EGGS   Usually 2, sometimes 1–3, non-glossy pale buffish eggs marked with darker browns and greys. 2.10 x 1.60in:55.9 x 41.1mm. Incubation, by both sexes but mainly the female begins early in laying of clutch and takes 25–30 days. The young are semi-precocial and downy, and are cared for by both parents until they fly at about 43 days.

BREEDING SEASON   Late May to June. Single-brooded.

Herring Gull

SIZE   26–22in:66–56cm.

DESCRIPTION   Large gull with grey back and wings, with black wings-tips spotted with white 'mirrors', white head and underparts, and flesh-coloured legs and feet. The large bill is yellow with a bright red spot near the tip of the lower mandible, and the eyes are yellow. Its heavy build and large bill give the bird a fierce look. Immatures are dusky, mottled brown, and take 4 years to achieve adult plumage of grey and white.

CALL   A loud 'kee-kyow-kyow' call, and a variety of wailing cries.

RECOGNITION   The Herring Gull is a common resident of Britain's coasts, and numbers increase still more in winter as Continental birds arrive to stay from September to April. It chiefly frequents coasts, estuaries and offshore fishing grounds, but is also found inland, on reservoirs, rubbish tips or arable land. Its behaviour is typical of large gulls and it has developed the skill of dropping mollusc shells from a height in the air to break them open. It is gregarious, noisy and aggressive, and can be regarded as a pest in some areas where colonies nest inland on buildings. It may also prey on other more endangered species, like Terns.

WATER & SEA BIRDS

PLATE 58

Common Gull (scale 1:8.2)

Kittiwake (scale 1:8.2)

Herring Gull (scale 1:7)

FRANCES FRY.

Fulmar (scale 1:7)

FOOD   A wide range of food, from fish, offal, carrion and garbage, to craustacea, molluscs, worms and eggs, and occasionally small birds and mammals.

NEST   The Herring Gull nests in colonies, on cliff ledges, in shingle or sand dunes, or sometimes by inland freshwater. In recent years it has taken to nesting on roofs of buildings. Both birds help to build the nest, which is quite substancial, and consists of grass, seaweed or plant material.

EGGS   2–3 olive coloured eggs are laid, speckled and blotched with dark brown or black. Colour tends to be very variable. 2.73 x 1.90in:69.8 x 48.2mm. Incubation, by both sexes but mainly the female, takes 25–33 days. The young are semi-precocial and downy, and are tended by both parents for about 30 days. They can fly at about 6 weeks.

BREEDING SEASON   Begins in late April. Single-brooded.

Fulmar

SIZE   18½in:47cm.

DESCRIPTION   Gull-like petrel that flies like a shearwater with stiff wings. The plumage is dove-grey on upperparts and wings with darker primaries, and white underparts, but the overall appearance is light grey. It has a large head and thick neck that give a 'bull-nosed' effect, particulary noticeable during flight. The bill is short and yellow, and has typical petrel tube-nose on upper mandible.

CALL   'ag-ag-ag-aar' call, together with various grunting and growling notes in the breeding season.

RECOGNITION   The Fulmar is now a common sight around sea cliffs where it spends most of the time wheeling round over the sea. It is mainly a summer visitor, although a few birds are seen in winter. Numbers have increased dramatically in the last 100 years, and from a remote colony on ST Kilda in 1878 a population over 3,000,000 pairs has now spread around the coasts. Part of this success may be due to their habit of following fishing fleets and feeding from discarded offal thrown overboard. Fulmars are gregarious birds and form large flocks and colonies on cliffs . They are slow maturers, and do not breed until 6 or 7 years old, but live long lives –17 years on average, although over 30 years has been recorded.

FOOD   Fish and squid, supplemented by offal and waste from fishing and whaling fleets.

NEST   The Fulmar is usually a cliff breeder, but may sometimes venture further inland to occupy a ruined building or rocky crag. Usually the eggs are laid straight on to a cliff ledge. It is a colonial nester.

EGGS   1 white egg is usual, occasionally 2. 2.95 x 2in:74 x 50.5mm. Incubation, by both sexes, takes 55–57 days, with each bird sitting for 3–4 days at a time. The downy young is fed and brooded by both parents until it can fly at 46–51 days. The fledgling

WATER & SEA BIRDS

will spend about 6 years at sea before it returns to land to breed. Fulmars that are disturbed at the nest can eject an evil-smelling liquid from their mouths to discourage intruders.

BREEDING SEASON From May to September. Single-brooded. If the egg is lost it is not replaced that year.

Other grey birds which are fully described under different sections.

GREY PHALAROPE, RED-NECKED PHALAROPE Both the above species are fully described in part two of this book, under WATERSIDE BIRDS: GREY BIRDS.

GREY BIRDS: BLACK-NECKED BIRDS The Black-necked Grebe is fully described under WATER & SEA BIRDS:BRIGHT COLOURED BIRDS, taking into account its bright plumage in the breeding season. However it is often seen in Britain in winter when its plumage is dull black and white that gives an overall grey appearance.

Other grey and white birds which are fully described under different sections.

BLACK (SOOTY) TERN The Black Tern only lives up to its name during the breeding season. In autumn its plumage changes to grey back and wings, white underparts, with black on head. But since it is mainly seen in Britain in the summer, it is fully described under WATER & SEA BIRDS: BLACK BIRDS.

RED-NECK GREBE Its summer plumage includes a bright reddish neck, white cheeks and black crown, and so this species is described under WATER & SEA BIRDS: BRIGHT COLOURED BIRDS. In winter plumage however it appears grey and white.

BLACK-HEADED GULL, MEDITERRANEAN GULL and LITTLE GULL are all fully described under WATER & SEA BIRDS: BLACK HEADED BIRDS, although their winter plumage is grey and white.

247

Ferruginous Duck

SIZE   16in:41cm.

DESCRIPTION   Chestnut brown and white duck, with distinctive white eye, that gives the species the alternative name of 'White-eyed Pochard' The male has rich chestnut head and breast, with darker brown back, and bold white undertail coverts; the female is dark brown with similar white rear end, and lacks the white eye. It also has a white wing-mark that is conspicious in flight.

CALL   The male has a wheezing call; the female sounds very like the Pochard, but quieter.

RECOGNITION   The Ferruginous Duck is a winter visitor from eastern Europe that is occasionally seen in Britain in freshwater habitats, or in winter on the sea. It is also kept as an ornamental wildfowl, so some of the birds seen may well be escapees. Its chestnut plumage with domed head and white patch under the tail are quite distinctive, but it is a retiring bird, secretive and shy and is difficult to observe closely, as it will often skulk in cover rather than take flight. It is not very gregarious, and does not mix much with other species. An expert swimmer and diver, it will also dive for cover as well as for food.

FOOD   Mainly vegetable matter.

The Ferruginous Duck does not breed in Britain or Ireland.

Garganey

SIZE   15in:38cm.

DESCRIPTION   One of Britains smallest ducks, similar in size to the Teal. The male has a broad white band extending from eye to nape on a dark brown head, with breast and back mottled brown, and grey flanks barred with darker grey and black, and mottled brown rear. The female resembles the female Teal, but has slighter build, longer neck and greyer wing. In flight both sexes are distinguished from other species by pale blue inner wings.

CALL   The male has a low crackling call, the female a 'quack' rather like the female Teal's.

RECOGNITION   The Garganey is a summer visitor to Britain, rather scarce, but occuring regularly in small numbers in south-eastern England, East Anglia and the Midlands. It has been recorded in Scotland, Wales and Ireland too, but is rarer there. Habitat preferred is shallow, fresh waters with plenty of vegetation. It is a gregarious species, but owing to its comparative scarcity, large flocks are rare here, and it is usually seen in pairs or small parties. Its general habits resemble those of the Shoveler. Its flight is rapid, but not twisting and turning like the Teal's.

FOOD Vegetable and animal food, taken from the surface or by 'up-ending'. Waterplants, crustacea, molluscs, worms, insects and young fish.

NEST The Garganey usually nests in long grass or tall vegetation near to water. The nest consists of a hollow lined with plant material, down and feathers.

EGGS 8–11, sometimes 6–14, creamy-buff eggs are laid. 1.77 x1.30in;45.3 x 33.3mm. Incubation, by the female alone, begins on completion of the clutch and takes 21–23 days. The young are precocial and active, and leave the nest soon after hatching, and are cared for by the female until they can fly at 5–6 weeks.

BREEDING SEASON Begins mid-April. Single-brooded.

Tufted Duck

SIZE 17in:43cm.

DESCRIPTION Small, freshwater duck with crested head. The male had dark metallic blue/green head that may appear black from a distance, black upperparts and black breast, and white belly; the female has brown plumage, with a shorter crest or tuft, and sometimes a little white at the base of the bill. Both sexes have a bold white wing-bar.

CALL A quiet whistle from the male; a more rolling note from the female or a Crow-like croak.

RECOGNITION The Tufted Duck is resident all year round, and quite widespread throughout the British Isles although sparser in northern and western hills. Fresh water forms the usual habitat, although in winter it may frequent estuaries. A gregarious species, often seen in large numbers, sometimes in association with Pochard although it prefers deeper water as a rule. It is an expert diver and can swim considerable distances underwater. British birds disperse coastward in winter, and are joined by birds from Scandinavia and Russia, swelling the population by almost tenfold.

FOOD Molluscs, crustacea and insects, also some plants and seeds. Tufted Ducks may often feed with the tame ducks on ponds and lakes.

NEST The Tufted Duck is a sociable breeder, often nesting in colonies by ponds or lakes. The nest consists of a hollow lined with grasses, down and feathers, usually well hidden amongst vegetation.

EGGS 5–12, sometimes more (up to 18 have been recorded); occasionally two birds may lay in the same nest. The eggs are large for the size of the bird, smooth but non-glossy, pale green to grey in colour. 2.29 x 1.60in:58.3 x 40.8mm. Incubation, by the female alone, takes 23–25 days. The young are precocial, downy and active, able to dive when a few hours old, and flying at about 6 weeks..

BREEDING SEASON Mid-April to June. Single-brooded.

Gadwall

SIZE 20in:51cm.

DESCRIPTION Introduced species, with male brown from a distance. Closer inspection will show that only the head is brown, the belly sides and back being finely marked with grey, with white speculum and black tail. The female is brown, and superficially resembles the larger Mallard or Pintail females, but is distinguished by orange sides to bill and white belly. Both sexes show conspicious white patches a rear of wing, borded with black and white bellies in flight.

CALL The male has a single low 'croaking' note, the female a quack like a Mallard.

RECOGNITION The Gadwall was first introduced into Britain in 1850, and has since spread to many parts of the country, with its main stronghold in East Anglia. The local population is swelled by visitors from the Continent in winter. Habitat is usually amongst inland fresh water, like lakes, reed beds, and flooded meadows in winter, but it may occasionally occur on the sea coast. It is gregarious by nature, but overall numbers remain small and large flocks are rarely seen in this country. However the species readily associates with other ducks and waterfowl.

FOOD Aquatic vegetation forms the main part of the diet, with plants and seeds being picked up from the surface of the water. Although, like most ducks, the Gadwall can 'up-end' to feed, it seems to prefer feeding from the surface, but it will sometimes associate with deeper water feeders like Swans or Coots and pick up food disturbed by them from the bottom.

NEST The Gadwall breeds by freshwater ponds or slow-running streams, hiding its nest amongst thick vegetation by the water, or more rarely in dryer vegetation like heather. In popular breeding areas nests are often placed in close proximity. The nest consists of a hollow lined with plant material, down and feathers.

EGGS 8–12 usually, 7–16 have been recorded, short oval eggs, cream or pale green in colour, and smooth, almost waxy. 2.12 x 1.52in:54.3 x 39.1mm. Incubation, by the female alone, takes 25–27 days. The young are precocial and very active, taking to the water immediately on hatching, and are independent at round 7 weeks.

BREEDING SEASON May or June. Single-brooded.

Ruddy Duck

SIZE 16in:41cm.

DESCRIPTION Small, stiff-tailed duck. The male is cinnamon brown, with white cheeks and white under tail, black crown and black tail that is often held stiffly upright. The short stubby bill is pale blue. The female has brown/grey back with barred underparts.

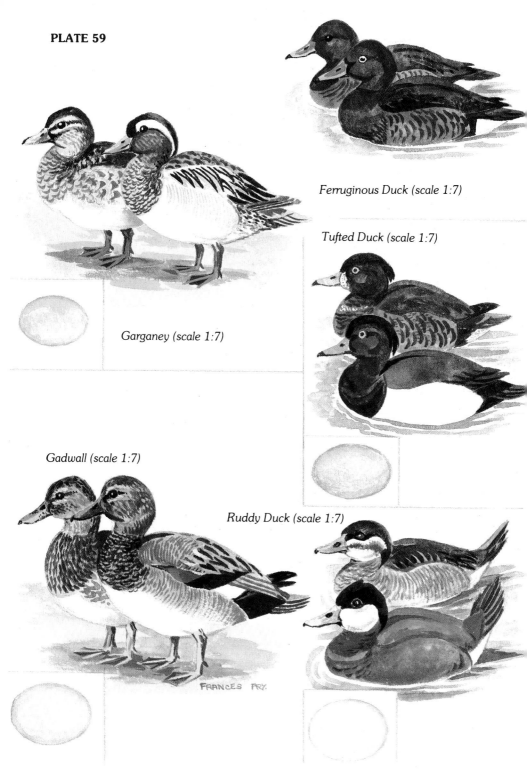

PLATE 59

Ferruginous Duck (scale 1:7)

Tufted Duck (scale 1:7)

Garganey (scale 1:7)

Gadwall (scale 1:7)

Ruddy Duck (scale 1:7)

FRANCES FRY.

CALL   Rather silent except in breeding season when it drums beak on chest making a rattling noise.

RECOGNITION   The Ruddy Duck is a native of North America, and was brought to Britain as an ornamental wildfowl. Young birds escaped from the Wildfowl Trust's collection at Slimbridge, Glos. and these formed the basis of a feral population which has gradually spread from the severn Valley to central Midlands and other areas. It is found mainly on inland lakes or ponds. In spring the male has a spectacular courtship display – he raises his tail and crown feathers. and inflates an air-sac in his neck, then drums on the swollen neck with his bill, producing a hollow sound and aerating the water with bubbles.

FOOD   Aquatic plants.

NEST   The Ruddy Duck breeds on freshwater lakes or ponds where there are tall reeds or other water plants. The nest is a partly floating structure attached to such plants, built slightly above water-level with plants pulled together over it for disguise. It is made of reed stems, weeds or other plants, and lined with down.

EGGS   6–10, sometimes more (up to 20 on occasion) white, with rough surface. 2½ x 1.60in:64 x 42mm. Incubation, by the female alone, takes 20–21 days. The young are precocial and active. Unlike most ducks the male helps tend the brood until they reach independence.

BREEDING SEASON   Late May to June. Single-brooded.

Goldeneye

SIZE 18in:46cm.

DESCRIPTION Small diving duck with triangular-shaped head. The male has predominently black and white plumage, black upperparts and white underparts with glossy dark green head with circular white patch by bill, and the golden eye that gives the species its name. The female has a brown head, a grey back, and grey/buff flanks, but has the characteristic golden eye.

CALL A silent species outside the breeding season, when the male has a harsh 'zeee-zeee' sound, the female a screeching call. Loud whistles are given during flight.

RECOGNITION The Goldeneye is a winter visitor to Britain, with a very few pairs remaining here to breed. It is found around most of Britains coasts and estuaries, and visits inland reservoirs and lakes too. It is most easily recognized by the perculiar head shape, or by the whistling noise of its wings in flight. Gregarious by nature they often form small flocks, and elaborate courtship displays occur in spring, or late winter. Groups of drakes gather round a duck or ducks and throw back their heads showing off their white breasts and making a low growling sound.

FOOD Molluscs, crustacea insect larvae and some small fish, also some aquatic vegetation.

NEST The Goldeneye is a rare breeding bird in Britain, with only a few pairs nesting in the Scottish Highlands, but the species has taken well to using nest boxes and numbers are increasing slowly. In natural conditions the nest is made in a natural cavity in a tree, or a large hole excavated by a woodpecker, or even occasionally in a rabbit burrow. The hole is lined with down.

EGGS 6–11 eggs are laid, at intervals of 1½ days. The eggs are pale green/blue. 2.40 x 1.74in:59.6 x 42.6mm. Incubation, by the female alone with the male remaining near-by, takes 27–32 days. The young are precocial and active, and drop down from the nest soon after hatching and make their way to water. The female tends them for about 7–8 weeks until they reach independence.

BREEDING SEASON From April to June. Single-brooded.

The Goldeneye is also listed under BLACK AND WHITE BIRDS.

Red-breasted Merganser

SIZE 23in:58m.

DESCRIPTION Sawbill duck with long, thin serrated red bill. The male has a dark green head with a ragged crest that forms two tufts, white neck with brown flecked black band below, vermiculated grey flanks and black back. The female has a rust-red head with two short tufts, white foreneck, grey back and buff-grey flanks.

CALL   A silent bird except in the breeding season, when the male has wheezing or purring notes, the female a harsh croaking.

RECOGNITION   The Red-breasted Merganser is found along the coasts of Britain and Ireland, and inland in Scotland, the Lake District, Northern Ireland and north Wales, and is increasing its range. In winter birds move to the coasts, and Scandinavian birds join them. Summer habitat is mostly rivers and ponds in wooded countryside. It is a gregarious species, and small flocks are often seen in favoured areas, larger ones in winter. Like all sawbills fish are taken by pursuit underwater, but Mergansers will sometimes hunt as a flock if a shoal of fish is discovered.

FOOD   Mostly fish, with salmon forming an important part of the diet in inland waters, but crustaceans are also taken and may form the dominent item when at sea.

NEST   The Red-Breasted Merganser may breed by freshwater or sea-lochs and off-shore islands. It is a ground-nester, concealing the nest amongst boulders or tree-roots, or in a thicket, or more rarely a burrow. The nest consists of a hollow lined with plant material and down and feathers.

EGGS   7–12 usually, although up to 21 have been recorded, creamy to greenish-buff in colour. 2.58 x 1.80in:65.6 x 45.2mm. Incubation, by the female alone, takes 29–35 days. The young are precocial and active, and are led to water soon after hatching. The female cares for the young, but several broods from different nests may band together with one or more females on creche duty. Able to fly at 59 days.

BREEDING SEASON   Mid-May to June. Single-brooded.

The Red-Breasted Merganser is also listed under BRIGHT COLOURED BIRDS.

Goosander

SIZE   26in:66cm.

DESCRIPTION   Largest of the British sawbills, with elongated rounded head and long slim outline. The male has dark green head, black back and white breast flushed with pink; the female has a rust-red head and superficially resembles the female Red-breasted Merganser but is distinguished by white throat and small drooping crest. Both sexes have the typical long thin serrated bill that gives the genus the name 'sawbill' and it is bright coral-red in colour.

CALL   A silent species except during the breeding season, when the male has a variety of croaks, the female a harsh cackle.

RECOGNITION   The Goosander is a relative newcomer in Britain, arriving in the late 19th century in Scotland. It has since extended its range to include England and Wales, and Scandinavian immigrants join local birds in the winter. It is found on lakes and rivers, particularly in wooded country, or on reservoirs or estuaries in winter. An

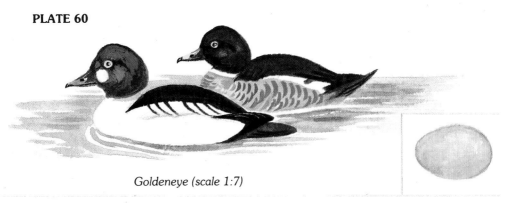

Goldeneye (scale 1:7)

Red-breasted Merganser (scale 1:7)

Goosander (scale 1:7)

expert fisherman, the Goosander chases its prey under water using its feet for propulsion, and the long serrated bill helps to hold the slippery catch. Although unpopular with fisherman for taking trout and salmon, it also takes the enemies of such fish too.

FOOD   Fish obtained by diving from the surface and pursuit. Salmon and trout and eels form a large part of the diet.

NEST   The Goosander breeds by freshwater lakes or rivers, usually in wooded surroundings. It nests in tree holes or natural crevices among rocks, and will use suitable nest boxes. The same nest site may be reused annually. The cavity is lined with down.

EGGS   7–14, rarely 15, elongated eggs are laid, cream to yellow in colour. 2.60 x 1.78in:66.4 x 46.4mm. Incubation, by the female alone, takes 32–35 days. The young are precocial and active, remaining in the nest for about two days, then going to the water. The female tends them until they reach independence at around 5 weeks.

BREEDING SEASON   Mid-March to June. Single-brooded.

The Goosander is also listed under BRIGHT COLOURED BIRDS.

Other green-headed birds which are fully described under different sections.

MALLARD   This common dabbling duck is fully described under WATER & SEA BIRDS: BRIGHT COLOURED BIRDS.

SHOVELER Dabbling duck with large spatulate bill fully described under WATER & SEA BIRDS: BRIGHT COLOURED BIRDS.

SHELDUCK   Colourful large duck that is fully described under WATER & SEA BIRDS:BRIGHT COLOURED BIRDS.

SCAUP   Sea duck that is fully described under WATER & SEA BIRDS: BLACK AND WHITE BIRDS.

Red-necked Grebe

SIZE   17in:43cm.

DESCRIPTION   Rather thick-set grebe with large head. In summer it has a black crown with a small crest, whitish cheeks and chin and deep chestnut red neck that gives the species its name. The upperparts are grey-brown, the underparts white. In winter the plumage is much duller, with no bright neck colouring, and a grey and white appearance. The bill is yellow tipped with black.

CALL   A wailing, neighing 'song', and a high-pitched 'keck'.

RECOGNITION   The Red-necked Grebe is a winter visitor to Britain, arriving in October from Denmark and north-east Europe, and returning in March. It is seen along coasts and estuaries, mainly on the east of England, although it may venture further inland and is sometimes seen on London reservoirs. Apart from the odd summer sighting it is usually only seen in Britain in dull winter plumage.

FOOD   Aquatic insects and their larvae, and small fish obtained by diving.

The Red-necked Grebe breeds in eastern Europe, and has not been recorded nesting in Britain or Ireland.

The Red-necked Grebe is also listed under GREY AND WHITE BIRDS, as this is how it appears in winter plumage.

Slavonian Grebe

SIZE   13in:33cm.

DESCRIPTION   Beautiful small grebe with bushy head tufts in summer, giving it the alternative American name of Horned Grebe. In summer the black head has two 'horns' of bright orange-gold, with dark chestnut neck and flanks and black back. The winter plumage is dark brown/black upperparts and white underparts, resembling the Black-nested Grebe.

CALL   A long, low trill, and a variety of breeding calls.

RECOGNITION   The Slavonian Grebe is a winter visitor to the coasts of Britain, and London reservoirs, with small numbers resident all year in Scotland where there is a breeding population of about 50 pairs. It may visit inland lakes also. Most of its food is caught underwater. Although this attractive bird is increasing in numbers it remains vulnerable to disturbance from holidaymakers, illegal egg-collecting, and changes in water levels.

FOOD   Small fish and crustacea, but aquatic insects and their larvae, obtained by diving, form part of the diet in summer.

NEST   The Slavonian Grebe nests in shallow waters where vegetation is present to give nesting cover. It is sometimes a solitary breeder, but often nest colonially, sometimes in association with the Black-headed Gull. The nests consists of a mound of aquatic vegetation built in shallow water and anchored to nearby plants, with a shallow hollow on top for the eggs.

EGGS   4 usually, sometimes 3–5, rarely 8, longish white eggs are laid at daily intervals. 1.75 x 1.25in: 45.6 x 31mm. Incubation, by both sexes although the female takes the major share, takes 22–25 days. The young are precocial and active, leaving the nest soon after hatching. Both parents tend the young, but occasionally it is left mainly to the male while the female lays another brood.

BREEDING SEASON   Late May to July. Single or double-brooded occasionally.

The Slavonian Grebe is also listed under BLACK AND WHITE BIRDS, as it is most often seen in winter plumage.

Black-necked Grebe

SIZE   12in:30cm.

DESCRIPTION   Small grebe with predominently black and white plumage in winter that gives a rather grey appearance. In summer the plumage changes to black upperparts and white underparts, seperated by the chestnut flanks, black neck that gives the species its name, and bright chestnut-gold tuft of fan-shaped feathers extending from the lores round the eye to form 'ears' behind it. The bill is slightly up-tilted, and is a good distinguishing feature.

CALL   A wide variety of chattering notes, and a low poo-eep' call-note.

RECOGNITION   The Black-necked Grebe is mainly a winter visitor to Britain, occuring around coasts along the south and east of England, but a few pairs nest here, chiefly in the eastern lowlands of Scotland. It is more likely to be seen inland than the rather similar Slavonian Grebe, and in winter may visit lakes and reservoirs even in urban areas and show little fear of man. In summer it prefers lakes and waterways with plenty of vegetative cover .

FOOD   Insects and their larvae, crustaceans, molluscs, amphibians and small fish.

NEST   The Black-necked Grebe breeds on freshwater lakes and waterways where there is lush vegetation or good reed cover. The nest is a mound of aquatic vegetation and plant material hidden amongst the reeds or other vegetation. It is often a colonial breeder where numbers are large enough, or it may associate with Black-headed Gulls.

EGGS   3–4, rarely 2–8, smooth white eggs are laid. 1.72 x 1.13in:43.1 x 29.7mm. Incubation, by both parents, takes 20–21 days. The young are precocial and active, leaving the nest soon after hatching, and are tended by both parents, sometimes in

PLATE 61

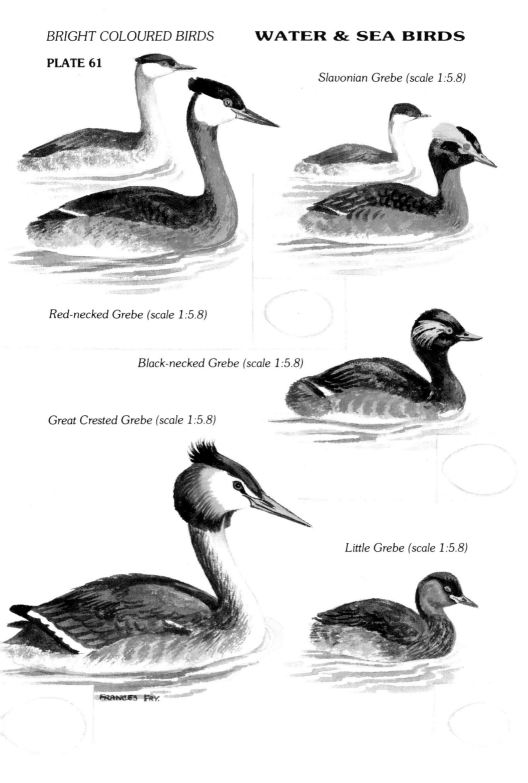

Slavonian Grebe (scale 1:5.8)

Red-necked Grebe (scale 1:5.8)

Black-necked Grebe (scale 1:5.8)

Great Crested Grebe (scale 1:5.8)

Little Grebe (scale 1:5.8)

FRANCES FRY.

company with other youngsters belonging to neighbouring pairs. The fledging period is short – sometimes as little as 21 days.

BREEDING SEASON   From April to June. Single, but occasionally double-brooded.

The Black-Necked Grebe is also listed under GREY BIRDS, taking into account the winter plumage more often seen in Britain.

Great Crested Grebe

SIZE   19in:48cm.

DESCRIPTION   Largest of the grebe family, easily identified by black ear-tufts, and in the breeding season by prominent chestnut and black frills on sides of head. These beautiful head plumes were much sought after in the 19th century and nearly endangered the species, but now it is protected by law numbers are increasing again. The back is grey-brown, the flanks buff, the belly and foreneck white, and the long slender bill is pink. Sexes alike.

CALL   Several strange groaning and barking calls, a 'kar-arr' and a 'er-wick' note.

RECOGNITION   The Great Crested Grebe is widespread in England, Wales and Lowland Scotland, and the northern half of Ireland, with numbers up from a desperate low of 32 pairs in 1860 to about 5000 pairs today. Resident all year, and found on lakes, reservoirs or gravel pits, or estuaries in winter. Gregarious birds, gathering in sizeable flocks in winter. In spring there is a remarkable courtship ritual, when the birds display to the opposite sex, raising their crests and shaking their heads, diving and bringing up weeds, finally rising almost upright, treading water and pressing their breasts together – an aquatic 'dance.'

FOOD   Fish, insects and thier larvae, crustacea and molluscs, and also some vegetable matter. They also eat feathers, and feed feathers to their young – possibly to help form pellets of indigestable matter like fish bones.

NEST   The Great Crested Grebe breeds on freshwater lakes or shallow waters with plenty of vegetative cover. Sometimes a solitary nester, at other times may nest colonially. The nest is an accumulation of aquatic vegetation and plant material, forming a mound near the waters edge or floating on the surface anchored to a nearby bush or reeds. A small hollow on top forms a cup for the eggs.

EGGS   4 usually, sometimes 3–6, longish white eggs, non-glossy, laid at 2-day intervals. 2.18 x 1.45in:54.8 x 36.7mm. Incubation, by both sexes, begins with the first egg and takes 25–29 days. The young are precocial and active, hatching over a period of days. When all have hatched they take to the water, and are frequently carried on their parents backs. They are independent at 12 weeks.

BREEDING SEASON   May to July. Single or double-brooded.

Little Grebe (Dabchick)

SIZE 10½in:27cm.

DESCRIPTION Smallest grebe, with dark brown upperparts and pale underparts with rich chestnut cheeks and throat, and yellow-green patch at base of bill. In winter the plumage becomes much duller, the cheek colour is lost, and the overall colour is brown-grey.

CALL A high-pitched trill rather like a whinny, and a short 'whit-whit'.

RECOGNITION The Little Grebe is resident all year round, and found throughout most of Britain and Ireland except in very hilly areas. For most of the year it is a freshwater bird, inhabiting lakes, ponds and rivers with good vegetative cover, but in winter it may frequent estuaries and coasts. It is easily identified from other grebes by its size, shorter neck, and rounded dumpy outline, and it tends to be more skulking in behaviour, more ready to take flight if danger threatens. At other times when alarmed it may sink very low in the water, leaving only head and neck visible. Often a solitary bird, but in favoured areas loose flocks may form.

FOOD Aquatic insects and their larvae, small and fish crustacea. Sticklebacks appear to be a favourite food.

NEST The Little Grebe breeds by freshwater ponds and rivers, and builds its nest – a shallow heap of vegetation – in shallow water or by the water's edge, well hidden by vegetation.

EGGS 4–6, more rarely 2–7, smooth white eggs are laid, soon becoming stained with brown. 1½ x 1in:37.8 x 26.2mm. Incubation, by both sexes, takes 19-25 days. The young are active and precocial, and leave the nest soon after hatching. Both parents tend the young, sometimes carrying them on their backs when tiny, but sometimes the female may build a second nest and leave the male to raise the chicks. They are independent at 44–48 days.

BREEDING SEASON Usually April to July, but very early nests have been recorded, some in February. Double-brooded, occasionally treble-brooded.

The Little Grebe is also listed under BROWN BIRDS taking into account its winter plumage.

Wigeon

SIZE 18in:46cm.

DESCRIPTION An attractive surface-feeding duck, with rounded head and small bill. The male has a mainly grey body, the darker upperparts being separated from the paler underparts by a white line, but the breast is a pinkish-brown, and the head is chestnut with a yellow forehead and crown. The tail is black with a white mark at the base. The female is a rather drab buff-brown mixture, distinguished from other similarly coloured females of different species by her small bill and rounded head.

CALL The male has a distinctive, loud, high whistle 'whee-oo', often given during flight.

RECOGNITION The Wigeon is present throughout the year, with many passage migrants and winter visitors joining the resident population. It is found throughout the country, breeding on lakes and lochs, moorlands or wooded countryside, and frequenting grassland, coastal saltings and open shorelines in winter. Gregarious birds, they often form large flocks offshore, and this close association is often seen during flight too. The Wigeon is a strong flyer, walks on land easily, and can even run well if the occasion demands. Strangely, it does not associate much with other species of duck, but if often grazes alongside 'grey' geese, like White-fronts, or Brent greese.

FOOD Molluscs, crustacea insect larvae and some small fish, also some aquatic vegetation.

NEST The Wigeon nests on the ground, amongst heather, grass or bracken usually near to the water. The nest consists of a hollow lined with vegetation, down and feathers.

EGGS 7–8, sometimes 6–10, creamy eggs, sometimes with a greenish-blue tinge. 2.08 x 1.50in: 53.9 x 38.3mm. Incubation, by the female alone, begins with the last egg and takes 22–25 days. The active, precocial young leave the nest soon after hatching, and are led to water by the female, who tends them until they can fly at about 6 weeks.

BREEDING SEASON Begins in April. Single-brooded.

Teal

SIZE 14in:35cm.

DESCRIPTION One of the smallest European ducks, with great flying agility. The male has chestnut head with broad green band edged with cream that runs from eye to nape. The back is grey, the flanks paler grey; the breast is spotted brown on buff, and the belly white. The dark undertail has a cream triangular patch. The female resembles many other female ducks, being mottled brown and buff, but remains distinguishable by her small size.

CALL   The female has a high-pitched 'quack', the male a double whistle 'krit-krit'. Flying flocks call continuously.

RECOGNITION   Teal are largely resident birds in Britain, although some birds may move south to France in the winter, and many other visit from the continent in the autumn. It is spread throughout the country, preferring marshes, pools and lakes in the breeding season, and reservoirs, floods, estuaries and open shores in the winter. Teal are very gregarious and form large flocks outside the breeding season. If disturbed they shoot straight up from the water in rapid flight, and are so agile on the wing that they often resemble waders, turning and wheeling in unison.

FOOD   Mainly vegetable matter, like duckweed or algae, but also seeds of aquatic plants, and some animal food like worms, insects and molluscs.

NEST   The Teal usually nests near to water, but sometimes choses a dry site some distance away. The nest consists of a hollow in the ground, concealed by vegetation, and lined with plant material and leaves, with an inner lining of feathers and down.

EGGS   8–12 usually, although clutches of 16 have been recorded. The eggs are cream or buff. 1.75 x 1.25in:45.5 x 33.5mm. Incubation, by the female alone, starts on completion of the clutch and takes 21–28 days. The precocial, active young leave the nest soon after hatching, and are tended by the female until they can fly at about 44 days.

BREEDING SEASON   Begins in late March. Single-brooded.

Red-Crested Pochard

SIZE   22in:56cm.

DESCRIPTION   A diving duck that is easily recognised by the bright chestnut head of the male that gives the species its name. The head is large for the size of the bird, rounded in shape, and shades to a more golden brown on the crown. The bill is bright red as are the legs and feet. Neck and breast are black, as is the rear end; and the back is brown, the flanks white. The female has brown upperparts and pale buffish under parts, with a distinctive pale cheek, and her bill is a slate-blue.

CALL   The male has a wheezing call, and the female a harsh 'churr' or 'kur-rr' that is seldon heard as they are generally silent except during the breeding season.

RECOGNITION   The Red-crested Pochard is quite a rare bird in most of Britain and Ireland, being mainly seen as an autumn visitor to large reservoirs in southern England. However it is widely kept in collections of ornamental waterfowl, and numerous escapees take to the wild and form feral popuations that breed. It seems to prefer large areas of water with good cover such as reeds, but occasionally takes to open, brackish lagoons. On the Continent where it is common it often forms large flocks, as it is a gregarious species, but it is unlikely to be seen in large numbers in Britain. It dives well and freely in deep water, but will also feed in the shallows by 'up-ending' like surface-feeding ducks; but it is also quite at home on land, walking easily, and it will sometimes graze on land.

FOOD   Largely vegetable matter, like aquatic vegtation, but occasionally some animal matter is also taken.

NEST   The Red-crested Pochard is not regarded as a breeding species in Great Britain or Ireland – the few birds that have bred are thought to have escaped from collections.

Mallard

SIZE   23in:58cm.

DESCRIPTION   The most common dabbling duck, widespread throughout the British Isles. The male has splendid breeding plumage of bright green head and neck bordered with white collar, with chestnut breast, and grey upperparts, and black rear with curled-up feathers on the uppertail coverts. The bill is yellow tipped with black. The female is mottled brown and buff. Both sexes have a bright blue speculum edged with white.

CALL   The familiar 'quack-quack' associated with ducks, although the male has a much quieter 'queek' note.

RECOGNITION   The Mallard is present throughout the year, and is found in virtually every type of habitat near water, ranging from open shores and country ponds to urban parks. It is even found in the heart of towns and cities, like the fountains of Trafalgar Square in London. Noisy and gregarious, often forming large flocks that rest on the water in daytime, feeding mainly at night. In the breeding season however the drakes form small parties while the female tend their young. It is a strong flyer, rising straight from the water when flushed, and it walks quite well on land, with less waddle than domestic ducks.

FOOD   Mainly vegetable matter, including aquatic plants obtained by 'up-ending'. Some animal matter is also taken, like insects, molluscs, crustacea, worms and frogs.

NEST   The Mallard has a noisy, violent courtship, with much vigorous chasing of the female. It usually nests near water, either on the ground concealed in vegetation, or in tree crotches or holes. Sometimes the old nest of another species is used, such as a Crow. Usually though the nest consists of a hollow lined with plant material, leaves and grass, with an inner lining of down and feathers.

EGGS   10–12, sometimes 7–16, greeny-blue eggs with a waxy sheen. 2.84 x 1.65in:52.2 x 41mm. Incubation, by the female alone, begins when the clutch is completed and takes 28–29 days. The young are precocial and active, leaving the nest and taking to the water soon after hatching. The female tends them until they are fully fledged and able to fly at 7–8 weeks.

BREEDING SEASON   Usually begins in March, although nests have been recorded in February. Single-brooded, but park and pond birds sometimes have a second brood.

Teal (scale 1:8.2)

Wigeon (scale 1:8.2)

Mallard (scale 1:8.2)

Red-crested Pochar (scale 1:8.2)

Pochard (scale 1:8.2)

FRANCES FRY

Pochard

SIZE   18in:46cm.

DESCRIPTION   Typical diving duck with smallish head. The male has a dark chestnut head and black neck and breast that is quite distinctive; with grey back and pale grey underparts, and black rear. The bill is steel-blue, tipped black. The female is brownish-grey with slightly darker head and neck, and grey-buff eye-ring.

CALL   The male has a rather nasel call and a soft whistle, and the female has a harsh croaking 'kur-r-r'.

RECOGNITION   Large numbers of Pochard are resident all year round in Britain, and many more join them in winter migrations from central and eastern Europe. Firmly established in eastern England, particularly East Anglia, the species has gradually extended its range over the last 150 years and is now found throughout most of the British isles. Pochard are very gregarious, and are usually seen in large flocks (or rafts as they are sometimes called) particularly in winter. As might be expected from a diving duck they are expert swimmers and divers, and are most at home on the water, seldom venturing onto dry land. Habitat includes lakes and reservoirs, marshes, and in winter estuaries and sheltered coastal waters, often in association with Tufted Ducks.

FOOD   Animal and vegetable material, usually obtained by diving from the surface prefixed by a leap. Pondweeds and stonewarts, insects, frogs and worms, crustacea etc.

NEST   Pochard nest at or near the waters edge, heaping up vegetation and plant material to form a mound, which is lined with feathers and down.

EGGS   6–11, sometimes up to 18, non-glossy greenish eggs are laid. 2.38 x 1.57in:60.7 x 44.2mm. Incubation, by the female alone, takes 24–26 days. The young are precocial and active, leaving the nest soon after hatching, and are tended by the female until they can fly at 7–8 weeks.

BREEDING SEASON   Mid-April to June. Single-brooded.

Shoveler

SIZE   20in:51cm.

DESCRIPTION   Colourful dabbling duck, with large spatulate bill that gives the species its name. The male has dark green head, with yellow eye, and chestnut belly, with white breast and scapulars, and a pale blue forewing noticeable during flight. The female is mottled brown and buff, rather like a female mallard, but heavier in build and easily distinguished by the large bill.

CALL   A typical quacking call, rather like the Mallard's. The male also has a low, guttural 'took, took' call.

RECOGNITION   The Shoveler is present all year round in Britain, although some birds may migrate south to France or Spain in winter, while others from northern Europe may overwinter here. In the breeding season it may be found on lakes or reservoirs, or bogs or sewage farms, but at other times it frequents fresh or brackish water, estuaries or even the sea. It is gregarious and often forms small flocks in favoured locations. An expert swimmer and active flier, it is at a disadvantage on dry land, being a clumsy walker.

FOOD   A wide variety of animal and plant matter. It feeds while paddling rapidly, dabbling its large bill in the water and filtering its food from the surface. Like other ducks it can 'up-end' or dive for food, but it is more reluctant to do so.

NEST   The Shoveler choses an open site near water for its nest, and lines a hollow in the ground with plant material or down and feathers.

EGGS   8–12, sometimes 7–14, cream-buff or olive eggs are laid. 2.05 x 1.5in:52 x 37.2mm. Incubation, by the female alone, begins with the last egg and takes 22–23 days. The young are precocial and active, and leave the nest soon after hatching. They are cared for by the female until they reach full independence at 6–7 weeks.

BREEDING SEASON   Begins late April or May. Single-brooded.

Mandarin Duck

SIZE   17in:43cm.

DESCRIPTION   Spectacular duck, first introduced into Britain as an ornamental Water Bird. The male has a gorgeous mixture of chestnut, buff, purple and blue plumage, boldly marked with black and white, a chestnut and green crest, bold white eye-line, and fan-shaped orange wing feathers that stand erect like sails when swimming. The female is much duller, with greyish upperparts and mottled underparts, and pale eye-ring.

CALL   A sharply rising whistling call for the male, a 'kett' from the female.

RECOGNITION   The Mandarin was first imported into Britain from China in 1747, and quickly gained popularity as an ornamental bird. Around 1930 escapees began to form a feral population and now the breed is quite well established in the wild in southern England, particularly in Surrey and Berkshire with around 400 breeding pairs. Habitat is usually well-wooded country with lakes or rivers nearby, and enough mature trees to provide suitable holes for nesting. It is a lively, active bird, and is usually quite tame.

FOOD   Largely aquatic vegetation.

NEST   The Mandarin Duck has an elaborate courtship display, involving much head-bowing and crest-raising. When paired the birds seem devoted to each other. A hollow tree or stump provides a suitable nest site, and the cavity is lined with a little down.

EGGS   9–12, creamy-buff or pinkish eggs are laid. 1.89 x 1.45in:48.8 x 36.3mm. Incubation, by the female alone, takes 28–30 days. The young are precocial and active, and drop down from the nest within a day of hatching, and follow their mother to the water. The female alone attends the young.

BREEDING SEASON   Begins early April. Usually single-brooded, but a lost clutch may be replaced.

Shelduck

SIZE   24in:61cm.

DESCRIPTION   Goose-like bird, with bold black, white and chestnut plumage. It has dark green head and neck, and a broad chestnut band around the upper back and breast. A bright red bill (crowned with a knob in the male) and pink legs and feet.

CALL   The male has a variety of whistling calls, the female makes chattering quacks. A 'ak-ak-ak' call is sometimes given.

RECOGNITION   The Shelduck is widely distributed around Britains coastlines, but is rarely found on freshwater, preferring estuaries and the muddy conditions found there between the tides, or sand dunes. Only during the breeding season does it resort to lakes or agricultural land inland from the sea. It is a good swimmer, but seldom ventures far from the shore. Shelducks are very gregarious, and are usually seen in flocks, rarely singly. In late summer this characteristic is put to good use, as one bird may take charge of many youngsters in a kind of 'creche' which can be up to 100 strong.

FOOD   Molluscs, crustacea and insects filtered from shallow water and mud.

NEST   The Shelduck usually nests in a rabbit-hole or similar burrow, but if none are available it may nest under furze or brambles, or under rocks, or in a concealed hollow. A little plant material is added to the hollow, and a lining of down and a few feathers.

EGGS   8–15, creamy-white eggs are laid. 2.56 x 1.90in:65.8 x 47.6mm. Incubation, by the female alone, takes 28–30 days. The young are precocial and active, and follow their parents to the water or the mudflat feeding sites soon after hatching, even if the journey is long. After the first few weeks they are left in a creche under the care of one or more adults. They achieve full independence at about 8 weeks.

BREEDING SEASON   Starts in May. Single-brooded.

Mandarin Duck (scale 1:7)

Shoveler (scale 1:7)

Shelduck (scale 1:7)

Egyptian Goose (scale 1:8.2)

FRANCES FRY.

Egyptian Goose

SIZE 27in:70cm.

DESCRIPTION Long-legged, rather upright goose, with two distinct colour forms. One is predominently buff-brown, the other grey. Both types have a pale head with dark eye-patch, and a dark patch on the breast, and bright blue fore-wing. Bill, legs and feet are pale pink.

CALL The female has a trumpeting call, but the male has only gusty breaths, sounding rather like laboured breathing.

RECOGNITION The Egyptian Goose is in some ways more like a Shelduck than a goose. Despite its name it came from Africa not Egypt originally, and was introduced into Britain in the eighteenth century. There is now a self-supporting feral population in Norfolk, and it also occurs in other parts of southern England, frequenting habitat with lakes and rivers with abundant vegetation, and trees to provide nest-sites. It is not very gregarious, particularly in the breeding season, when couples pair off and seek solitude for nesting.

FOOD Grass and vegetable matter.

NEST The Egyptain Goose nests in trees, on rocky ledges, or on the ground concealed under bushes or by vegetation. The nest is built from vegetation, and is lined with down and feathers.

EGGS 5–8, sometimes 9–10, oval, creamy-white eggs are laid. 2.75 x 2in:70.5 x 50.5mm. Incubation is shared by both sexes, and takes 28–30 days. The young are precocial and active, and are led to water soon after hatching. They reach full independence at about 3 months, but tend to stay with their parents in a family group for sometime afterwards.

BREEDING SEASON March or April. Single-brooded.

Other bright coloured birds which are fully described under different sections.

GOOSANDER This colourful sawbill is fully described under WATER & SEA BIRDS: GREEN-HEADED BIRDS.

RED-BREASTED MERGANSER Colourful sawbill fully described under WATER & SEA BIRDS: GREEN-HEADED BIRDS.

BRITISH BIRDS AND THEIR FAMILIES

DIVER FAMILY
Black-throated Diver
Great Northern Diver
Red-throated Diver

GREBE FAMILY
Black-necked Grebe
Great Crested Grebe
Little Grebe
Red-necked Grebe
Slavonian Grebe

PETREL FAMILY
Fulmar
Great Shearwater
Leach's Petrel
Manx Shearwater
Sooty Shearwater
Storm Petrel

GANNET FAMILY
Gannet

CORMORANT FAMILY
Cormorant
Shag

HERON FAMILY
Bittern
Grey Heron

IBIS FAMILY
Spoonbill

DUCK & GOOSE FAMILY
Barnacle Goose
Bean Goose
Brent Goose
Canada Goose
Eider
Egyptian Goose
Ferruginous Duck

Gadwall
Garganey
Goldeneye
Goosander
Greylag Goose
Long-tailed Duck
Mallard
Mandarin Duck
Pink-footed Goose
Pintail
Pochard
Red-crested Pochard
Red-breasted Merganser
Ruddy Duck
Scaup
Scoter, Common
Scoter, Velvet
Shelduck
Shoveler
Smew
Teal
Tufted Duck
White-fronted Goose
Wigeon

SWAN FAMILY
Bewick's Swan
Mute Swan
Whooper Swan

HAWK FAMILY
Buzzard
Golden Eagle
Goshawk
Hen Harrier
Marsh Harrier
Montague's Harrier
Osprey
Sparrowhawk
Red Kite

FALCON FAMILY
Hobby

Kestrel
Merlin
Peregrine

GROUSE FAMILY
Black Grouse
Capercaillie
Ptarmigan
Red Grouse

PHEASANT FAMILY
Golden Pheasant
Grey Partridge
Lady Amherst's Pheasant
Pheasant
Quail
Red-legged Partridge

RAIL FAMILY
Coot
Corncrake
Moorhen
Spotted Crake
Water Rail

OYSTERCATCHER FAMILY
Oystercatcher

PLOVER FAMILY
Dotterel
Golden Plover
Grey Plover
Kentish Plover
Lapwing
Little Ringed Plover
Ringed Plover

SANDPIPER FAMILY
Bar-tailed Godwit
Black-tailed Godwit
Common Sandpiper

BIRDS AND THEIR FAMILIES

Curlew
Curlew Sandpiper
Dunlin
Green Sandpiper
Greenshank
Little Stint
Knot
Purple Sandpiper
Redshank
Ruff
Sanderling
Spotted Redshank
Temmink's Stint
Turnstone
Whimbrel
Woodcock
Wood Sandpiper

SNIPE FAMILY
Jack Snipe
Snipe

AVOCET FAMILY
Avocet

PHALAROPE FAMILY
Grey Phalarope
Red-necked Phalarope

STONE CURLEW FAMILY
Stone Curlew

SKUA FAMILY
Arctic Skua
Great Skua
Long-tailed Skua
Pomarine Skua

GULL FAMILY
Black-headed Gull
Common Gull
Glaucous Gull
Great Black-backed Gull
Herring Gull
Iceland Gull
Kittiwake

Lesser Black-backed Gull
Little Gull
Meditterranean Gull

TERN FAMILY
Arctic Tern
Black Tern
Common Tern
Little Tern
Roseate Tern
Sandwich Tern

AUK FAMILY
Black Guillemot
Guillemot
Little Auk
Puffin
Razorbill

PIGEON FAMILY
Collared Dove
Feral Pigeon
Rock Dove
Stock Dove
Turtle Dove
Woodpigeon

CUCKOO FAMILY
Cuckoo

BARN OWL FAMILY
Barn Owl

OWL FAMILY
Little Owl
Long-eared Owl
Short-eared Owl
Snowy Owl
Tawny Owl

NIGHTJAR FAMILY
Nightjar

SWIFT FAMILY
Swift

KINGFISHER FAMILY
Kingfisher

HOOPOE FAMILY
Hoopoe

WOODPECKER FAMILY
Great Spotted
   Woodpecker
Green Woodpecker
Lesser Spotted
   Woodpecker
Wryneck

LARK FAMILY
Shorelark
Skylark
Woodlark

SWALLOW FAMILY
House Martin
Sand Martin
Swallow

PIPIT FAMILY
Meadow Pipit
Rock Pipit
Tawny Pipit
Tree Pipit

WAGTAIL FAMILY
Grey Wagtail
Pied Wagtail
Yellow Wagtail

SHRIKE FAMILY
Great Grey Shrike
Red-backed Shrike
Woodchat Shrike

WAXWING FAMILY
Waxwing

DIPPER FAMILY
Dipper

WREN FAMILY
Wren

ACCENTOR FAMILY
Dunnock

BIRDS AND THEIR FAMILIES

FLYCATCHER FAMILY
Pied Flycatcher
Spotted Flycatcher

WARBLER FAMILY
Aquatic Warbler
Blackcap
Cetti's Warbler
Chiff-chaff
Dartford Warbler
Garden Warbler
Grasshopper Warbler
Marsh Warbler
Lesser Whitethroat
Reed Warbler
Savi's Warbler
Sedge Warbler
Whitethroat
Willow Warbler
Wood Warbler

GOLDCREST FAMILY
Firecrest
Goldcrest

THRUSH FAMILY
Blackbird
Black Redstart
Bluethroat
Fieldfare
Mistle Thrush
Nightingale
Redstart
Redwing

Robin
Ring Ouzel
Songthrush
Stonechat
Wheatear
Whinchat

BABBLER FAMILY
Bearded Tit

TIT FAMILY
Blue Tit
Coal Tit
Great Tit
Long-tailed Tit
Marsh Tit
Willow Tit

NUTHATCH FAMILY
Nuthatch

TREECREEPER FAMILY
Treecreeper

BUNTING FAMILY
Cirl Bunting
Corn Bunting
Lapland Bunting
Reed Bunting
Snow Bunting

FINCH FAMILY
Brambling
Bullfinch

Chaffinch
Crossbill
Goldfinch
Greenfinch
Hawfinch
Linnet
Redpoll
Siskin
Scottish Crossbill
Twite

SPARROW FAMILY
House Sparrow
Tree Sparrow

STARLING FAMILY
Starling

ORIOLE FAMILY
Golden Oriole

CROW FAMILY
Carrion Crow
Chough
Hooded Crow
Jackdaw
Jay
Magpie
Raven

PARROT FAMILY
Rose-ringed Parakeet

273

GLOSSARY OF TERMS

ALTRICIAL: Helpless newly hatched young, naked or near naked with only a little fine down, confined to the nest until fledged.

BROOD: Young birds in nest, or birds all hatched from one batch of eggs.

CERE: Bare, sometimes swollen skin in which nostrils are situated at the base of the beak – a prominent feature in hawks.

CLUTCH: Eggs in a nest laid by one bird.

COCK: General term for a male bird.

CRECHE: Group of birds from several different families which are in the care of adult bird or birds, not necessarily their own parents.

CREPUSCULAR: Of creeping habit.

DISPLAY: Visual signals given by birds, usually during courtship.

DUIRNAL: Active living and feeding during the day.

FERAL: Living wild, but not originating in the wild, usually released by man, or escaped from captivity.

HABITAT: Area with distinctive vegetation or terrain that suits a particular bird species.

HAWKING: Fast, harrying flight while chasing prey, derived from the habits of hawk family.

HEN: General term for a female bird.

IMMATURE: Young bird that has left the nest but is not yet in adult plumage. In some species a bird may take up to 4 years to acquire adult colouring.

INTRODUCTION: A bird deliberately released by man, but now breeding in the wild.

INVASION: Sudden large movement of birds into a particular area, usually for a short period of time.

IRIS: Coloured portion of the eye.

IRRUPTION: Irregular movement of large numbers of birds in search of food, or away from over-populated areas – i.e. Waxwings.

JUVENILE: Similar to immature – young bird that has left the nest but not yet attained adult plumage.

MANDIBLE: The jaw.

MIGRATION: Movement from one area to another at a certain season, followed by a return to the original area at another season.

MOULT: Natural loss and replacement of feathers.

NOCTURNAL: Active hunting or feeding at night.

PASSAGE MIGRANT: A bird that passes through an area on migration, but does not stay for any length of time.

PLUMAGE: The feathers of a bird.

PRECOCIAL: Nestling that is thickly covered in down, and is active from birth, leaving the nest soon after hatching, and able to feed itself.

RAPTOR: General term for day-flying bird of prey.

RESIDENT: A bird that remains in the same area throughout the year.

ROOST: Communal sleeping quarter of birds.

SPECIES: Bird of one particular sort that can reproduce an identical new generation to itself.

SPECULUM: Coloured patch on a duck's wing.

SUBSPECIES: Subdivision of a species, when birds are basically the same in build and behaviour, but may vary a little in plumage or in habitat.

TERRITORY: Area where birds live and feed, which is defended by individuals or pairs from other birds of the same species.

INDEX

INDEX